# THE ATLANTIC COMMUNITY

# THE
# ATLANTIC COMMUNITY

*A Study in Unity and Disunity*

By DREW MIDDLETON

CHIEF CORRESPONDENT, *New York Times*, PARIS

DAVID McKAY COMPANY, INC.

New York

THE ATLANTIC COMMUNITY

COPYRIGHT © 1965 BY DREW MIDDLETON

Library of Congress Catalog Card Number: 65-24699

MANUFACTURED IN THE UNITED STATES OF AMERICA

VAN REES PRESS  •  NEW YORK

This book is for

"THE DOCTOR"
WILLIAM H. STONEMAN,

Guide, counselor, and friend to two generations
of American correspondents in Europe

# FOREWORD

I have never finished a book in so pessimistic a mood. Since the writing of it began, a procession of melancholy events has amply demonstrated the decline of cooperation within the Atlantic alliance and the strength of the opposition to European unity. It seems quite possible that within a year the situation in the Western community will have degenerated into a series of squalid squabbles over national interests, with the United States moving steadily away from involvement—and leadership—in Europe. The lesson of collective security, learned at such high cost between 1935 and 1945, has been forgotten. It is highly unlikely that the West will relearn it in time to deal with the next phase of the global struggle with Communism.

For some time it has been unfashionable in Washington and London, although highly popular in Paris, to draw attention to the weaknesses of NATO or to the grave obstacles delaying any further progress toward political unity in Europe. No apologies are necessary for doing so. America will emerge from her preoccupations with Southeast Asia to find that the foundations of her policy, and her security, in Europe have been eroded to the point where they cannot be restored. By then it will be too late.

Most of the material in this book has been gathered as part of the daily work of a foreign correspondent. All my gratitude is directed not to anonymous researchers, but to the cabinet ministers, ambassadors, and officials, the politicians, economists, sociologists, and generals who found the time to talk about the crisis in our affairs. They are too numerous to mention individually, but I hope they will understand how much I value their help and their friendship.

The reader perhaps may conclude that I have painted a gloomy picture. If he does, I am satisfied. We cannot begin to deal with the issues of tomorrow until we understand the situation of today. I have worked in Europe for over a quarter of a century. I am convinced that the present situation there and the American attitude to it represent a juncture more dangerous for the future of the West than any since the end of World War II. We are moving into a period when national interests are exalted over international security, when appeasement is presented as common sense. This time we do not have even the excuse of ignorance.

DREW MIDDLETON

PARIS, APRIL 23, 1965

# CONTENTS

ix

# THE ATLANTIC COMMUNITY

# Chapter I

## TWENTY YEARS AFTER

The Solutions of Yesterday and the Problems of Today •
Transatlantic Understanding • The New Appeasement
and Communism • "Pactomania" and Personal Diplomacy

Twenty years after the victory over Nazi Germany, America has reached a crisis in her relations with the chief beneficiaries of that victory, the old and famous states of Western Europe that, in theory at least, are our closest allies. The leadership of the United States is rejected or bitterly criticized. Administration policies are denounced. Alliances supported by America to safeguard the freedom of Europe, and of the Middle East and Southeast Asia, are crumbling. The process widens and accelerates with each passing month. Yet each day sees new pressures and ominous threats building on every continent.

In the largest sense the crisis reflects, on the American side of the Atlantic, the failure of the policy of the Forties and Fifties to meet the vastly different problems of today. Successive administrations have modified and adjusted policy in Europe, but the basic concept behind the policy remains unchanged: the belief that the United States, by virtue of unrivaled military and economic strength, is the leader of the West.

1

Leadership on that basis cannot be reconciled with the Europe of today. In that Europe the need for immediate military protection by the United States is receding. The sovereign states of Western Europe, whether or not they desire nuclear weapons, consider United States control of ninety-nine percent of these weapons inconsistent with their equality within the North Atlantic alliance. A combination of a nuclear stalemate between the United States and the Soviet Union and the recovery of their old political dynamism by Western Europe's leading states has led their governments to adopt independent and, in some instances, anti-American policies.

This situation is the primary cause of the crisis that affects American relations with individual governments and with the great international organizations such as the North Atlantic Treaty Organization and the European Economic Community.

The secondary cause has been a grievous lack of understanding on both sides of the Atlantic. The American people have been slow to recognize the sweeping changes that have occurred in Western Europe in the last ten years. In view of the public's ignorance it is not surprising that governments, Republican and Democratic alike, have been slow to fashion new policies that would suit the dramatic alteration in Europe's economic and political status.

This process of change began in the late Forties with the rebirth of European prosperity. It accelerated in the late Fifties when a nationalist leader of genius, Charles de Gaulle, came to power in France, geographically the heart of Western Europe. In the last five years the changes have been multiplied by continued prosperity, the revival, in other countries besides France, of nationalism, and, since 1961, by the easing of Soviet pressure upon the eastern boundaries of Western Europe.

In discussing this area and its relations with the United States, the focus is on seven countries: the six of the European Economic Community—France, the German Federal Republic, Italy, Belgium, the Netherlands, and Luxembourg —and Britain. These are the countries in which American political and economic interests are most deeply involved. All are members of the North Atlantic alliance. If there is ever to be an Atlantic community, bound by something stronger than pious hopes, it will be because these countries together form its eastern base. Finally, these are also the nations that have changed most, politically, economically, and socially, in the last ten years.

Why don't Americans, with rare exceptions, understand this change? Why do we cling to a dangerously outdated view of Europe? Knowing your friend is as important as knowing your enemy. Until America does know its friends abroad, it cannot be expected to support the changes in policy that will prove necessary in dealing with the new Europe.

The present American attitude toward Western Europe is rooted in the rather recent past of 1945–1955. But it also is affected by older attitudes that have survived two decades of Western leadership. Americans, naturally proud of their material progress, have not yet grasped either the extent or the significance of European progress in industrial expansion in the last ten years. It is no answer to say that European industry isn't as big as American. This is perfectly true. To the European, however, it is very big.

European corporations cannot rival the giant American industrial complexes in size. Throughout Western Europe, however, and especially in France, long the home of the

3

small, family company, there is an intense effort to merge existing firms in preparation for the contest with the transatlantic giants. In the last ten years, the smaller European corporations have, in addition, rivaled their American competitors in adaptability, inventiveness, enlightened labor-management relations, and, in some cases, marketing.

There is a fundamental problem arising from the different attitudes of Americans and Europeans toward size; size in industry, size in nations. The individual European, German or Briton, Italian or Belgian, knows that the United States is bigger and richer than his country. He rejects, however, any suggestion that our size and wealth make the average American abler, more intelligent, or more industrious than the average European. And, in moments of candor, the European will sometimes add that each encounter with the American proves him right.

America's view of Europe still is heavily shadowed by the experience of the postwar years. Most accept the fact that Western Europe has recovered from the war and its aftermath, but few appreciate how far and how fast recovery has taken Europe or understand the influence of prosperity on national political outlooks. And Americans often are convinced that this prosperity is due entirely to United States aid. They seek gratitude where international cooperation is the most that can be expected.

The flow of tourists to Europe has not visibly improved our understanding of the continent. Tourists of any nationality are more attracted by the past than the present. Who wants to visit an automobile plant in Turin when one can go to Florence? The myth of an aged, decaying Europe is maintained by returning tourists who have seen cathedrals, castles, and quaint old villages but very little of the modern industrial technology that is changing a continent. The diplomats of the State Department and, to a lesser degree, the Departments of the Army, Navy, and Air Force are better acquainted with contemporary Europe than the mass of Americans. But the inertia that a mistaken popular idea of Western Europe must inevitably impose upon government action surely has delayed the development of bold new policies. The fault, to be sure, is not all on one side of the Atlantic. With the gradual abandonment of the old European world empires, the governments and peoples of the continent have tended increasingly to look inward rather than outward.

The United States now is the only NATO power that has both global responsibilities and sufficient military and economic power to meet them. Britain's overseas responsibilities have shrunk with the transformation of an empire into a commonwealth. Although members of the latter, Malaysia and Tanzania, for example, have asked for, and received, military help from the United Kingdom, Britain's power to assist in a major crisis, such as a Chinese invasion of India, would be severely restricted by her comparative economic and military weakness.

For members of EEC, now comfortably free of colonial preoccupations, foreign policy to a very great extent is European policy. Consequently there is a lamentable lack of understanding, especially in France and Italy, of what the burden of leadership entails for the United States. Policies, such as those in Southeast Asia, that most Americans recognize as part of the defense of freedom seem to Europeans, and often to their governments, as mischievous meddling with affairs that do not concern the United States and certainly should not affect Europe.

If the American in most cases has failed to recognize Europe's material progress and its results, the European shows an appalling lack of understanding of the growth of

5

American responsibility toward peace and toward her allies.

Most Europeans would agree that a repetition of the folly of appeasement would be dangerous in Europe. But they seem perfectly willing to follow a policy of appeasement of the Communist powers in Asia. They cannot understand why the United States should be concerned over the freedom of, say, Thailand. Europe welcomes American assistance in holding the line against Communism in central Europe. But many European statesmen seem blind to the danger of Communist advances elsewhere. General de Gaulle set the fashion in this respect, but Europe's loss of interest in the rest of the world hastened the development. It is odd that Europeans, who, more than most, should realize the smallness of the world of today, are those who dismiss Western setbacks in other continents with the comforting thought that it's all very far away. And those who are interested can always blame the reverses on the clumsy Americans.

In this respect Europe, also, is the prisoner of past attitudes. The old ideas die hard. American governments still are stigmatized as irresponsible in international affairs and amateurish in the diplomatic implementation of policy.

Up to a point, governmental and popular concern over United States policy is natural and even flattering. The European knows in his heart of hearts that, in the clutch, his freedom would depend on the military power of America. We should not become irked when Europeans express their fears about American policies or politicians. After all, we have been telling them for twenty years that their liberty depends on us, that we are, quite evidently, the leaders of the free world.

Still, some aspects of European attitudes toward the United States are disquieting. Even if we grant that the conspiratorial approach to history is deeply ingrained in Europe, the willingness of many otherwise sensible people to accept the story that President Kennedy's death was engineered by a vast right-wing conspiracy was alarming.

In a less sensational way, the American resident abroad is concerned by the popular attitude that almost anything done by an American president is "politics." Certainly politics plays a part in the policy calculations of an American administration. But are Dr. Erhard or General de Gaulle above politics?

Even more serious is the fundamental difference of outlook between Western Europe and the United States on the essential nature of Communism. European attitudes toward Communism differ from country to country. We can take it as a rule, however, that neither the man in the street nor the official in the government recognizes the Communist threat to the same extent as do the Americans.

To be sure, Europe has its violent anti-Communists. One finds these in Paris as in Pasadena. But they are a minority. The masses do not fear Communism as an ever-present, ever-dangerous threat to their liberties. Nor do they regard it as treasonable, as would most Americans, for a neighbor to support and vote for a Communist candidate. Large Communist parties flourish in France and Italy. The socialist parties in these countries, and in West Germany and Britain, have a Marxist tinge.

To people who live with Communism in their own countries and who see all of neighboring Eastern Europe in the hands of Communist governments, the popular American attitude seems exaggerated, even faintly ridiculous. This very considerable gap between American and European thinking on a central issue has existed for years. It has become a serious problem now because, at the moment when new American policies for Europe must be molded, there are political and economic inducements that lead a more independent

Europe to reject the basic United States view of Communism as a continuing danger to peace.

New American policies for Europe are urgently needed, but they must be really new and positive. NATO, for example, must be remade, not revived. And new policies toward Europe should not stop at Europe. This is the moment to enlist Europe's support in framing what might be called "Atlantic policy" to deal with present or potential crises elsewhere in the world. The first step is greater frankness in dealing with the United States' European allies. The failure to provide adequate information to trusted friends was one cause for the flood of sharp and often ill-informed criticism of American operations in South Vietnam. Clearly, the multilateral United States approach, so successful in an economically precarious and militarily weak continent, cannot be expected to succeed in a prosperous and increasingly powerful Europe. The North Atlantic alliance was what Europe needed in the late Forties. It was organized to meet a clear danger, that of Soviet military aggression into Western Europe, when Europe was not only unable to defend herself, but could provide only a marginal reinforcement to American forces deployed on the continent.

In 1949 when NATO was established, European governments *had* to follow American direction to insure their survival. The fact that this direction was given by a series of able secretaries of state and was issued with discretion did not make it easier for some Europeans to take. But they were too weak to protest or to continue an argument.

For example, there was a good deal of opposition among West European governments to the United States proposal to bring Greece and Turkey into the alliance. This opposition, based on the knowledge of the deep-seated animosity between the two countries and their known differences on key

8

issues such as Cyprus, did not, however, develop into success-ful obstruction. Uncle Sam had the power and the money, and what he said was law.

In the related fields of planning for military and political action, most European governments now feel they no longer must invariably follow United States policy. This may be an error on their part, but it is one of the facts of international life, and it is a basic cause of weakness to NATO, America's most important multilateral approach to Europe and her problems.

The harsh truth is that NATO, designed to deal with West-ern Europe's military defense and political stability in the anxious period of the Korean War, is inapplicable in its orig-inal form in 1965. Some Americans may wish for the return of the good old days when an administration's fiat ran from London to West Berlin. Such wishful thinking is a waste of time—as is deploring the ingratitude of Europeans. What we have to consider is the way things are, not the way we would like them to be, and frame new policies to meet new conditions.

It is not only the NATO policy that seems irrelevant to the Europe of today. American policy also must adjust to the new situations in every country in Western Europe. This process can be best begun by simply coming to terms with the fact that the statuses of these countries differ greatly from those for which present policy was framed.

Germany is one example. The basic United States attitude toward the Federal Republic was adopted between 1949 and 1955, the first years of Dr. Adenauer's chancellorship. Even before Dr. Adenauer departed from the Schaumburg Palace, however, the Germany he had led so long and so single-mindedly was changing. This change will be discussed later at length. It is pertinent here to observe that the change in the last three or four years has been political, just as the change in the earlier period of recovery and boom was economic. The political change was largely a product of the economic change, but successive administrations in Washington were very slow to realize that the economic and social changes of the Fifties would exert a drastic effect upon policies and politicians.

German politics already are beginning to show this effect. Note that politics in Germany, today, are affected quite as much by what happens in Paris or London as they are by changes of course in Washington. Chancellor Ludwig Erhard and his foreign minister, Dr. Gerhard Schroeder, remain faithful allies of the United States. West Germany is a member in good standing of NATO and the European Economic Community, or Common Market. Yet both government and people are conscious that their republic now is the most powerful economic entity in Western Europe and that, although thus far denied nuclear weapons, she is fast becoming the most important military power in Europe west of the Elbe.

Whatever the reason—self interest, a sharp eye for the main chance, or gratitude—Germany remains a firm ally of the United States. Can we expect this to continue? Not, I fear, without an adjustment of American policy to take into account Germany's economic power and the Republic's rising political influence in Western Europe. Do we really believe that the Germans will be content forever with the role of economic leader in Europe? Or that, with their country divided, they will wish to leave the great question of reunification to others?

At the moment, of course, West Germany is included in all the consultations among the Americans, British, and French on the long struggle with the Russians over unification. Will this suffice? Only if the consultations deal with a developing

10

policy that has progressed from the rigidity of the early Fifties. It is up to the United States, as the most powerful of the Allies, to take the initiative in framing a policy for the future of Germany that reflects the interests and ideas of contemporary Europe as well as of the United States. To leave this policy problem unanswered is to court disaster.

Germany will never be content to remain economically powerful and politically inhibited. Indeed, by the very nature of things, this is an impossible role for any German government. Twice in the past, in 1914 and 1939, Germany's economic expansion was such that it appeared she had only to continue this expansion to become, without war, the central economic power in Europe and, perhaps, the Western world. East Europe, the Middle East, Africa would have become her commercial fiefs. Yet in each instance the Germans, moved by political considerations, chose not continued economic expansion but the road to war.

I am not suggesting that Chancellor Erhard's Germany is aggressive or militarist. I am suggesting that if this powerful nation is to continue a loyal member of the Atlantic alliance, she must be offered something more than a policy on unity, framed when Germany was painfully clambering back to economic health. The United States must rethink and redraft policies for central Europe that will take into account West Germany's new political status. Americans are aware of Germany's great contributions to the alliance. They must also understand the disastrous consequences to that alliance, and to the whole West, if, once again, Germany is moved by internal political pressures to act independently on an issue that affects her deeply.

Britain is another country to which policy patterns of the past no longer apply. Americans tend to think of Britain in two ways. Either she is the firm friend, the loyal ally of two world wars, or she is the decadent, shiftless family dependent, combining adroitness in sucking gold from the United States with a mysterious, never fully explained, ability to influence American policy to British advantage. American policy toward the United Kingdom has been formulated largely on the basis of the first proposition. This process was accelerated because those making policy, in both London and Washington, knew how frequently and how intimately the interests of the two countries are virtually identical in world trouble spots like Southeast Asia and Malaysia.

I do not believe that American policy toward Britain should be framed on any other basis than the simple fact that the British, in the clutch, or what Sir Winston Churchill called "the crunch," are our most dependable allies in Europe. Even so, it is time for an American government to understand the alteration in Britain's popular and governmental outlook. We are only too aware that Britain's world power has been drastically reduced. Again, as in Germany, we do not understand the effect of this reduction upon public opinion. Both the sensational rise of the Campaign for Nuclear Disarmament in the late Fifties, fortunately short-lived, and the growth of a kind of British Gaullism in the Tory and Labour parties result from the change in Britain's world role.

The British are making their own adjustment to this role. Its course at the moment is unknown. They may decide to abandon their positions in Malaysia or Aden. They may let their nuclear force fade into obsolescence—it is very near that now. Or they may experience a revival of political nationalism comparable to that of France. What the United States must do is to frame long-term policies for dealing with Britain that are in accord with the development of that country since 1955. We cannot afford to lose our most loyal ally because we fail to understand her present situation.

To be sure, the United States has tried to adjust her policy to meet a changing situation in one field, that of NATO. The proposal, first developed during President Eisenhower's second Administration, for a multilateral force was a project that met some of NATO's political needs. Its establishment was intended to bring Western European powers, particularly Germany and Italy, more closely into nuclear partnership with the United States by allowing them to share in a fleet of surface vessels armed with A-3 Polaris missiles and manned by mixed crews drawn from the participating countries.

Naturally the American proposal generated a great deal of controversy in Europe. Inevitably the United States was attacked for trying to force upon the Europeans a nuclear role they did not want. Such controversy is the result of bold and imaginative leadership at any time; the MLF was and is both controversial and imaginative.

Opponents of the proposal, and they were and are plentiful, object that the fleet is militarily unnecessary. They have an argument. But it is outweighed by the political considerations: Europe, and especially Germany, must have some share in nuclear strategy if she is to remain a loyal contributor to the Atlantic alliance.

This has been clear in Washington since the last years of the second Eisenhower Administration. But, having taken the initiative, the United States backed away from the consequences. By the close of 1964 President Johnson had decided to ease the American pressure on our NATO allies for a positive acceptance of the proposal. It was left to the British and the Germans to negotiate on a basis of the original American proposal, what the Labour government called an Atlantic Nuclear Force. This was an abandonment of the American initiative, at a critical moment, in an area in which only the

United States can lead because only the United States has the nuclear power that entitles it to leadership in this key area. To fail to lead from strength is the negation of leadership.

It was General de Gaulle, leading from weakness, in his case an infant nuclear force, who succeeded, by sheer force of personality and by an adroit use of publicity, in forcing the Administration's retreat. MLF had been conceived to give Europe a share in nuclear strategy and thus perpetuate the vital element of military integration in NATO, this time at the highest weapons level. The assumption was that this would stimulate support for NATO, already flagging.

De Gaulle's diplomatic riposte was that MLF would kill NATO by, he hinted, driving France out of the alliance. Whether he would have taken France completely out of NATO is a matter of conjecture. He has said repeatedly that France relies on the alliance for protection until Europe is able to defend herself in the nuclear sphere, which is never. No one apparently even thought of calling the General's hand. Instead, there was an ignominious scuttle away from the MLF that embittered some of its firmest advocates among our European allies and left many an American diplomat with a red face. The affair was, however, a brilliant example of how an able man like De Gaulle, commanding only limited military power, can force a change in American policy in the present phase of United States leadership.

The point to remember is that Gaullism, as we shall see, is not confined to France. Something very like it would have developed somewhere in Western Europe. This form of nationalism developed in France when it did because of the existing combination of a crisis in public confidence in the government and the availability of a truly great, although often misguided, man.

14

The Gaullist program contains many fallacies. It often reflects the prejudices of the General, prejudices that have been encouraged by years of virtually unchallenged rule in France. But the United States will have to recognize that this program or policy responds to something deep within the French people and, indeed, within all European peoples: the demand for a reassertion of national identity in a world dominated by the super-powers, the United States and Russia.

This demand is the product of long experience. Nations that for hundreds of years have been accustomed to deciding their own foreign policies and arranging their own defenses cannot be expected, once they have regained political stability and restored their economies, to dance to another's tune, no matter how suitable the music. When European governments act on the basis of national interests they do something to which Americans have become unaccustomed since the war. But we should not consider that they all are animated solely or even largely by anti-Americanism. Rather, they are acting within the framework of European historical experience. And, it might be remembered, Europeans care a great deal more for history than Americans.

Any new American policy toward Western Europe must be developed on the basis of Europe's current needs and changed situation. We must understand that such a policy can no longer be imposed, no matter how great our diplomatic finesse, as it was in the days of the continent's military weakness and economic chaos. The time has come to frame a policy that through compromise satisfies both our needs and Europe's. And this includes, among much else, a sure understanding of Western Europe's political and economic approach to the countries of Eastern Europe, Poland, Czechoslovakia, Hungary, Rumania, Bulgaria, Yugoslavia, even East Germany. The American people must realize that, as far as

15

the countries of Western Europe are concerned, there are no longer any "outlaw" states.

I am sure that an effort to frame a new American policy will be met more than halfway by Europe's peoples. And it is the peoples, not the governments, that endure. Despite all that governments have done, this is especially true in France, where the sentimental basis for cooperation between Europe and America remains very strong.

France is, indeed, the best example of a country in which the government's rancor and hostility toward the United States has not been reflected by public opinion. Parenthetically, it should be noted that the anti-American tone of French television and radio, very cleverly presented, may in time shift public opinion against the United States. But traveling around France in the summer of 1964, I was struck by the deep, universal good feeling toward the United States. The French, at that juncture, could not understand how the Republican party had happened to nominate Senator Goldwater for the Presidency. But there could be no doubt that they regarded the American people as friends and that they believed American leadership of the West, on the whole, to be informed and tolerant.

One night in a café in Carcassonne I listened to a schoolteacher and the proprietor argue the position. There were many points of disagreement between them; the schoolteacher, for example, was against a nuclear force for France, the proprietor was for it. But both agreed that it was madness for France to adopt a policy that brought her into constant conflict with the United States on international issues. Nor did they think that General de Gaulle's recognition of Communist China was a feat of statesmanship. They thought it was a shabby trick to play on the United States.

When in the future America fashions a new policy for

Western Europe, it will have to face another political situation—the presence in Europe of social democratic governments. It is easy to argue that this has not been a problem in the past, that the Labour government of Clement Attlee was in many respects a more malleable ally than the Tory regime of Anthony Eden. This, again, is not the point. The point is that social democratic leaders of today and tomorrow represent countries far stronger, far more individualistic in a national sense than those of a decade ago.

Their opposition to American policies, new or old, however, is likely to be interpreted in the United States as an expression of anticapitalism. This is nonsense. Anticapitalism may be strong on the hustings in West Germany or Britain. But, when it comes to the great issues of defense or economics, it stops at the frontier. Those who say that the socialist content of European government bars the formulation of an effective joint policy for the Atlantic community are simply raising bogey men to divert policy-makers.

The problem for American policy-makers in the last half of the Sixties is to draft a statement of principles on which policies will be based, rather than a succession of policies designed to meet specific situations. This statement of principles should meet two criteria. First, it must be explicit; that is, it must go beyond the customary emphasis on a desire for peace and control of nuclear weapons and the containment of Communism; it must, to use these instances, explain what sort of peace, what sort of control, what sort of containment the United States envisages not as the optimum solution but as the most possible solution.

The second criterion is that these principles relate to the objectives not solely of the United States but to those of the Atlantic community. Once Europe is educated to the need for an Atlantic policy to cover Africa, Asia, and Latin America, a difficult but not impossible process, agreement on mutual objectives will be easier. In view of the growth of national independence in Europe, no blanket policy for Europe, covering its own problems or problems on other continents, would be acceptable. NATO was, and to some still is, an inspiring instrument for mutual protection. But American influence will lose still more ground in Europe if it concentrates on "a new NATO" or "a stronger NATO."

Despite the progress of EEC, American administrations will have to deal in the foreseeable future with Europe on a country-by-country basis. It may, of course, be necessary, too, to deal with EEC as a separate entity. But these aspects of policy-making will be easier on both sides of the Atlantic if the principles on which the United States is operating are spelled out. Nor are these principles likely to alter greatly with changes in administrations. The problems America faces are going to be the same whether there is a Democrat or a Republican in the White House. The difference will be in emphasis and style when policies based on basic principles are announced and implemented.

Any change in the present policy of papering over leaks from the Communist into the non-Communist world will require a considerable effort on the part of both government and people. Our "all or nothing" philosophy will have to be forgotten, as will contemporary attitudes toward Europe. And the Europeans will have to rid themselves of many of their misconceptions of United States objectives. This will be easier for them if they are fully aware of the basic principles on which American policy is based.

The American diplomatic disease of the Eisenhower-Dulles years was pactomania. It was believed that a pact, a treaty could resolve any international issue, no matter how grave. Pacts and treaties have great usefulness in some areas of international policy when they are used to legalize an existing situation accepted by both parties to the issue. They are, however, of relatively little lasting value unless they are related to a well-understood set of principles. New treaties, multilateral or bilateral, and new alliances, no matter how imposing in name, will not meet our requirements until the world knows the basic concepts on which policy is made and implemented.

The strong belief in the magic virtue of personal contact with foreign leaders pervaded the Kennedy era. Judging from the stream of foreign dignitaries visiting Washington in this administration, President Johnson shares this belief.

Anyone who has been exposed to the euphoria generated by the meeting of two heads of government and who has then remained in the capital of one of the powers knows how little application the exchanges of courtesies, the after-dinner speeches, the carefully contrived "contacts with everyday people" have to cooperation between the nations involved.

Early in 1956, for example, Sir Anthony Eden, the British Prime Minister, visited Washington for talks with President Eisenhower. Neither man really understood the other, but there was a record of shared danger and achievement during the war and enough respect to form a basis for successful cooperation. Both men certainly believed the visit had been remarkably successful. Yet before the year was out they were bitterly divided over Suez. Whatever else may be said about that episode, it is clear that most of the difficulties between Washington and London arose from sheer inability to see the other fellow's point of view.

The reader can properly complain that immunity to pactomania and doubts about personal contacts leave precious little with which to fashion a new American policy. Both pacts and handshakes can be helpful in international relations. But America will not achieve the sort of relations she should have with her allies in Western Europe, indeed the crisis we now face in those relations cannot even be approached, until America understands the Western Europe of today and its attitude toward the United States and toward other key areas of international relations: the Soviet Union, Eastern Europe, China and Southeast Asia, and Africa.

Such understanding in foreign policy is impossible without an equal understanding of the nations themselves as they are today. We must look first at the Western Europe of communities, treaties, and alliances, and second at the countries that compose it. Nations, like people, differ quantitatively, not qualitatively. They all have the same qualities. It is the quantity of, say, internationalism or racism in a national society at a given moment that differentiates one from the other. These quantities increase and decrease within the body politic. In what follows we see how they affect both individual nations and international organizations.

Much of this book is about the Europe with which the United States must deal. But the same developments that make a new American policy for Europe necessary and, indeed, mandatory are influencing Western Europe as a place where 300,000,000 people live and work. The Twenties was the period of the big change in the United States. The big change in Europe, in her way of life, her ambitions, her politics, began in the Fifties. But it is far from finished. Great areas of Western Europe, Spain and Portugal for instance, have not been affected by the change to any great extent. Elsewhere there are pockets within changed communities that have not yet experienced the change; Eire and southern Italy are examples.

It is superficially correct to say that one effect of the great

20

change in Europe has been to make the great industrial nations—West Germany, Britain, and France—more alike. True
though this may be, it is a dangerous basis for the formulation
of foreign policy. One need look no farther than the Europe
of communities and alliances for proof.

## Chapter II

# EUROPEAN UNITY vs. NATIONALISM

The Strength of European Unity in History • Half-Steps
and Missteps: EEC, EFTA, WEU, NATO • The Easing
of Soviet Pressure and the Decline of NATO • The
Revival of Nationalism

The ideal of a united Europe has attracted some of the
noblest, and some of the basest, of men. The Roman emperors, ruling over a continent then half-unknown, for a time
imposed unity. Charlemagne tried and failed. Throughout
the Middle Ages, before the development of nationalism,
emperors and kings, often using the Church, or being used by
it, strove to unite the continent.

Napoleon made himself the master of Europe. But he was
undone, in the end, by that very nationalism he had aroused
in France and which, spreading to other European nations,
raised new armies to replace those he had defeated. He also
had to contend with England, in those days an equally advanced national state, run, not by some bumbling monarch,
but by William Pitt, a hard-headed Irishman named Castle-
reagh, and led in war by tough professionals like Moore,
Nelson, and Wellington.

In our day Hitler and the Nazis tried to impose their New
Order in Europe. There may be a lesson for contemporary

nationalists in the fact that they were defeated not by a great revolt of Western European nationalism, but by the efforts of three powers from outside Western Europe, the United States, the Soviet Union, and Britain and her Commonwealth.

The dream of unity, nevertheless, has a striking vitality. Over the centuries Europeans have seen the day when Gaul and Teuton, Italian and Austrian could be diverted from their petty squabbles to membership in a union that represented all, that spoke for all.

The impulse to make this dream come true was strongest when Europe lay ruined in the years immediately after 1945. There was, however, one important difference in the approach. In the past the impulse toward unity came from above, from ambitious national leaders. Significantly, the present movement toward unity is the work of hundreds of men of different nationalities doing different jobs—politicians, professors, government officials, industrialists—who began the struggle for unity against the background of the derelict Europe of the immediate postwar years.

Nationalists nowadays denigrate the enthusiasm for European unity that swept the western half of the continent then. They argue that it was the product of the despair that overtook Europe in that time of troubles. They say, too, that it was the concept of dreamers; a strange description of Winston Churchill and Konrad Adenauer, two hard-headed politicians who shared the idea of a United States of Europe.

The movement generated genuine emotion. Men looked across a wasteland, the result of unbridled nationalism, to the day when all the West European states would be members of one federation speaking to the world with a single voice; a Europe that would be the peer of America and Russia. Despite the revival of nationalism, the faithful still

23

propagate this noble concept. There are many in each country who see in the supranationalism of a politically united Europe the ultimate, indispensable answer to the national rivalries that have torn Europe apart in the last three hundred years. Europe, in Harold Macmillan's words, cannot afford another civil war.

The first steps toward European unity, however, were in the economic field. This was as it should have been—peace to the advocates of political unity. Europe must have a foundation of economic cooperation if that unity is to be developed. It is highly unlikely that European economic unity would have progressed to its present stage were it not for the attraction of the ultimate idea of political unity. The steps toward economic unity basically are the means toward the end of political unity. Without that ideal the whole movement would founder.

The organizations aimed at political unity in Europe or assisting its growth have no common parentage. The European Economic Community, for example, owes its conception almost entirely to Europeans, although it has received over the years considerable encouragement from successive administrations in Washington.

The EEC or, as it is often called, the Common Market, is in reality three organizations; the Community itself, the European Coal and Steel Community, and Euratom, an agency for the joint development of the peaceful uses of atomic energy. Their establishment represents the most important steps Europe has ever taken toward unity because, although basically economic, they provide solid foundations on which a political union can be constructed.

The establishment of EEC and its growing economic strength resulting from a grouping of France, West Germany,

Italy, Belgium, the Netherlands, and Luxembourg produced a natural reaction by the "outsiders": the creation of the European Free Trade Area. EFTA, formed at British instigation when Prime Minister Harold Macmillan realized that a counterbalance must be struck, included, in addition to the United Kingdom, Norway, Denmark, Sweden, Switzerland, Austria, and Portugal. Although EFTA had a certain economic validity, its true importance was its indication of the strong beliefs of countries of strikingly different political, economic, and social structures (compare Portugal and Norway) that they must organize and thus ultimately induce EEC to widen its frontiers. EFTA, in essence, means that these seven countries want to join the Common Market.

Naturally there are difficulties. Some of these are caused by the inability of individual countries to make the concessions required for membership. Others arise from the "Little Europe" concept that pervades political thinking in the Common Market. Finally there is General de Gaulle's veto on the entry of any member unwilling to accept and follow his somewhat archaic and highly nationalistic view of the development of European unity.

To General de Gaulle, Britain is the great outsider. This view is not shared completely by the other governments of The Six. Barred by the General in January 1963 from joining EEC, Britain still remains on the horizon of most other governments. Whatever the political complexion of her government, many Belgian and Dutch leaders want Britain included in the planning for political unity. An active and powerful minority in West Germany feels the same way. The Italians are favorable. Only the French, of the major nations, are in opposition.

General de Gaulle and Maurice Couve de Murville, his foreign minister, say Britain can enter the Common Market

once she accepts all the conditions of the Treaty of Rome.*
There is a strong impression that even if a British government
were to do this, De Gaulle and his diplomatic messenger
would find some new reason to veto a British application.
They may not be afraid of Britain's political influence within
an enlarged EEC—in fact, they stoutly insist they are not—but
they act as though they were.

Things may be different "after the funeral." This is the
professional diplomats' rather macabre way of referring to the
new situation they expect to arise in relations between EEC
and the other European powers, notably those in EFTA, after
the death of General de Gaulle.

Possibly because of the stimuli resulting from the progressive reduction of customs duties within EEC, the economies
of the six partners have flourished since its establishment.
Although cynics argue that Europe was due in any case for
an era of prosperity, the lowering of tariff barriers within the
Community accelerated the boom. Industrial output by the
six members has risen by more than forty percent since the
Common Market was established. All barriers to trade in industrial products within the Community will be eliminated by
July 1, 1967.

Progress toward the harmonization of agricultural programs has been slower, largely because of the difficulty of
reconciling the interests of Germany, the Common Market's
factory, with those of France, its farm. The agreement on
grain prices and the progress made toward an agreement on
dairy and beef prices, however, point toward further progress
in this most difficult problem.

A recurrent theme in the evolution of a politically united

* The Treaty of Rome established the European Economic Community. It was signed in Rome on March 25, 1957, by representatives
of the six powers.

Europe is the connection between progress toward this goal and agreements in the economic field. France has twice, once in 1964 and again in 1965, made agreements on agriculture the price of her cooperation in talks on political unity. But even when France discusses this unity, she is talking about a specific Gaullist concept that has very little to do with proposals for a federal union, such as the United States of Europe.

An important change will overtake the balance of power within EEC on January 1, 1966. From that date onward unanimous voting will no longer be required in the Council of Ministers. This means that from that date neither France nor Germany, the two dominant states in the history of EEC, will be able to veto major proposals.

This situation will affect the political as well as the economic future of the Common Market. In the political sphere there will be a major conflict between De Gaulle's concept of a confederation of Europe of fatherlands, that is, a confederation of sovereign states, and that of a federation, a United States of Europe, under which each nation will gradually relinquish sovereignty to a supranational organization. While De Gaulle is at the helm in France, his government will do its utmost to block any move in the latter direction. But he will not be there forever.

EEC is thus moving ahead at varying rates of speed on three fronts, the industrial, the agricultural and the political. The reasons why Britain should seek union with it are even stronger today than they were in 1963. Nowhere are they stronger than in the political sphere, where the decline of British political influence and military strength in the home islands and the gradual dissolution of the multiracial Commonwealth, beloved of Labour party theorists, is progressing rapidly. From the standpoint of the United States, British entry into EEC seems more desirable than ever. A new Europe with new policies and new attitudes is evolving. Without British participation in that evolution, the result may be disastrous to American political interests in Europe, to say nothing of the interests of the United Kingdom.

At the moment Britain has two means of maintaining her interest in the development of European political unity even while she remains outside the Common Market. The first is the diplomacy of an experienced and skilful foreign service working directly on the governments of The Six. The second, and more important, from the standpoint of publicity for an abiding British interest in Europe, is the United Kingdom's role in an organization called the Western European Union, composed of Britain and the members of EEC.

Originally designed as a military alliance—it was a forerunner of NATO—WEU has been revived as a communications channel between Britain and EEC on the development of political unity. WEU's importance does not arise solely from the British use of the channel. Other members of EEC, the Italians, the Germans, the Dutch, the Belgians, want to maintain contact with Britain on so important a development. The British know this. Consequently, there is seldom a meeting of the Council of Ministers of WEU at which the British Foreign Secretary fails to emphasize his government's abiding interest in the development of political unity. As surely as night follows day, there will be a German or a Dutchman or an Italian following with a statement that his government hopes Britain will play a role in this process.

This annoys the French. They believe that De Gaulle settled the whole business on January 14, 1963, when he vetoed British entry into the Common Market. Their view is that Britain should play no role in the discussions of political unity until she unequivocally accepts all the clauses of the Treaty of Rome—which no member has done—and shows she is prepared to sever her economic obligations to the Commonwealth.

WEU must be accounted an important instrument for keeping open the political exchanges between EEC and Britain on the political development of Europe.

NATO is another organization that, in a rather roundabout way, exercises great influence upon the development of political unity, for it was founded upon a basic requirement of all governments: the necessity of defending their peoples from aggression. The North Atlantic alliance was born in 1949 as a defense treaty at a moment of maximum peril for Western Europe. The Putsch in Czechoslovakia, the Berlin blockade overshadowed the minds of statesmen. It was urgently necessary to create a military and political alliance that would defend Western Europe on both fronts.

It is difficult today to recapture the sense of urgency that animated the original discussions that led to the formation of NATO. In the summer of 1950, the American and British generals, who represented the only credible Western military strength on the continent, were telling their political masters that it was a toss-up whether the Russians would strike across the north German plain, in the north, that is, on the front of the British Army of the Rhine, or through the Fulda Gap in the south against the hastily reorganized United States Seventh Army.

The North Atlantic alliance was born in this atmosphere. As it grew stronger, there was a sensible easing of the emergency. One explanation is that Stalin died and, for a few years, Soviet foreign policy lost its dynamism. But the other explanation, which the West has forgotten with a characteristic willingness to dismiss its own achievements, was that the alliance did establish in Western Europe a formidable defense. By about 1955 one no longer heard gloomy forebodings that the Russians would be in Frankfurt and Düsseldorf on D-plus-3 and across the Rhine and into the Low Countries and France three days later.

Having established itself as the military shield for Western Europe against any but nuclear attack, NATO began to develop into a political forum. This was quite natural. The alliance was concerned with the central issue of defense. And day-by-day defense, even in conventional weapons, became more complex in the research, development, and production of weapons and in the supply and maintenance of armies in the field. These became international rather than national problems.

Superficially these were military questions. But, as the NATO delegations soon learned, they affected the economics and politics of the European partners. If the British made a superior tank, why should it not be acquired by the other partners? And if it was, what should the French government tell the industrialists who thought they had built an even better tank? Issues like this hypothetical one could not be settled by the Atlantic Council, NATO's permanent political body, but had to be sent upstairs to the foreign and defense ministers of the alliance.

Starting with such politico-military questions dealing with the internal workings of the alliance, NATO gradually developed into a political forum for the discussion of international problems that affected its stability. The "watching brief" given the NATO Secretary-General on Cyprus in May of 1964 is a recent example of the alliance's involvement in an issue that involves two of its members, Greece and Turkey, and hence the stability of Western defense in the eastern Mediterranean theater.

NATO is much more than a Western Europe defense mechanism. The United States is its most powerful member. Canada, Greece, and Turkey are members who, geographically, are far removed from Western Europe. But the focus of the alliance, both in defense and politics, is Western Europe. It is in NATO and in the field of defense that Western Europe has learned to cooperate in one of the essential tasks of government. Cooperation in such an important field naturally encouraged the European members of NATO to favor the development of political unity in Western Europe. The organ had to develop outside NATO, essentially a military alliance. But the spirit of cooperation, of intergovernmental discussion and give and take that developed in meetings of the North Atlantic Council, argued powerfully to Europeans for the practicality of political union.

NATO's involvement in political and economic questions had an application beyond the recognition of the feasibility of political union. The North Atlantic Council, the alliance's permanent political body, extended its interest to such issues as the dispute between two members, Greece and Turkey, over Cyprus. Inevitably the practice of consulting NATO on issues arising far beyond its military responsibility developed. The United States involvement in Vietnam and the British difficulties in Malaysia were discussed by the Council. In each case the Atlantic allies demonstrated a deeper understanding of the relationship between these crises and European security than could have been anticipated on the basis of soundings of public opinion.

The four organizations, the North Atlantic Treaty Organization, the European Economic Community, the European Free Trade Area, and the Western European Union, differ sharply in purpose and structure. Each, however, has contributed to the growth of European political union. Each, to some degree, is a battleground between European and Atlantic policies on the future development of Europe. Of the four, NATO is the most important for the future because it deals with the vital issue of defense and because the principles of integration have been carried further there than elsewhere.

If the battle is lost in NATO, that is, if the alliance declines into a loose association of governments as De Gaulle wishes, the concept of Europe as a confederation of national states will have been strongly reinforced. In that situation it is doubtful if EEC will ever open its ranks to other powers. The triumph of nationalism will be nearly complete and the establishment of an integrated Atlantic community will be a dead letter. For the General clearly sees "his" Europe as a third power in the world rather than as an integral part, with the United States, of the Atlantic community. He wants a Europe, as he wants a France, independent of the "hegemonies" of America and Russia.

The battle is not yet lost, although the odds are now on the side of nationalism. But the four organizations exist. They have power and influence. They can be used to further the cause of the Atlantic community. But progress within them toward either a European political federation or a true Atlantic community is at "Dead Slow."

On New Year's Day 1965 De Gaulle was asked if he expected any progress toward European political unity in the new year. There would be, he said, a lot of talk but not much progress. In the first half of the year, French policy did its best to make the General's prediction come true. The French were ready to confer on both the foreign ministers' and the heads of states or governments' level—but. Progress had to be made first in the talks to fix agricultural prices at Brussels and there had to be adequate preparation for the conference suggested by the Italians. In each condition, the French made it clear, they would be the judge of whether conditions were ripe for a talk on political cooperation. And they used the word "cooperation" rather than "unity" to emphasize that De Gaulle's proposal of a loosely knit confederation of the six governments of EEC remains their objective.

Individual governments have watered down their policies and reduced their moral and material commitments to NATO. The Common Market no longer offers the promise of becoming the basis for a United States of Europe. Events outside Western Europe have helped the erosion of cooperation in these organizations.

The foremost cause, affecting all the members of these groups and the United States as well, has been the easing of Soviet pressure on Europe. As far as Western Europeans were concerned, this pressure began to ease after the last Berlin crisis of 1961–1962. But it is more exact to date Europe's salvation from recurrent Soviet crises, usually focused on Berlin, from the Soviet-American confrontation over Cuba in the autumn of 1962. This was the great divide in East-West relations since the war. The Soviet leaders were forced, as they had never been forced before, to recognize that nuclear war would mean the destruction of the Communist state.

If my information on this point from East European sources is accurate, the motivating factor in the calculations of Nikita Khrushchev, the Soviet Premier, was not defeat but the hopelessness of life for Russia, or indeed for any other East European country, after a nuclear war—win or lose. The Soviet leaders realized (again East European sources must be cited) that, granted the resolution of any American administration, no local nuclear confrontation, over Cuba or Berlin or anywhere else, offered any hope of ultimate Soviet victory. The relaxation of Soviet military pressure in the Caribbean was accompanied by a sensible relaxation of political pressure

33

in Germany and West Berlin. In a shrunken, nuclear world, a nation that backs down in one area backs down in all.

Western Europe, then, has been encouraged to believe that the Soviet military threat, the armed invasion that NATO was organized to repel, is now a negligible danger. This contributes seriously to the difference between the American and the European attitudes toward Communism, referred to in the previous chapter.

The movement toward unity in Europe originated and developed partly from revulsion. The survivors of 1945 saw what rampant nationalism had done under Hitler and Mussolini and decided that union was their only salvation. But an equally powerful factor was the Soviet threat that developed immediately after the end of World War II. Temporarily, Soviet pressure has relaxed. There is no immediate, pressing argument for political union or even for intimate cooperation.

Those who, like Jean Monnet, the father of European unity, retained their belief in the need, indeed in the inevitability, of that unity, found their ideas opposed by the resurgent nationalism of men like De Gaulle; a nationalism based in part on the conviction that Europe, protected by the United States, need not fear a resumption of Soviet pressure. In the event of such resumptions, Europe had all the time it needed to develop cooperation. But had it? Certainly De Gaulle has acted as though it had. However, the period between 1949, when NATO was founded, and 1964 was marked by progress toward union and cooperation in the political field.

Another factor, often overlooked by officials in busy departments, was working steadily to promote European unity during this period. The mass urban populations of Britain, France, Germany, northern Italy, and the Benelux countries began to evolve along the same social lines. Workers in Turin or Amsterdam or Lyons or Birmingham were wearing very much the same sort of clothes, driving the same sort of cars, seeing the same movies, Italian, French or British, and, often, watching the same program on television through Eurovision, which links the television systems of West Europe. The united Europe idea has made its greatest headway among both the employers and workers in the industrial cities because the business planner discounts national boundaries and thinks in terms of a European market, and the factory worker, now that he can travel, finds little difference between his way of life and that of workers in other countries.

The belief of this group on unity in Europe, often only dimly seen, conflicts with the second factor that has reduced the prospects for a European political federation and an integrated Atlantic community—the revival of nationalism. General de Gaulle is its foremost exponent. But ideas are stronger and more enduring than men.

Had De Gaulle not returned to power in 1958, it can be assumed that some leader would have emerged in Europe to proclaim first his country's independence and sovereignty and second Europe's independence, political at least, of the United States. Nationalism is the foe of federation with its linked concept of supranationalism.

There is a clear relationship between the external factor, the relaxation of Soviet pressure, and the internal revival of nationalism. Were the Russians today hammering at the gates of West Berlin, as they were a decade ago, there is little doubt that De Gaulle would be a stalwart upholder of cooperation and NATO's military integration would have no greater champion.

Americans should understand that De Gaulle and the national leaders elsewhere in Europe who follow his policies have strong support. In the present crisis of relations between the United States and Western Europe, Europeans are preoccupied, in this period of East-West détente, with their own internal problems. Some of these may seem trivial to us: the price French farmers are paid for their milk, the closing of branch railway lines in rural England. But they are desperately important to those concerned. Much more important, for example, than whether the Soviet Union or the United States can put three, four, or a dozen men into space.

It is quite true that the future of the human race may rest upon the amount of cooperation that can be established within the Atlantic community. But Americans should never forget that Western Europe is going through a phase of economic expansion and social change very like that the United States experienced in the years 1924–1929. Who, in those years, cared whether the Germans and Russians were cooperating in the development of tanks? Who gave a damn what the Japanese were doing in Manchuria? A few Americans, a very few. If the average European is now chiefly interested in buying his first car, his first home, his first washing machine, he is merely following the pattern set by us a generation and more ago.

This attitude, blending indifference to the outside world and support for any leader who maintains prosperity, is a powerful factor in the growth of nationalism. We are accustomed to thinking of the Fifth Republic of Charles de Gaulle as the most nationalist of European states. And so it is, in some respects. But we must realize, if we are to understand and solve the present crisis, that nationalism is present to some degree in the political attitudes of all the Western European states.

France in 1958 was ripe for a nationalist renaissance. She had endured, from the homeland in 1940 to Algeria in the late Fifties, a series of humiliating military defeats. A wavering economy never seemed able to fulfill its rich potential. Government followed government with bewildering rapidity and, although the French made wry jokes about the changes, they knew, and bitterly resented, the spectacle of political instability that this presented to the world. Later we can study how De Gaulle exploited this situation. For the purpose of this chapter it is enough to emphasize that from the point of patriotic self-respect France had the most to gain from a revival of national independence even if this came at the cost, as it did, of estranging her two best friends in World War II, the United States and the United Kingdom.

France was first in the nationalist field. But other situations have worked on other peoples. We are accustomed in the United States to taking Britain's continued adherence to the Anglo-American alliance for granted. Too much so, for there is a potential for nationalism in Britain almost as strong as that in France a decade ago. If Britain were to follow the French lead, the consequence would be much more serious for America and for the Atlantic alliance. In military strength, in ability to assist and support United States policy in far corners of the globe, and in willingness to assume the burden of Western defense in other areas, Aden to Singapore, for example, Britain has been a far more important ally than France.

For the moment it is enough to say that there exists in Britain, in both the Conservative and the Labour parties, a strong undercurrent toward national reassertion. A new British nationalism can develop only at the expense of the United States and of the transatlantic cooperation that has been such a formidable factor in keeping the peace.

The problem was difficult but manageable during the thirteen years of Conservative rule from 1951 to 1964. There was a brief, bitter Tory protest late in 1956 after the United States had arraigned Britain before the United Nations for her role in the Suez adventure. The "anti-Europeans" of the Conservative party resented American pressure on Britain to join the Common Market. The right wing of the Tory party still contains many who resent the manner in which successive American administrations have pressed Britain to relinquish her holdings in Africa. And there is a lingering resentment, less strong than it was a decade ago but still potent among Tory primitives, over the manner in which the United States has taken over Britain's old position as leader of the West.

This anti-Americanism never became dangerous, largely because all four Tory Prime Ministers, Sir Winston Churchill, Sir Anthony Eden, Harold Macmillan, and Sir Alec Douglas Home, were devoted to Anglo-American solidarity and enforced support of the alliance upon an often restive party. It was not always easy.

A cabinet minister told me during one difficulty between London and Washington, "I was brought into government by Winston Churchill and his lesson to all the young newcomers to the Cabinet was the same. It was that we must get along with the United States on matters of high policy. We would find it difficult at times, as indeed we have, but our survival and the survival of the West depended upon it. But it's not always easy, you know."

Tory nationalism was rooted in fading dreams of Britain's imperial state. It was controlled for thirteen years not so much by wise Washington handling of the British but by the growing recognition among the younger generation of Tory leaders that the world had changed and that they must come to terms with Britain's new role in that world. Nationalism on the Labour side is a less simple development, one that poses a more difficult problem for the United States.

The majority of the Labour leaders are "Little Englanders." Their party never shared the Tory veneration for the Empire.

Under the Labour governments of 1945–1951, Labour cabinets did much to disband the old Empire and lay the foundations for the multiracial Commonwealth of today. The Labour party thus is not offended by the fact that the United States has taken over Britain's old position as the leading Western power. It sheds no tears for the Empire. Even its somewhat ingenuous enthusiasm for the multiracial Commonwealth has been strained by the establishment of something very like a police state in Ghana.

Labour is frequently at odds with Washington on the manner in which that leadership has been exercised. But its chief preoccupation is with the internal direction of the British economy and society. This form of nationalism can be as disturbing a factor in the Atlantic community as the jingoism of right-wing Conservatives. A Labour government that abandons British responsibilities around the world will be a more serious problem for Washington than a Conservative government that desires more than its share of responsibility and of authority in allied councils.

Labour is intent on maintaining the connection with Washington. It is a powerful supporter of NATO. But the question is not of intent, but of means. Can a Labour government, can any British government, maintain the transatlantic alliance while reducing the United Kingdom's overseas commitments and its nuclear forces? A British policy that developed along these lines would conflict with the growing conviction in Washington, among men of all parties, that the allies of the United States must accept more, not less, responsibility. Such a policy by a British government would result in a drastic alteration of the alliance.

The United States probably would be forced to assume many British responsibilities; the protection of Malaysia, for example. In those circumstances, no administration could be expected to pay the same attention to Little England as to Great Britain. Nor would it be as interested as it now is in the United Kingdom's economic health and ability to defend itself.

Certainly the nonpolitical ties would remain: a common language, a common literature, a common political heritage. But without the day-to-day cooperation between the two governments, the importance of the alliance as a political instrument would wither.

It seems entirely probable that a Labour government that reduced its overseas and defense commitments would at the same time remain hostile to British involvement in Europe. With a few exceptions, the Labour party does not believe that Britain's future economic and political development lies in greater involvement in Europe, either the Europe of the Common Market or the Europe of the Free Trade Area. To British socialism it is the Commonwealth that offers the more attractive opportunities in both fields. This, of course, is true of some vocal but not particularly powerful sections of the Tory party.

A Britain that looked inward instead of outward would force the United States to recast policy toward the Atlantic community.

This could happen in Britain. Were the "Little Englanders" of the Labour party to triumph, no great stretch of the imagination is required to envisage a Britain that, divested of her remaining overseas responsibilities, Aden for example, and of her nuclear weapons, might embrace a policy that placed less and less emphasis on international cooperation and more and more upon the interests of developing socialism in a "Little England."

A Tory nationalism is equally threatening to the Atlantic community, for the right-wing party still contains the greater potential for British "Gaullism." A Conservative leader who campaigned on a Gaullist policy of independence of the United States would have "swept the country" in 1964, in the words of one of the most astute politicians in Britain. This politician, and many like him, are too honorable to betray the principles of cooperation with the United States, drummed into them by Winston Churchill. But will they always lead the Tories?

Nationalism is only too clearly at the helm in France. It has a potential in either party in Britain. What of Germany, whose name was associated with nationalism, to Europe's woe, from 1860 to 1945? Here again we are dealing, as in the case of Britain, with potential rather than actuality.

The first two West German chancellors, Dr. Konrad Adenauer and Dr. Ludwig Erhard, were aware of the political risk to them and to their country's international good name of any revival of German nationalism. There was a good deal of nationalism, some of it a crude imitation of Hitler's National Socialism, in the Federal Republic during the first five or six years of its life, that is, from 1949 through the middle Fifties. It was kept in check partly through the efforts of the Federal government but mainly through the intelligence services of the American, British and French High Commissions. Dr. Adenauer, of course, always took a strongly antinationalist, anti-neo-Nazi line. But I have never been able to decide in my mind the extent of his knowledge or the depth of his motivations.

The Chancellor in some ways was remarkably ingenuous —or remarkably good at dissimulation. For example, Dr. Adenauer swore to the then French High Commissioner, the experienced André François Poncet, that he had never heard of Oradour sur Glaine, the site of one of the most terrible mass killings of Frenchmen by Germans during the occupation. Repeatedly the Chancellor expressed his surprise that anyone in the United States should be concerned at a revival of nationalism in Germany. He was quite willing to accept the results of surveys by the United States High Commission that showed a revival of nationalism as late as February 1953. What he could not understand was why this should cause any alarm.

The Chancellor was walking a tightrope in those days. He had continually to reassure his new friends in Washington that Germany, or at least his part of it, had found salvation in democracy. At the same time he depended upon officials and diplomats who had been more or less intimately connected with the Nazi party and the government under Hitler. And finally, he had to maintain at all times a ferocious anti-Communism satisfying to Washington.

Since the Fifties the steady growth of German prosperity, the admission of Bonn into NATO and the political councils of the West, the establishment of a German army, navy, and air force have served to remove some of the causes of the nationalism of that period. The Federal Republic is treated as an equal partner, the occupation is over, the nationalist-minded refugees from East Germany and from Eastern Europe, principally Czechoslovakia, are being assimilated into the population. But public opinion is never static. The internationalist of today may become the nationalist of tomorrow.

General de Gaulle has provided interested Germans with an example of a nationalism that cannot be condemned, at the outset at least, as fascism or neo-Nazism. He preaches independence: independence of the United States in deciding the great issues of state, from the formation of a national nuclear striking force for the protection of the state, to the establishment of economic policies that serve the state first and the European Economic Community a bad second. De

42

Gaulle, as we shall see, has never liked EEC. It is a good bet that had he then been President of France, his government would not have signed the Treaty of Rome.

Elements of the German Federal Republic are understandably attracted by the Gaullist formula of independence, for in one important area of German national affairs, the interests of millions of Germans clash directly with their country's position as an ally of the United States. This vital area is the complex and dangerous issue of Germany's reunification. To many patriotic Germans it is only too clear that their country cannot be unified as long as the United States, the United Kingdom, and France are her partners in any negotiation with the Soviet Union. Nearly twenty years of futile negotiations have convinced these Germans that only an independent Germany allied not with the United States and Britain but with the other five members of the EEC has a possibility of negotiating unification with the Russians.

Thus the quest for German unity through greater independence for the Federal Republic leads them back to the Little Europe idea, also favored by General de Gaulle. The General, naturally, sees France as the most influential member leading The Six, with himself or his successor marching in the van. The German nationalists, although they make profound obeisances to De Gaulle's greatness, do not see things developing in quite this way. They see Germany becoming the most powerful national entity in the small, tightly knit European community, a state that, once it establishes its independence of the United States, will be able to take military and political initiatives forbidden her since the Federal Republic was established in the autumn of 1949.

There is no lack of experienced and able politicians in Germany prepared to embrace a new nationalism thinly disguised as independence. Franz Joseph Strauss, the former Minister of Defense, leads a strong "Gaullist" group in the Christian Socialist Union, the Bavarian branch of the Christian Democratic Union that has ruled Germany, alone or in coalition, since 1949. There are other politicians of like mind, less experienced but more vocal. But in estimating the strength of this development in Germany and its effect upon the present crisis between America and Europe, our concern must be over the men who eventually will replace Strauss and his colleagues.

The development of German nationalism must contend, however, with a very strong counterattraction. This is the view, long held by resolute democratic leaders like Chancellor Erhard and Foreign Minister Dr. Gerhard Schroeder, that Germany's true interests over the long or the short term lie in the assiduous cultivation of the connection with the United States. German politicians have an acute sense of where power resides. They are courteous about the French nuclear striking force, but they are realists enough to know that it is a puny weapon compared to the nuclear forces deployed around the world by the United States. The Germans have been content to conclude arms deals with the French and the British for what are today relatively minor items of military equipment. But when the question arose of gaining a share in nuclear power, the German leaders went straight to Washington.

They were exploiting not only the realities of the situation —the United States was the only country that could provide Germany with a share in an up-to-date nuclear weapons system—but also a favorable political opportunity. General de Gaulle's hostility to American military policies and Britain's recurring economic and financial crises culminating in the near disaster of late 1964 have led many in Washington to conclude that the old special relationship with these long-time allies could be transferred eastward to Germany. The Federal Republic, they argued, has been prompt in fulfilling its defense commitments. It has displayed its appreciation of America's defense of German soil. Without undue prodding, Bonn has endorsed United States policies in distant areas like South Vietnam, where the Federal Republic has no direct interests.

These are all factors that strengthen German allegiance to the bonds already existing with the United States and thus argue against the establishment of German independence on the Gaullist pattern. But it would be foolish, in the present fluid state of Europe, to consider that these are decisive factors. The best that can be said—and, considering Germany's past, it is a great deal—is that the Federal Republic, despite the well-nigh intolerable emotional burden of territorial partition and the blandishments of De Gaulle, has remained loyal to international cooperation within the Atlantic alliance.

Nevertheless, the political situations in the three strongest members of that alliance, France, Britain, and Germany, harbor the seeds of a virulent nationalism. Already in the case of France such nationalism has virtually ended French integration in NATO. Tomorrow it may be Britain's turn. And, the day after, Germany's.

Yet even without the rapid growth of nationalism, other circumstances tend to delay the development of unity between Europe and the United States. The easing of Soviet pressure on Western Europe is one. The gradual movement of national Communist parties toward independence and away from obedience to the Kremlin is another. There are the discords that arise between members of the European Economic Community; the one between France and Germany over wheat prices in 1964 was a good example. These delay the attainment of economic cooperation among the closest of allies and thus contribute to the general disarray of the Atlantic community.

A final factor in the crisis is the doubt about American intentions on the protection of Europe in the event of a nuclear war. This doubt is well established. As long ago as 1952, the first leaders of NATO had to contend with the fear that, if war came, the United States would not endanger its own population to save that of Europe. In the last three years General de Gaulle has strengthened this doubt by offering the uncertainty of the American nuclear response as a reason for establishing France as a nuclear power.

The General's arguments and the conclusions he draws from them obviously are a good deal more complicated than this simple reason put forward to justify spending huge sums for what is, in the context of Western nuclear strength, a superfluous force. The General's basic reasoning apparently follows this sequence:

(1) The United States will protect France in any nuclear or conventional war because by doing so she is protecting herself.

(2) But should an American government hesitate, France, in her independent nuclear force, has the means of defending herself and, by doing so, precipitating the nuclear war in which the United States would have to participate.

(3) In view of this assumption, this unspoken guarantee of American protection, De Gaulle can act as independently as he wishes within the Atlantic alliance even to the extent of assuming policy positions that conflict directly with those of the United States.

These arguments are understood in Germany and Britain by those who make high policy. But the popular argument, which is used to justify nuclear forces, has a much more direct application to the present crisis in relations between the

46

United States and Europe. Embroidered and repeated, these doubts about American readiness to protect Europe can have a serious influence on the development of public opinion in the United States. There are plenty of Americans ready to say, "If they don't trust us, to hell with them." The Fortress America concept, as the followers of Barry Goldwater demonstrated, has an astonishing vitality.

We must conclude that the crisis in cooperation between Europe and the United States will worsen. Unless there is a sudden revival of Russian pressure upon the West, progress toward the political unity of Western Europe will dwindle into speeches by impotent gatherings of enthusiasts whose dreams bear no relation to the realities of nationalist policies. The United States will have to do more than deplore this situation. It must act to restore the old cooperation, the old faith in the solidarity of the Atlantic community. But where is the start to be made?

## Chapter III

# DE GAULLE AND *LA GRANDE NATION*

The Roots of French Nationalism • De Gaulle and
How He Rules His Republic • Is He a Dictator? •
France's Role in the World as He Sees It • A Booming
Economy • The High Cost of Nuclear High Life

The political discord in the Atlantic community started in
France. Independent European nationalism was bound to
develop in the old continent once prosperity and political
stability were reestablished. The development began in
France because the climate was favorable.

To begin, there was the historical experience. Americans,
coming from many nations, often discount the effect of history on a homogeneous people. The French remember that
their country was for centuries the center of Europe. *La
Grande Nation.* The richness of her farms, the skill of her
artisans, the mastery of the arts no less than a succession of
great rulers, kings, emperors and premiers, renowned generals and admirals made France the greatest of continental
countries. She was not only the seat of power but also the
capital of the intellect.

This French primacy in Europe had a long life. It lasted
far longer than the bright but brief high noon of Britain's
Victorian Empire. The memory of France and her glory is

part of the French heritage. Few escape it. I have met French Communists as chauvinistic as British Tories. Consequently, the impact of the sorry history of the last quarter of a century has been very deep. From 1940 until the very recent past, French history has been scarred by ugly defeats, weakness and inefficiency in government, corruption, subversion, and disaster. A people sensible to a great past has found this intolerable, an affront to national pride.

Suddenly events conspire to create recovery. Prosperity, its foundations laid by the Fourth Republic, now much abused by the Gaullists, returned to France in the late Fifties. General de Gaulle, France's greatest living son, returned to power. And this time De Gaulle ruled not over a wasted country and a staggering economy, as he did immediately after the war, but over a prosperous state and a people to whom confidence was fast returning. The one serious drain on France's economy, the long, bitter war in Algeria, was liquidated by De Gaulle. France faced the world without debilitating foreign involvements and cleansed of embarrassing colonial obligations.

Contemporary France of the Fifth Republic is inseparable from De Gaulle. He is the only out-sized leader in Europe, perhaps in the world. He has survived his great contemporaries of the World War II era, Franklin Roosevelt, Winston Churchill, and Joseph Stalin. Most of the men who ran the world when he took power a second time, Dwight D. Eisenhower, Nikita Khrushchev, Harold Macmillan, Nehru, have left the stage.

Charles André Joseph Marie de Gaulle was born at Lille in the north of France on November 22, 1890. He graduated from St. Cyr, the French military academy, and joined the army as a *sous-lieutenant* in 1911. When World War I began he was a full lieutenant of the 33rd Infantry regiment commanded by Colonel Philippe Pétain. De Gaulle was wounded and taken prisoner during the fighting at Douaumont in the Verdun battlefield in 1916. A *commandant,* that is, major, when the war ended, he served under General Weygand in Poland in 1920 and 1921 when that wily tactician set the trap that sent Marshal Budenny's Soviet forces fleeing back to the Russian frontier.

At first De Gaulle's life between the wars followed the usual course of the young professional officer. There are many men who now profess to have glimpsed genius in the gangling, serious, rather abrupt young officer. In 1921 he married Yvonne Vendroux, the daughter of a solid, no-nonsense, bourgeois family. By all accounts the marriage has been supremely happy, as marriages of two shy, introspective people often are.

The General early showed a turn for military study. He was a professor of military history at St. Cyr and a student at the Ecole Supérieure de Guerre. Like most of the survivors of the holocaust of 1914–1918, he early turned his military thinking to the lessons of that war and to the means of avoiding another such blood bath. Out of this came perhaps his best-known military work, *Vers l'Armée de Métier.* In this he foresaw the future dominance of the tank on the battlefield and pleaded, in vain as it turned out, for French concentration upon a smaller, more highly trained, mechanized mobile army. He was, of course, ahead of his time; the commanding figures of French military life, Pétain, Weygand, Georges, and the rest, paid little attention to his theories.

By the outbreak of war in 1939 he was commanding tanks in the French Fifth Army. When in May 1940 the fighting in the west really started, De Gaulle had an armored division and, as its commander, fought one short, brilliant action that stands out like a beacon against the murky tale of French disasters of those days. Premier Paul Reynaud, casting about desperately for new men with new ideas, made De Gaulle Assistant Secretary for Defense.

When, on June 17, the French government led by his old chief, Marshal Pétain, surrendered, De Gaulle refused to give up. He flew to London, and, in Winston Churchill's memorable phrase, "De Gaulle carried with him, in this small airplane, the honor of France." The next day he launched his appeal to France to continue the battle. On that June 18, De Gaulle entered history. He has been a towering figure in the history of our times ever since. He knows it.

This is not a biography of De Gaulle. But his pre-1940 history is almost as important as his experience since he emerged from the war as the dominant figure in French politics. Disgusted with parliamentary intrigue and partisan chicanery, the General left the government in January 1946. For twelve years he stayed in the wilderness, in his case a comfortable but rather bleak country house at Colombey-les-Deux-Eglises in eastern France. There he wrote his memoirs of World War II, including a detailed record of his long, bitter fight to impress upon Roosevelt and Churchill that France was a full combatant and entitled to be treated as such. Here was the beginning of a familiar theme; France must have her own identity or she is not France. De Gaulle made an abortive attempt to regain power. After his failure he waited.

Then in 1958, with Algeria in a rebellious turmoil and the national confidence in the Fourth Republic exhausted, France, the despair of her sons and the joke of her allies, called again. Such, in brief, is the history of the most remarkable Frenchman of our times. But here we are concerned with how De Gaulle rules and how he forms the policies that have restored France's independence of action and reminded her people of that glory that has played so important and so costly a part in her past.

To an extent unequaled elsewhere in the Western world, the making of policy in France is concentrated in one man, President Charles de Gaulle. A chosen few among his ministers are aware of the policy situation on which his mind is currently dwelling. They may even be asked for their views. But there is no evidence that these in the end count for more than the studies and statistical analyses that are furnished to the Presidential office in the Elysée Palace by France's corps of highly skilled civil servants.

The General takes his time. The description of him as a ruler who thinks of the day after tomorrow and the day before yesterday is accurate. When, after weeks, or it may be months, of consideration, De Gaulle reaches a decision, his intimates, including the Premier and perhaps the Foreign Minister, are informed. But they are informed in order that they may be better prepared to execute the decision, not because the General is seeking their agreement.

The decisions, however, are not usually a surprise to the inner circle. The leaders of the General's government and the small group of Gaullists whose loyalty and discretion are alike unimpeachable are familiar with the thought patterns that guide his policy-making. For example, they are aware that he dislikes NATO because he believes that through it the United States retains control of Europe's defense. Consequently the inner circle is able to anticipate a new move by the President against NATO whenever American influence in the organization appears to him to be growing, or when NATO, for some reason, often trivial, has annoyed him.

The General takes a poor view of parliaments, even one so subservient to his wishes as the Gaullist-dominated National Assembly of the Fifth Republic. He believes that the National Assembly comes between him and the French, that his charisma is strongest when he is addressing the French people directly in a televised news conference. Great decisions of policy are not announced to the National Assembly but to a news conference.

The reader should not confuse such conferences with those given by a President of the United States or with a British Prime Minister's biweekly ordeal of question time in the House of Commons. The General's entourage solicits questions. The General answers those he selects, and only those, in a series of speeches devoted to specific subjects: Asian affairs, the future of Europe, the French economic situation. No one rises to say, "Yes, but," and there are no supplementary questions.

In the United States, Britain, or West Germany a great decision in foreign policy excites a great debate, in the legislature, in the press, and on television or radio. The General and his government are adroit at avoiding these, as they see them, time-wasting and superfluous airings of public opinion. Why bother? The General knows best.

As we have seen, the General's intentions are hidden from all but the inner circle until shortly before his decision is announced. The National Assembly, due to its complicated schedule and to shrewd parliamentary manipulation by the Gaullist majority, seldom debates the President's decisions until weeks or months after they have been made and announced. Moreover, as Michel Gordey has pointed out, the French people "hear little about these debates and care less."

The emotional repudiation of the parliamentary process in France, kept alive by the General's frequent criticism of the Third and Fourth Republics, has created an antiparliament psychology. There has been a revival recently of political discussion among the French, and the size of audiences for antigovernment politicians is growing. But little attention is paid to what politicians, often the same ones who have drawn large crowds a week before in the provinces, say in the chamber of the National Assembly.

Political opposition, therefore, is not powerful in the place where it should count the most in a parliamentary democracy, the National Assembly. Opposition under De Gaulle has tended to concentrate in the newspapers. In Paris and the provinces there are a half dozen well-informed, responsible newspapers that have criticized cogently the General's foreign and internal policies. But newspaper critics, no matter how well-informed and responsible, are not political opponents. Nor do they have the field to themselves. General de Gaulle can count upon the unwavering support of a large number of other newspapers. But, these, unlike the critical papers, do not devote a great deal of space to international affairs. They announce the General's policy decisions in a manner that gives the reader the impression that these are unquestioned at home and acceptable abroad.

After France's recognition of Communist China, the French press's self-censorship was most efficient. Except for stories in *Le Monde* or *Figaro* and the Parisian intellectual weeklies, whose circulation is small, it was difficult to learn from the French press that recognition had been widely criticized by France's allies. Nor was much space given or attention paid to the well-reasoned arguments against recognition that were deployed by Washington.

French critics rightly complain that the people are poorly informed about the world's view of General de Gaulle's France. They are quite right. But the blame does not lie entirely with the press or with the government's manipulation of television and radio. Much is due, too, to French xenophobia. The French, more than any people in Western Europe, are convinced that they and their country are the center of the world. Even if they knew of the hostility aroused abroad by some of the General's policies, methods, and aims, it is doubtful that they would be affected. It would not be resented, as foreign criticism often is in the United States or Britain or West Germany. The French just wouldn't care.

This is part of a basic nationalism that makes France an arid field for internationalist agitation. For every Jean Monnet, laboring for the vision of a united Europe, there are ten thousand like the industrialist declaiming upon the virtues of his country.

"Why should I, or any Frenchman, worry about what you Americans or the British or anyone thinks of us and the General?" he said. "Evidently he will not be here forever. Here we have a sweet country, fine food, the best of wine. What is it to us, this NATO, this unity with people we don't especially like, the Germans and the Italians."

In this situation it is not surprising that the General's foreign policies have received and, predictably, will continue to receive popular approval as long as they emphasize the importance—which, in Gaullist terms, is another word for independence—of France. Interestingly, and typically, the French do not regard these policies as the most important parts of his program. Like people in other Western countries, they are far more interested in their own day-to-day problems: jobs, taxes, housing, roads, and schools. But when they are induced to air their views on such Gaullist policies as the hostility to NATO, the banning of Britain from the Common Market, the recognition of China, the majority approve De Gaulle's actions.

There is naturally a minority, composed largely of people with business or other ties abroad, who are unable to praise these actions as demonstrations of France's importance or independence. They view them as steps toward France's isolation and as measures that someday may invite harsh countermeasures by more powerful Western governments. But these critics are in the minority and politically ineffectual.

Before returning again to the General and his government, one additional point about his popularity should be stressed. The end of the Algerian war brought peace to France for the first time since 1939. The French, and especially Frenchwomen, are grateful. During a 2,000-mile tour of France in the summer of 1964, I heard much criticism of the Gaullist government—but seldom from a woman. And often wives would hush their husbands' criticisms with a sharp, "But we have peace, have we not?"

In 1965, after seven years of steadily growing ascendancy over the French government and people, General de Gaulle's extraordinary career was at its zenith. During the previous year he had recognized Communist China, visited Mexico and South America, bullied his German allies and the other members of the European Economic Community, flouted the United States' desire to bring Europe into a nuclear partnership through the multilateral force, and shaken the foundations of NATO. None of this was spontaneous. All of it was rooted in De Gaulle's triumphs and rebuffs of the past. Before we can understand France today, we must understand what De Gaulle has done in her name and, naturally, the man himself.

In his case it is not oversimplification to say that he has one goal: to establish France as a great power in such a manner that *no* successor can modify her greatness or independence. This is based on his consistent view that the nation-state, a category in which he regards France as preeminent, rather than an ideology is what endures in international affairs. If we accept this as his guiding aim and principle, and on the record we must, then we see De Gaulle as a rebel against the internationalist thinking that has been popular in the Western world since the end of World War II. He has little use for European unity, except in the unlikely event that Europe unites on France's terms; he regards supranationalism as unworkable and, more important, dangerous to France's independence; and he considers parliamentary democracy an inefficient way of running a great state.

The course of Gaullist policy supports this view of the General. His first major international act set the tone. On September 17, 1958—he had been in office less than six months—De Gaulle sent a memorandum to President Eisenhower and Prime Minister Macmillan. The General proposed that France, the United States, and the United Kingdom should form an international directorate over the defense and diplomatic policies of the Western world, taking joint decisions on strategy including, of course, nuclear issues. This implied, in the context of the General's memorandum, a French vote over the use of nuclear power by either the United States or Britain.

Washington and London discussed the memorandum. In the end they rejected it. President Eisenhower made it clear to De Gaulle that because NATO was an alliance of sovereign and equal states bound by the interests of collective security, no group of governments within the alliance was entitled to assume the direction of other sovereign states. To do so would break the spirit of NATO and subvert the principle of equal, collective responsibility. The French have since contended that Eisenhower's rejection was abrupt to the point of discourtesy. This is not true; it was comprehensive and fair. But the French exploit its rejection as a reason for the pursuit of independent policies within the North Atlantic alliance, policies that are hostile to that alliance.

A year later the General exposed another of his favorite stratagems. This might be called "the feint to the East." In form it is an indication, by word or action, that France knows she can find friends in the Soviet Union or in Communist China or in Eastern Europe, that she is not dependent politically or economically on her position in the Atlantic community.

In 1959 De Gaulle drew attention to the fact that Russia was "a white European nation" with "the yellow multitude which is China" at her back door. The international uproar resulting from so little effort must have been gratifying. There was a spate of talk about a Paris-Moscow axis.

The United States was warned further that there could be no joint American-Russian settlement of Europe's affairs, no new Yaltas. The idea that the United States and the Soviet Union intended to get together and settle Europe's affairs has long haunted De Gaulle and his party. Indeed the French have warned the West Germans about it so often, they no longer take them seriously on this point.

It is almost axiomatic that when De Gaulle has suffered a particularly sharp, and public, rebuff in the West, his thoughts turn eastward. Early in 1965 it was painfully clear that, despite the General's eloquent appeals for a negotiated settlement in Vietnam, the United States wasn't paying the slightest attention. Few thought it a coincidence that De Gaulle was soon able to disclose that France and the Soviet Union thought the same way on Vietnam and that on this issue, as on German unity, there was a new "understanding."

De Gaulle's idea of Europe is a Europe led by France and not by the United States. EEC is not his chosen medium for establishing that leadership. The Treaty of Rome, establishing the Community, had been ratified before the General's return to power; it is significant that the Gaullist deputies in the National Assembly opposed the treaty. Periodically there are indications that the General feels that France cannot fulfill her destiny while bound to the Community. Then again, there are signs that he believes Europe will come around to his concept of political unity, which is cooperation on confederal lines, and establish herself, with France in the lead, as a rival of the United States.

So great is his concentration upon replacing American leadership that the General appears blissfully ignorant of the danger of German economic leadership and consequent political influence in Europe. If he were aware of this, French policy probably would seek an integrated, federal Europe rather than the "Europe of Fatherlands." For it is only through an integrated Europe that Germany's massive economic power can be controlled for the benefit of all by supranational institutions. As it is, De Gaulle appears to think that in his confederation France and Germany will balance each other.

Christian Fouchet, a gifted diplomat who later became a cabinet minister, was given the task of planning for a Europe that would follow Gaullist policies. The result was a proposal that seemed curiously anachronistic to governments and peoples talking of a United States of Europe and of supranational authorities. Fouchet suggested a loose union of the sovereign states of the Economic Community in which the governments would be supreme and in which cooperation would be attained through frequent meetings of government leaders and ministers. By April 1962, the plan was dead.

Here we encounter a constant element in Gaullist tactics. Policies, such as the Fouchet plan, are born and reared in the midst of resounding publicity. They make their international debut. The world rejects them. Nothing more is heard. The

General salvages what he can and prepares his next exploit. Cervantes said it all: "Patience and shuffle the cards."

In this case the next great maneuver was the French-German Treaty of Cooperation signed in January 1963, shortly after De Gaulle had barred Britain and, very important to him, the insidious American influence inherent in the British-American relationship, from EEC.

Dr. Konrad Adenauer, then the German Chancellor, wanted the treaty. He saw it as crowning his life's work of reconciling France and Germany. De Gaulle, at first, was lukewarm. Then, perhaps miscalculating the strength of Adenauer's hold on the reigning Christian Democratic Union, he embraced the treaty. One important reason was that its procedures for consultation followed those laid down in the rejected Fouchet plan: twice-yearly meetings between the heads of government; more frequent encounters between leading ministers; economic, technical, and cultural cooperation. If the rest of Europe had been so foolish as to reject the Fouchet plan, perhaps the workings of the Treaty of Cooperation would prove how wrong they had been.

So the treaty was signed in Paris, adorned with diplomatic razzmatazz more suitable to a pact ending a world war. Within a year the treaty was torn at the edges and gaping at the seams. De Gaulle soon made it clear to the Germans that he expected them to see that by signing the treaty they had chosen France and Europe, rather than the United States and the Atlantic community.

Although such an approach was clearly in keeping with the General's views on French, and European, independence, it clashed with the German outlook. Chancellor Adenauer, during his last months in office, feared that "that young man," meaning President Kennedy, would be beguiled by Prime Minister Macmillan into making a deal with the Soviet Union on German unification. In view of the pledges and aid given Dr. Adenauer by both the Eisenhower and Kennedy Administrations, this was a queer position for *der Alte*. But "old men forget."

Dr. Erhard, and his foreign minister, Dr. Gerhard Schroeder, were much tougher about Bonn's relations with Paris than Dr. Adenauer's government. They placed more emphasis behind the American proposal for a multilateral force. They supported, with words rather than men, money, or material, the United States effort in South Vietnam. They signed the nuclear test ban treaty that De Gaulle scorned. The new German rulers became, in De Gaulle's coldly furious phrase at a diplomatic gathering, "American satellites."

Such outbursts illustrate a curiously feline aspect of a great man's character. Although his comments are retailed as elegant *mots* by the faithful, they also frequently touch the sensitivities of France's allies. Midway through the Cyprus crisis in early 1964, a French diplomat told me, the General had remarked gratuitously that if it came to war, "The Turks will have no trouble with the Greeks. The Greeks made their military reputation fighting the Italians." Sharp, but not particularly diplomatic. When the remark made the diplomatic circuit, it wounded the pride of two of France's allies.

Having concluded the treaty with West Germany, the General widened his field of fire. One act was the recognition of Communist China. This was taken five weeks after De Gaulle had assured Secretary of State Dean Rusk that no early action was contemplated in this field. Of course, an argument can be made on the meaning of the word "early." The Americans accepted it, at the time, as meaning that there would be no recognition for at least six months.

But the recognition of Peking was only a part of the General's policy for Asia. By August 1963, he was advocating neutrality and independence for South Vietnam. The announcement of recognition was followed by the assertion that China must participate in any Asian settlement. This, coming after De Gaulle's description of the Chinese as "a great people" with "a capacity for patience, labor, and industry," emphasized France's independent policy. So did trading with Cuba, his government's conclusion of a long-term credit deal with the Soviet Union, and the General's patient cultivation of what one of his ministers termed the "claustrophobia" in Latin America caused by overwhelming United States influence in that area.

"Having settled all the great problems of her past, France has today a freedom of action that no other nation enjoys," said Maurice Couve de Murville, foreign minister of the Fifth Republic, in April 1964. It is hard to conceive of a more fatuous statement. In the pressing interdependence of the modern world, no country, not even the United States, enjoys freedom of action. But the remark must stand as typical of the grotesque overconfidence of Gaullism, the sort of illusion that is nourished by the absence of serious political opposition and year after year of unchallenged power.

Is this the picture of a dictator and a dictatorship? Certainly not, if we think of De Gaulle as a possible successor to Hitler and Mussolini. But if we consider the powers he has gathered into his hands, if we mark the decline in authority of the legislature, if we note the control of television and radio by the government, we must conclude that France today is ruled by an authoritarian government centered on one man. But, and this is very important, France is not a police state. There is an opposition, albeit a weak one. The Communists are active and vocal. Portions of the press, notably *Le Monde, L'Express, Le Canard Enchaîné,* and *Figaro,* criticize the government.

Even so, the National Assembly is a debating society, and not a particularly lively or pertinent one at that. De Gaulle makes a policy on foreign affairs, defense, and the national economy. Under his rule also some strange changes have been made in the French system of justice. For example, between 1810 and 1939 the idea of what constitutes a crime against the state was modified only once. Since De Gaulle's rule began in 1958 it has been changed four times.

Does the ordinary Frenchman care? Again, as in the conduct of foreign affairs, he is inclined to trust the General. He does not *think* of him as a dictator—a condition that could encourage a government toward arbitrary action. There has been some victimization of loyal servants of the Fourth Republic. But there does not exist in France that fear of a ruthless state apparatus that is common to dictatorships.

The average Frenchman, like the average American or Briton or Russian, wants a quiet life. De Gaulle has given him this. If "Jean Dupont" does not worry about the future after De Gaulle, it is because the present authoritarian high summer seems destined to last. What will happen to De Gaulle's France "after the funeral" is, however, a subject of the widest interest to France's allies.

Certainly his passage from the scene would lead to a revival of political action. But, although it is easy to become mesmerized by life in the Gaullist climate, it is difficult to believe that France would slip back into the chaotic policies and rapid changes of government that characterized the Third and Fourth Republics. France and her people have regained their self-confidence, and this may ultimately be De Gaulle's greatest gift to his country. Nor will France soon abandon the independence the General has established and maintained. In fact, as we noted earlier, one of his chief objectives has been to establish that independence in international affairs, in the defense of the motherland, so strongly that no successor can undo his work.

De Gaulle's powerful advocacy of European independence of the United States has won support in France and in the rest of Western Europe as well. His idea of a Europe independent of the super-powers, the United States and the U.S.S.R., will not die with De Gaulle. Whether Americans like it or not, General de Gaulle and his ideas have had a powerful impact on political thinking among our allies as well as in his own country. His successors may wish to take advantage of this. Or, if the climate changes, they may conclude that it is time to take France back into the Atlantic community as a contributing member.

France's political situation in Europe is both a good deal higher and a good deal lower than the French themselves realize. General de Gaulle's policies have impressed his contemporaries in other governments. But those policies have made France no firm allies, no warm friends among her closest associates, the members of the European Economic Community. In some capitals, notably Bonn, London, and Rome, they have made enemies. France, however, can afford this. De Gaulle's identity with France, the appeal of his more assertive policies to the nationalism of the average Frenchman and Frenchwoman, the political quiet and economic stability of the country have given him a firm base for his forays in foreign affairs.

But France, under De Gaulle, aspires to the leadership of Europe. When a country leads, however, there must be followers. There are none.

Britain took a long time to recover from the shock of the General's veto. Governments, Conservative or Labour, may take different views of Gaullist policy now or French policy in the future. But it is very difficult to believe that the diplomats of the Foreign Office or the civil servants of the Treasury will be prepared to cooperate with the French on any basis of trust. This is one of the legacies of January 14, 1963, when De Gaulle cast his veto against Britain, that the French overlook.

West Germany, of course, was the chosen ally. But that was when Good King Konrad reigned in Bonn and listened attentively to De Gaulle's every word. The Treaty of Cooperation was to have been the guide for the rest of Europe in the movement toward unity. Instead it became, in a little more than two years, a source of friction rather than amity.

The others, the Italians, the Dutch, the Belgians, have all been affronted for one reason or another by Gaullist policies. They may at times find themselves in agreement with the French, but the reason is not acquiescence to basic Gaullist policies. It is that, on a given issue at a given time, they find their national policy on the issue coinciding with that of France. This may look like leadership in Paris, but it is not.

Why has De Gaulle, despite all his talk about Europe for the Europeans, been unable to lead? Primarily, I believe, because of the extension of his ideas on France to his policy for Europe. It is easy and quite popular to stress the independence and importance of France to the French. But having done so, having emphasized France's position as a leader in Europe, it is more difficult to induce other governments and people to follow France. Europeans have had quite enough of being led by European states (Nazi Germany's New Order is a case in point), and their aspirations toward European unity are influenced by a belief in equality.

Consequently, the reaction to the Fouchet Plan for European Union, De Gaulle's only detailed proposal on the matter, never had much of a chance. France is the only independent nuclear power in Europe. True, her nuclear power is derisory compared to that of the United States and far weaker than Britain's. But the "have nots" did not relish the idea of being members of a European union, without supranational authority, in which France, the only nuclear "have," was bound to boss the rest.

By May 1965 a stalemate had developed. France refused to dilute her nationalism to the point of accepting federation and supranational organizations. The other five members of EEC objected, especially Belgium and the Netherlands, to a Europe of Fatherlands led by De Gaulle's France.

The General's preoccupation with independence for France is at the root of the problem. To surrender any measure of her sovereignty would amount to the abandonment of his ideal: France as a great independent power. For De Gaulle, France as an interdependent power, either in a United States of Europe or in a slowly developing Atlantic federation, is the negation of everything France should be and for which he has fought.

De Gaulle, remember, thinks in terms of decades rather than years. The present stalemate is a temporary check rather than a final surrender of his hopes for a Europe organized along his lines. Always granting that he expects France to be the leader, the General does see a form of unity developing. It can be developed, in his view, only on the basis of truly national states. Which are? France, naturally. The West Germans but, more truly, all the Germans, meaning the German Democratic Republic in the east as well. Even the British! For when the General talks of national states, he thinks of those with a single language, culture, and history established as states within their own frontiers for a considerable period of time. By this definition the Belgians, who speak two languages, and the Italians, who have been a nation for less than a hundred years, fail to qualify.

How do the true nations develop toward unity according to the Gaullist doctrine? Development begins by the assertion of independence of the United States and any other foreign power. Thus to De Gaulle, the West and East Germans, the one tied to Washington and the other to Moscow, have failed as yet to establish the basis of independence. So, of course, have the British, who persist in their Anglo-Saxonism.

Never forget, however, that the General is convinced of the historical inevitability of his views. These things will happen. The spirit of the nation-state will break the chain of interdependence. Then, as real nations, they can unite and build a Europe of interlocking alliances. It is at this point that De Gaulle and his ministers see the development of a European nuclear force that will free the continent of its dependence on the nuclear armament of the United States.

The General's support for an eventual European nuclear defense reflects his willingness to see the end of NATO as it now is. This is part of his campaign against American involvement in Europe. To De Gaulle, NATO now embodies the principle of American control of Europe's defense through integration of command. While that exists, there can be no true independence for any European member of NATO and, consequently, no true progress toward an independent Europe. Nor can there be a European strategy for the continent's defense. These are objectives that the General values more highly than the continuation of NATO in its present form.

But he does not go too far. As Maurice Couve de Murville has pointed out, the General wants an alliance that would connect the United States and an independent European confederation. He wants American protection but not through an integrated command. In other words, he wants to have his cake and eat it, too.

We must remember that the French challenge is made by the leader of a country that in the last ten years has moved into a period of affluence equal to that in any of its neighbors. De Gaulle is operating from an economic base that, although smaller than America's or West Germany's, is remarkably stable and has an undeniable capacity for growth. As was pointed out earlier, one American handicap is thinking of France, and of Germany or Britain or Holland, as they were in 1945 and not as they are today.

Just as the German economic miracle was the great European wonder of the Fifties, so the French revival impresses the Europe of the Sixties. Here we might note that, although the foundations for it were laid before De Gaulle's return to power, their benefits are to his advantage politically. He has presided over the most opulent period of the boom and, in common with all politicians, he has been quick to take the credit.

It is commonplace to say that France is a rich country. It would be more accurate to stress the balance of her economy. The growth of France's economy between 1959 and the end of 1962 was rapid and relatively well balanced. In 1960, using 1953 as the base of 100, industrial production stood at 167. By 1963 the figure had risen to 201 and in the first quarter of 1964 to 215. This was accompanied by a sizable increase in freight traffic on the railroads and in the turnover in consumers' goods.

But 1963 also saw the beginning of economic difficulties and of vigorous government action to end them, especially the expansion of credit and of the money supply. The general index of wholesale prices, using 1949 as the base of 100, rose from 179.4 in 1960 to 195 in 1963. Farmers' prices, using 1955 as the base of 100, were 139.8 in 1960 and 164.6 in 1963. The nation's wages also rose rapidly. The hourly wage rate for all private activities was 141.9 in 1960, using January 1956 as the base, but it was 180.8 in 1963. Despite these increases, France's world trade continued to progress. Both exports and imports rose steadily from 1960 through 1964, but by the latter year France no longer had a favorable balance of trade. However, the balance of payments situation remained satisfactory.

The economic thrust of Gaullist France was made possible partly by intelligent national planning and partly by technological advances in industry and agriculture. French industries began to attract able young executives, many of whom moved in and out of government posts. This cross-fertilization of the official class benefited both the national economy and the national government. The old wall between politics and business was breached. Georges Pompidou, probably General de Gaulle's most successful premier, worked for the Rothschilds. To a degree unknown in the Third and Fourth Republics, there was a far greater understanding in both camps of the other's problems and objectives.

This did not give France immunity from the problems that beset any booming economy. It did insure a mutual recognition of the main problem of maintaining a rate of growth that would permit full employment while preserving price stability. The problem, of course, is not peculiar to France; it is endemic in Western Europe, and several other countries, notably Britain, suffer more acutely.

No one, certainly no one in the Gaullist government, expected any quick or complete solutions. The Price Stabilization Plan of 1963 slowed the rise in prices and also impressed the public with the government's determination to act. The government also maintained agricultural prices, much to the indignation of the farmers, and overhauled distribution channels, long a prime difficulty in the economy. It would be fair to say that the action of the government in this area showed a good deal more foresight and skill than some of its more spectacular ventures in the field of foreign affairs.

Early in 1965, the expansion in the French economy slowed down. In the previous year the increase in industrial expansion was about four percent, among the lowest rates of recent years. Officialdom took this, as it usually does, with complacency. It saw the bright side. The slowdown insured, it said, that the economy would not "overheat."

This complacency was not shared by either industrialists or workers. By February 1965 they were faced with the beginnings of a recession in the consumer goods industries. Textiles, automobiles, household appliances, home furnishings all felt the strain. Production dropped, unemployment rose, overtime virtually disappeared in many plants. Only the market for agricultural machinery remained fairly steady, a reflection of the revolution that is continuing in French agriculture. Steel production was a bright spot. It rose by thirteen percent in 1964 over 1963 because of an expanding market in Western Europe and the demands of a building boom.

On the whole, the most pessimistic note in the French economic outlook is the shortage of capital investment in France. Orders for machine tools have been static in the last two years. The spending on capital improvement and expansion has not progressed as rapidly as an expanding economy demands.

The French economy has one built-in problem in industrial relations: the difference between wages in the industries run by the state and those in the private sector. The nationalized industries are one area in which the government can act directly to check the wages-prices inflationary spiral. It does.

But by so doing it invites the continuation of the industrial unrest of the last two years.

France sits on a comfortable cushion of foreign and gold reserves. By early 1965 these were at a record figure of more than $5,000,000,000, of which about $1,350,000,000 was held in dollars. At that time the government announced that it would trade $150,000,000 for United States gold and that up to $200,000,000 would be sold for gold later. A month later General de Gaulle proposed the end of a world monetary system that depended on the dollar and the pound as the two reserve currencies.

The Gaullist adventures in the gold market and the General's rather woolly desire to return to the gold standard, announced in his news conference of February 4, were as much political as economic in their origins. The General resents what he considers American economic domination of Europe and the supposed inferiority of the franc as an international currency. Why he should be so troubled about the latter is a mystery. The franc's solidity, compared to the pound, is recognized.

Here we encounter the General's "European Europe" thesis working in a field unfamiliar to him. Most diplomats with whom he comes in contact do not believe that he has ever really understood the tremendous economic power of the United States. Nor, clearly, does he understand that the Administration could take measures in international finance that would harm the French economy very seriously. It has been fortunate for him, and for France, that thus far he has dealt with American presidents who understand their international economic responsibilities.

The foreign policy of General de Gaulle's government keeps the needs of the French economy very much in mind. The welcome given to cabinet ministers and trade missions from Western Europe and Latin America, the Franco-Soviet trade pact of 1964, General de Gaulle's visit to Mexico in March of that year, and his tour of South America in the autumn all emphasized the regime's recognition that there is an economic aspect to French grandeur.

This search for new markets, especially in heavy industrial equipment, became more pronounced throughout the last half of 1964 and in early 1965 when the French economy showed signs of lagging. General de Gaulle and his ministers are aware that the political stability of the early Sixties owed quite as much to the national prosperity as it did to the liquidation of the Algerian war and to constant reassurances of France's independence and importance in the world.

The economic thrust of France produced a revolution in French living, one very similar to that in Britain in the late Fifties. The city-dweller was the first to benefit, and the industrial worker, in nonnationalized industries, benefited most. The most obvious results of the revolution were new housing, a rapid increase in the purchase of home furnishings from furniture to television sets, the boom in car sales, and the growth of a demand for the more expensive foods.

Yet housing remains a serious problem. Statistics published late in 1964 showed that one French family in three lived in a house that was at least one hundred years old. The position is worse in the country, where more than half the houses have been lived in for over a century. But it is in the cities that the housing situation is the most critical, and prices higher.

Housing is a common European problem. But the French suffer more acutely than most. The drift from the country to the cities, a part of any industrial revolution, is greater in France than in the other major industrial powers largely because the revolution began later in France. In 1954, the active agricultural population was 5,200,000. The estimate is that there will be a fall of forty percent to 3,130,000 by 1970. Moreover, France has had to find housing for about a million repatriates from Algeria and for foreign labor brought in to feed an expanding economy. The government program under the fifth economic plan set a target of 470,000 houses to be built yearly. The majority of these will be constructed in and near the cities to accommodate the growing population. Along the Rhone valley, for example, cities that for hundreds of years have showed only a modest growth in population are now bursting out into the countryside as new industry, powered by electricity from the hydroelectric plants in the Alps, spreads up and down the river.

One of the pleasantest impressions the foreigner gets in France is the sense of willingness, indeed eagerness, to cope with new problems. Like all the countries of Western Europe, France has a rising birth rate and a steady flow of population from the country to the cities. Government, national and local, is busily preparing for the day when the nation's population may be seventy or eighty million, much of it in the cities.

An authority called the Central Group for City Planning has been established to deal with the problems of nine principal urban areas, including that of Paris, and three large towns. Representatives of the Ministries of Finance, the Interior, Construction, and Public Works are represented on the Group. Planning, however, is not taken entirely away from local government. But the residual authority left to the local councils is likely to be overridden by the authority of these ministries, increasingly important in a highly centralized government.

The imagination, the spaciousness of the planning reflects the dynamism that is one of Gaullism's greatest gifts to France. Paris, of course, is the most urgent problem. Parks by the dozen, new highways, new schools, new hospitals, new housing projects are now being planned. There may be a certain touch of ruthlessness in government planning. An official retorted, "Of course there is; we must be hard or Paris will become one immense industrial slum."

The government intends to avoid in Paris and elsewhere the growth of sprawling conurbations. A central problem in the provinces is the Lyons-St. Etienne area in southeast France. This area will also include Chambery, Vienne and, ultimately, those other cities south along the Rhone whose light industries have attracted tens of thousands of workers from the countryside. Here the primary problem is communications. Railroads are to be improved and new highways built. Work is being pushed on the superhighway along the east bank of the Rhone. A new airport will be built. Simultaneously the city center of Lyons will be expanded, and in St. Etienne the older industries will be moved out of the city and a modern business quarter constructed.

The other urban areas whose development is under study by the Group are Lille-Roubaix-Tourcoing, Marseilles, Nancy and Metz, Nantes and St. Nazaire, and Bordeaux, Toulouse, and Strasbourg with their satellite towns. The three large towns whose development will be guided by the central planning agency are Grenoble, Rouen, and Nice.

The planning and the implementation of the plans, officials concede, are part of a race against time. But the fact that the government has entered the race testifies to its vigor and foresight. Often there is the impression that the fierce energy generations of Frenchmen poured into the development of distant colonies now is being concentrated on France. And, as the critics of the government insist, not a moment too soon.

The transformation of country life has been slower. There is a striking difference between the energy and obvious prosperity of towns like Toulouse or Valence or Carcassonne and country villages and farms. Partly it is caused by the flow of investment into industry, particularly light industry producing consumer goods, and the realization by the authorities that if the boom is to continue, the industrial worker had to be cosseted with better housing, schools, and utilities.

"My family lives near Avignon," a young man in Montpellier said, "and the farm, although good, is nothing very great, you understand. When I first came here to work, five years ago, I was always given a package of food, a terrine, a good bottle, when I visited. Now, as things are, it is I who bring them something. The income is about the same. But it costs them more to live and, my friend, life for my father and mother and for my elder brother and sister-in-law is just as hard as it ever was."

France, like any country, cannot be truly prosperous while it operates on a two-nation basis. In the countryside there is continued agitation for improvements and against what the peasant considers government extravagance in other fields, including aid to French-speaking African countries and to Latin America. The argument, driven home in *Paris Match* by Raymond Cartier, a gifted writer, was that in many respects France herself is an underdeveloped country and that the money to be distributed abroad would be far better spent at home. This was popular among the French in the low-income groups generally and more popular in rural areas than in the cities. Inevitably any complaint concluded with the query, "And where is the money to come from for this famous nuclear force?"

Out of a prosperous national economy, says the government. But the present growth rate of the economy will have to continue, for the sums the government plans to spend are very high for France or, indeed, for any state except for a super-power like the United States or the Soviet Union.

The total defense expenditure planned between late 1964 and 1970 is estimated in the government's program at 140,000,000,000 francs, or approximately $28,571,430,000. Of this sum 80,000,000,000 or about $16,300,000,000 will be spent on equipment alone. Since the end of the Algerian war, the French have been successfully reducing the yearly running costs for defense, largely by reducing manpower in the armed services. The expectation is that the yearly bill for running costs can be kept to 10,000,000,000 francs a year, or about $2,040,080,000.

Of the sum assigned for defense, 27,400,000,000 francs or about $5,590,000,000 is for the nuclear strike force, including 6,700,000,000 francs (about $1,320,000,000) for nuclear materials. Very large sums have been assigned for the complex job of nuclear testing. The tests of the atomic bombs, France's passport into the nuclear age, were carried out in the Sahara. But an extensive and expensive test site is being built in the South Pacific for the test of France's first hydrogen, that is, thermonuclear, bomb. While the bomb itself is tested, developed, and produced, France must proceed with the necessary research, development, and production of the missiles to carry it. Meanwhile France continues to build the expensive Mirage IV bombers to carry her atomic bombs, bombers that will be obsolete by 1970.

To assess the impact of such a program upon the national economy, two circumstances must be kept in mind. The first is that once France begins to build the atom-powered submarines that will launch the Polaris-type missiles of her second phase of nuclear armament, actual spending is likely to spurt far ahead of estimates. This has been the experience of every Western country engaged in the production of nuclear arms, and there is no reason to believe that the French experience will prove any different.

The second circumstance is the assertion by opposition politicians that the published estimates do not tell all the facts. They claim that a great deal of military spending is concealed in the budget under other, more pacific, headings, and that the overall bill will be much higher than the government is prepared to admit.

Finally, the De Gaulle government does not intend to end its nuclear expansion when the atom-powered submarines become operational. It is already planning the installation of ground-to-ground missiles in underground sites on French soil. The missiles themselves may be produced relatively cheaply under the program for the submarines. But the construction of underground silos is an expensive business and a delicate political issue.

The defense program is very close to De Gaulle's heart. Its critics, who early in 1965 were beginning to question its usefulness, were challenging the General in a sensitive area. Primarily the criticism is on the basis of expense. But the sophisticated politico-military world of Paris doubts the nuclear force on defense grounds. The force, it is charged, is called a deterrent but it is too weak to deter.

The opposition has an issue on both military and economic grounds. But, unless the French economy nose-dives sharply in the immediate future or there is some international development that discloses the relative unimportance of the French nuclear force in deterring the Communists, De Gaulle's opponents are unlikely to do very much with their argument.

There is much criticism of this and other aspects of the government program in France. But criticism is not coherent, powerful political opposition. One of the most astute political tactics of De Gaulle and his ministers has been the consistent denigration of the "old parties" of the Third and Fourth Republic and the warnings that any return to the tumultuous politics of those days would endanger the economic and social gains of the De Gaulle era. Consequently various unhappy groups in French society, the farmers or the workers in the nationalized coal mines, appear psychologically unable to take the plunge into active political opposition. Their memories are long enough. They remember the chaos of the years before De Gaulle.

For years the Socialists, the Communists, the parties of the old center have done their utmost to revive political dynamism in the electorate. But such dynamism as one finds is that of the protest against a single aspect of the government policy, not against the government or the whole policy.

Nor do the various areas of discontent have much in common, politically or socially. The De Gaulle government moved into the middle of 1965 solidly entrenched in power. A mild economic recession had not shaken popular confidence in the government. Foreign policy provided opposition politicians with little ammunition in a country where the masses were largely content to believe that "the General knows best." There were, it is true, those both in and out of the government who saw the storm clouds on the horizon. They doubted, for example, whether enough had been done to prepare the economy for the day when the last trade barriers fall in EEC and French industry stands naked to competition from the German industrial colossus. There were others who felt that the General had gone so far in alienating the United States that should some great crisis arise overnight, France would not receive the support from America it expects and on which the General, for all his talk of independence, obviously counts. But France entered the last half of the decade prosperous and complacent.

An economic depression of major proportions or the sudden disappearance of De Gaulle, individually or both together, could create the conditions for the development of a serious political opposition. The effect of the General's passing, of course, will grow less with each year De Gaulle remains at the head of the state. The momentum given the continuation of *his* kind of France by a long period of the General's rule should not be minimized. If De Gaulle continues as President until the mid-1970's, it seems highly likely that France will accept whomever he designates as his successor.

The Fifth French Republic of Charles de Gaulle represents the major European element in the crisis in Atlantic leadership. In the years since he took power, the General often has seemed to be leading both positively and negatively. The positive aspect is his exaltation of France, his search for "a European Europe," constructed along lines he approves, his conviction that what he calls "the third world" of Asia, Africa, and Latin America is a field for French, and European, assistance and guidance. The negative aspect is De Gaulle's hostility to the two great Atlantic organizations developed in the postwar years, NATO and the Common Market, and his consistent challenge not simply to the leadership of the United States within the Atlantic community but to America's continued influence on policy-making in that community.

While these two contradictory elements of Gaullist France exist, it is impossible to see the country playing the role assigned her by De Gaulle, that of leader of a united Europe of the Common Market countries. Even if the other countries were willing to accept that leadership, which they are not, the base from which France would lead, although stable and prosperous, lacks sufficient power.

There is a great deal of justification for the General's assertion that Europe must lead herself, if she is ever to realize her full political and economic potential. But that leadership can only be collective, and it must have a wider base than any single country or the six countries of the EEC. Let us look now at Europe's great outsider, Britain, and her relation to Europe and America.

## Chapter IV

# BRITAIN, DECAY OR REVIVAL?

The High Cost and Meager Results of Nuclear Independence
•   The Urgency of Change and Resistance   •   The Not-
So-Special American Relationship   •   Europe Again?

Does the British road lead to revival or decay? This is the central question in any assessment of the future of the Atlantic community. It can no longer be avoided, it can no longer be glossed over, certainly not by the British themselves. It is useless to talk to the world of the mid-Sixties of the glories of 1940. The British, whether they know it or not, have reached a crisis in their affairs, one that affects every member of the Atlantic world and, indeed, every member of the British Commonwealth.

Let us begin by recalling what many apologists have said, that Britain's present plight might have been avoided had she been able to join the European Common Market. I say "might" because I am by no means sure that entry into the Common Market would have stimulated the British to make those changes in the national economic structure that are so long overdue. Three years ago, when writing a book about Britain and the Common Market * I was convinced that entry

* *The Supreme Choice: Britain and Europe,* New York: Alfred A. Knopf, Inc., 1963.

81

into Europe would indeed be, in Harold Macmillan's phrase, "the cold shower" that would reawaken and reinvigorate the British people. Now I am not so sure. Membership in the Common Market was not a cure-all. Some of the problems that beset the British economy, some of the weaknesses of British society are not susceptible to external remedies. It is highly doubtful whether the trade unions could be modernized or traditional industries rationalized simply because the economy exchanged a domestic market of 50,000,000 for a continental market of 220,000,000.

There is a school of writers that begins any discussion of Britain with the remark, "We must make allowances for the British," and then mentions the war and postwar austerity, the loss of the Empire, General de Gaulle's veto of British membership in the Common Market. These are all historical facts. But I question whether it is good for the British for these facts to be used again and again to explain the present plight of the United Kingdom. For they do not explain what seems to be the outstanding lack in British life: a sense of purpose and object.

To be fair, the facts stand. The British did suffer terribly in the war, but less than the Germans. The British were brave and they fought longer than any other ally. The British continued their sacrifices during the years of austerity under a Labour government that sometimes seemed to glory in austerity for austerity's sake. They did try to enter the Common Market and were barred by De Gaulle in what still seems to me one of the most irresponsible and narrow actions ever taken by a national leader in peacetime.

Yet the reasons why Britain has become the new sick man of Europe have little to do with these past events. Nor has it anything to do with the surrender of the Empire.

The blunt fact is that the British economy, under both

Tories and Socialists, has not developed as rapidly as that of neighbors of comparable size, France and Germany for example. There has been a monotonous cycle of expansion and stagnation. Nothing that the British governments have done since the economic revival of Germany and France encourages the belief that Britain and Britons can show the vigor and the enterprise necessary to keep pace with modern economic development.

For twenty years the British have been attempting to come to terms with the contemporary world. So, of course, have other peoples, including the Americans. But the British took upon themselves a heavier psychological burden than any other European people. Some Britons were obsessed with the golden dream of nineteenth century empire. Not even the shock of Suez wakened them entirely. Others—and this is very important in understanding Britain's slow postwar economic development—were haunted by the nightmare memories of working-class life in the industrial revolution, a history of recurrent crises in the long, dark night of unemployment. If we are making allowances, we are also indicting the British for their failure, on every level of society, to come to terms with the present.

Let us examine what might be called the Empire trauma and its effect on Britain's ability to compete with her neighbors. The granting of independence to India may have been an act of enlightened statesmanship, just as premature withdrawals from Kenya and Northern Rhodesia may prove to be acts of unmitigated folly. But the question is not reproach or blame, but the manner in which Britain, having given up what made the Empire, continues to cling to the trappings of a nonexistent world position.

The Labour party was quite right, while in opposition between 1951 and 1964, to emphasize that although Britain was not able to remain a world power, she could and should be a world influence. Yet what was Harold Wilson's first comment on this position after he had become Prime Minister? "Britain is a world power, a world influence, or she is nothing." Which sounds like any Tory statement.

The fact is that the retention of a façade of world power costs Britain too much in money and manpower. When Labour took over in October 1964, the total defense expenditure was around $5,600,000,000 a year, of which about $1,000,000,000 was spent overseas. This amounted to about thirty percent of the national budget and a yearly expenditure of $280 for each family, higher than in any other industrial nation except the United States and the Soviet Union. These figures, however, are only part of the story. Defense employed directly four and a half percent of the working population, including about one quarter of the country's qualified scientists.

This tremendous diversion to defense naturally reduced Britain's competitive commercial position vis-à-vis her rivals. There was a heavy cost in men and money for research and development, particularly on nuclear weapons and missiles. Where did the money go? The nuclear deterrent, of course. But also on maintaining the bases in the Middle and Far East. Some of these, Singapore for example, were part of a system of Commonwealth defense. Other bases defended economic interests, oil in the Persian Gulf, rubber and tin in Malaysia.

The question, however, is not whether Britain was right to retain these responsibilities within the framework of the defense of her own and American interests, but whether she could do so and still continue to compete as an industrial power. Both the Kennedy and Johnson Administrations encouraged the British to maintain these bases. Did this advantage to the United States in terms of world stability outweigh the risk of encouraging a steady decline in the British economy? It is doubtful that this question ever troubled the Kennedy or Johnson Administrations because British Conservative governments, although complaining bitterly about the loss of foreign exchange arising from the maintenance of the Army of the Rhine in West Germany, were prepared to shoulder these imperial burdens.

British ministers of defense in the years 1951–1964 invariably argued that one section of the defense budget, that devoted to research and development, paid off in terms of technological advance in industry. The claim just does not bear examination. The British did pioneer in certain fields of aircraft, the vertical-takeoff plane in particular, but the British aviation industry was not large enough, and not well-organized enough, to compete with the huge American companies.

There is a great reservoir of technological ability in the United Kingdom, and, properly employed for industry, it should have been able in the Fifties to put British industry well ahead of that of either France or Germany. The tragedy was, as *The Observer* has pointed out, that postwar governments "fostered technology not, in the first place to make Britain rich, but to make her powerful."

However, any comparison of the industrial structures of the United States and the United Kingdom will show that the British nuclear force was never more than a marginal addition to overall American strength. Certainly, the Chiefs of Staff in Washington were pleased to have British V-bombers on their side and to encourage the building of British atom-powered submarines. No general in history has ever had all the strength he thinks he needs. But this does not change the marginal nature of the British nuclear deterrent in the mid-Sixties.

It was argued that the British nuclear armory would make the country "independent" of the United States. This argument had a definite appeal to two closely allied groups, whose power in British society is still considerable. One group is composed of the remaining sufferers from the Imperial trauma, those who still believe, in the face of the history of the last quarter of a century, that Britain, or indeed any power, can act independently in the world. These people are psychologically akin to General de Gaulle. The second group is made up of Britons who for one reason or another detest any form of dependence on the United States because of mistrust or envy of America. To give them credit, they are perfectly prepared to make the sacrifices necessary to retain nuclear forces independent of America.

Despite its enormous cost in material and trained manpower, however, the British nuclear force never gave the United Kingdom that military independence it was supposed to promote. No situation arose in which Britain, and only Britain, was the object of direct military pressure by another power that also had nuclear arms. Considering Britain's membership in the Western system of alliances, NATO, CENTO, and SEATO, it is almost inconceivable that such a situation would arise. It might, of course. But such a remote contingency hardly seems worth all the billions spent to assure possession of nuclear arms for independent use.

The British nuclear force, that is, the V-bombers of the Royal Air Force, was efficient. But its strength was so small, compared to the thousands of American bombers, missiles, and warheads, that somehow the British nuclear force never gave the country quite as much prestige as Tory ministers believed. Possession of nuclear power, however, did have an important political consequence. As a nuclear power, Britain participated as the theoretical equal of the United States and the Soviet Union in conferences on nuclear disarmament and on banning nuclear tests. At best these were marginal advantages, useful to Tory politicians in impressing voters but not of lasting benefit to the country. Britain's importance in the West rests on much more than the possession of a small stock of nuclear weapons.

In the end Britain's devotion to a high defense budget, and particularly to an independent nuclear deterrent, inhibited the national economy without conferring any real benefits in prestige or power. There must have been a cut-off point somewhere along the way, a moment when it was apparent that the vast expenditures on new weapons were not producing the desired results. Did the abandonment of the Blue Streak missile in 1960 (cost, $235,200,000) or of Skybolt in 1962 (cost, $64,800,000) sound the alarm bells? There is no sign they did.

We can accept, I believe, that the money and effort spent on an independent British nuclear deterrent could have been better spent on the modernization of British industry. We can expect that in the future even the sufferers from the Imperial trauma will see the futility of trying to compete with the United States and the Soviet Union in this field.

What is uncertain is whether Britain will turn this technological know-how to the service of its ailing industries, particularly the bread-and-butter industries that enable Britain to live by exports. There is a glamor about electronics that is absent in a familiar, established industry like shipbuilding. But Britain has lost her old preeminence in this industry largely because of failure in technological improvement. The new methods and the new machinery that this and other British industries need are not so novel. What is needed is their application to ailing industries. Design is old-fashioned in many areas. Production is slow. One method of overcoming these problems is through the application of the new technology.

But here we encounter what I consider to be the core of the British problem: the refusal to accept change under normal conditions. This resistance to change is everywhere. In my experience it is strongest in the industrial working class. There one will meet the shop steward or the white-coat industrial technician who understands clearly that the whole national economy is suffering because British industry refuses to use modern equipment and techniques. Yet, if this general proposition is accepted, the specific proposal of doing something about the plant in which the shop steward or the technician is employed, all sorts of arguments are raised. In many cases the changes suggested by management or by experts are not particularly radical. It can be demonstrated that in the long run they will benefit both the individual worker and the company. Change is opposed, however, by arguments as primitive as "We've always done it this way," or by more technical discussions of wasted time and production while new machinery and new techniques are being installed.

British resistance to change, of course, is not confined to industry. However, that is where it is now having the most damaging effect on the nation's prospects for the future. What is its origin? Is it the result of being a homogeneous, island nation still deeply isolationist in many of its thought patterns? Is it a belief that the slow, cautious approach is the best course for a nation? Is it the conviction that stable government, which the British prize, is best secured when there is a consensus for any progressive step?

One could say "yes" to all three questions and yet be faced with the record to the contrary. For here are a people who, when moved, can invent and improvise in industry and politics with breathtaking rapidity and startling success. Europe, especially the French and the Germans, likes to think of the British as a rather dull, conformist people and, superficially, so they are. How then does one explain the bewildering array of brilliant eccentrics in every field from guerrilla warfare to nuclear physics spawned by modern Britain?

There certainly are arguments, not only in Britain but elsewhere, for the painstaking, tentative approach to change. Reflection is necessary to government and economics. Change for the sake of change can be dangerous. The danger, in Britain's case, is that only a very small percentage of the thinking population seems to recognize that reflection and caution, indispensable though they might have been to the government of a worldwide empire, are not paramount virtues in a Britain facing the world today. The British, unless they pay more attention to the necessity for change, stand a very good chance of following the road to decay rather than the one to revival.

Acceptance of change, the application of technological advances to industry, the abandonment of the Imperial trauma, all demand of the British people sacrifices not of well-being but of time-honored attitudes. The question, then, is whether the morale of Britain in the present circumstances is good enough to enable the nation to break with tradition and change.

The circumstances of Britain in 1965 are not those that favor a great national effort. The years since 1951 have seen a great rise in the living standards of the people. These new home-owners, these proud possessors of cars and television sets, these takers of continental holiday include hundreds of thousands of the class that, thirty years ago, hardly aspired beyond a subsidized municipal apartment, a bicycle, a cheap radio, and two weeks at Blackpool. Their answer is: change? why change things, look what we've got. They claim that they have worked for what they have, and so they have. They assert that things are all right as they are, and so they are —for the moment.

This moment will not last. So few, so very few Britons understand this. To anyone who, like myself, has known Britain in war and peace, in triumph and disaster for a quarter of a century, the moral climate of Britain today is profoundly depressing. What is happening in Britain is not a choice between one course and another but a rejection of choice.

There can be little doubt that the Labour party leaders who ruled Britain in the winter crisis of 1964–1965 understood the gravity of the country's predicament. The Tories, out of office but retaining great power in the economy and the Establishment, were equally aware. Where both failed was in impressing upon the people the terrible seriousness of the situation. Any assessment of the moral climate must start from there.

We are not discussing an insensitive or illiterate people. But we are dealing with a nation so cocooned by years of comparative economic ease that the scare-heads in the newspapers or the grave warnings of political leaders make almost no impression. It may be argued that the British have been over-propagandized, that they have been told for a quarter of a century that they must do this or that to survive. Build Spitfires, Save Coal, Export or Die, Save for Victory; the slogans no longer have any impact. When Harold Wilson asked a renewal of the spirit of Dunkirk, he might just as well have appealed to the spirit of Trafalgar or Agincourt. The British people in their present state are beyond that sort of appeal.

The aversion to change, in this case change from the steady job and the steady employment, which the unions assure the workers can never be changed, is the first problem. But place must also be given to what must be considered as a decline in morals. I am not talking here about the Profumo case. The British upper classes have always been remarkably free in their sexual morals. Nor have I ever noticed any marked difference between the working classes in Britain and those in France and Germany in this respect. I am discussing the decline in the morals of everyday work.

A British exporter told me he reckoned that one out of every ten cases of consumer goods exported by his company would be "accidentally" damaged and then systematically looted on the London docks. A taxi driver told me that his firm was increasingly employed in carrying goods of small bulk and high value to ports because truck crews also "accidentally" damaged the crates and looted them. This seems to me as serious an indictment of the failure of the British workman to grasp the seriousness of his country's situation as any number of wildcat strikes on the docks.

The strikes, the slow-downs, the working to rule, the disputes between unions on demarcation of labor have been part of the Trades Unions' strategy against the employers and against the government, in the form of the nationalized industries, since 1945. They are liable to remain so for years to come, for the simple reason that the men who sit complacently at the top of the Trades Union pyramid and a high proportion of the men who are the actual leaders of the unions have no more control over the working members of the union than you do.

Control, in the critical sense of deciding when to strike, when to accept mediation, when to go slow, when to accept change is in the hands of the shop stewards, the floor bosses of labor. It is impossible to indict a whole group. I have known shop stewards, sometimes in rather hide-bound industries, who were alert and welcoming to change, eager to increase production. But my own observation, confirmed by many on both sides of industry, is that the shop steward is the foremost opponent of improvement and progress in much of British industry.

Most of them accept, albeit somewhat unwillingly, the basic precept that productivity must rise and exports increase if the national affluence is to continue. But they are also unable to realize, or so they say, that increases in productivity and exports will benefit both the bosses and the workers. This is not an echo of Eugene V. Debs' belief that all must rise together. Rather, it is a conviction that any improvement should benefit *only* the working class. Why accept automation in factories? It may benefit the workers in the long run. But it will also benefit the bosses. So let's keep on as we are, we're all right, Jack. But for how long?

Some critics of the shop stewards and the unions charge that the Communists and the Trotskyites have taken over as the decision-makers. Clearly, there are too many Communists and Trotskyites in the key industries, those that could paralyze Britain by strikes in a moment of international crisis. But I doubt if this is a satisfactory answer. The reason has been the timidity of the leaders of the Labour party since 1955, always excepting Hugh Gaitskell, in attempting to educate the great mass of the working class in the realities of the economy of Britain in the present.

It can be argued, as some Labor politicians have argued, that this was the job of the Tory governments that ruled Britain. From 1953 to 1962 I attended the annual conferences of the Labour and Tory parties. These are held, usually, during the first two weeks of October. They offer the observer an unrivaled opportunity to learn at first hand the thinking of the two great parties on the critical questions of the day.

One of the critical questions in those years, and certainly today, is the rationalization of British industry to meet the challenge, not simply of German or Japanese or French competitors, but of a rapidly changing pattern of industrial organization. This, one would have thought, would have been the topic closest to the hearts of Labour's leaders.

The memory, substantiated by my notes, however, is of interminable arguments over priorities within the labor movement and of long, windy debates on nuclear arms. Occasionally some bright spark like Ray Gunter would suggest that labor should adjust itself to the demands of new industrial techniques. But such interjections were drowned in the sea of words about whether the bomb should be banned or how far nationalization should go. Of course, these affairs had their bright moments. Nothing can eradicate from memory the sight of Harold Wilson trying to discourage the applause that greeted Hugh Gaitskell's speech at Blackpool in 1959. And no connoisseur of political inanities should forget Frank Cousins' remarks a year later that Britain didn't need the atomic bomb because she had won the last war without one.

It was only at the Conservative conferences and at the Liberal assemblies that one heard thoughtful speeches about the urgent need for modernization in British industry to meet the challenges of change. Often these were made by pretty dull speakers like Selwyn Lloyd or Reginald Maudling. There was nothing in them to warm the blood, nothing of Labour's 'Nye Bevan or Michael Foot. But they got a great deal closer to the primary ills of Britain than any of their Labour opponents.

Herbert Morrison told me once in 1947, "We've been standing about on street corners for thirty years saying we ought to 'ave a go at running the country. Well, 'ere we are." And there Labour was again, after thirteen years in the wilderness, late in 1964, assuming the rule of Britain. (It is well to remember here the axiom that, although in Britain Labour may form governments, the Tories are always in power.)

Any discussion of Mr. Wilson's government must avoid the obvious pitfall: to talk of long-term policy. The British, except in a few instinctive areas, balance of power, for example, are not given to long-term policies. They are not a doctrinaire people. They are pragmatic.

In opposition Harold Wilson and his henchmen often acted as though they were the true guardians of socialism. In office they did what they believed needed doing to keep the ship afloat. If some of their measures, like raising the bank rate, were indistinguishable from those taken by recent Tory governments, they were operating at least in the mainstream of British pragmatism. If some other measures, like the imposition of a fifteen percent surcharge on imports, offended friends and allies and, incidentally, broke some agreements, they were merely reflecting that trait of Little Englandism that runs so strongly through the policy of what is in theory an international, social-democratic party.

What was most disappointing about Mr. Wilson's government was its inability or unwillingness to come to terms with the basic problem. This is the need to raise, over a long period, Britain's overall output, and especially her exports, to enable her to compete with the other great exporting powers. The Prime Minister and his colleagues made a great to-do about this, impressing in the process some American seers and continental pundits. But George Brown's Declaration of Intent in December 1964? For twenty years Britain has had declarations of intent, not all, admittedly, dressed up in such fine language. And what have they produced? The balance of payments crisis is still there, as it was under Mr. Churchill and Mr. Butler in 1954 and under Mr. Macmillan and Mr. Lloyd in 1962. The economic predicament exists and neither party has solved it.

Both the employer and the employed are at fault in this predicament, but the main burden of blame must rest with the Trades Unions or with what Americans call organized labor. It is unlikely that the issue can be solved under Britain's present form of government because it is difficult to foresee any economic debacle serious enough to force labor to accept the present.

Mr. Wilson's first government was one of all the talents and all the concessions. Within it, the Prime Minister accommodated all the warring factions that, until the virtual collapse of Tory government, had kept Labour from regaining power by dividing the party and reducing its credibility as an alternative. This is not an inquiry into British politics. Our interest here is the effect of the installation of this government on Britain's role in the Atlantic crisis.

Any British government, Labour or Tory, begins life with an advantage, one often discounted, frequently unrecognized but always there. It is that from 1940 onward United States administrations have been forced by circumstance to work more closely with those of Britain than with any other Western government.

This intimacy of operation has had some bad effects on the British side. It has led many politicians and civil servants to expect too much of the relationship. It has encouraged, certainly among the more light-headed London newspaper publishers, a belief, unshaken even by Suez, that Britain can *always* count on American support. It has induced among cabinet ministers a rather too sensitive attitude to what the current administration in Washington thinks and does.

At any rate the situation exists. It is not, however, a question of what we Americans make of it, but of what the British make of it. The community of interests, from the Rhine to Hong Kong, that the two nations share to a degree unparalleled elsewhere, certainly not by China and Russia, offers them great advantages. It also inhibits them to a remarkable degree.

The British have been at fault in two respects. Upon a basic loyalty to the American alliance they have built a tactical diplomatic process they would describe as "too clever by half." This consists of supporting, publicly, the leadership within the alliance of the American Union while privately seeking means to divert the use of that leadership, and power, to the ends of British policy. This is not the rule, but it has been an important exception. And I fear it will become even more prevalent among coming generations of cabinet ministers who, unlike my friend mentioned earlier, missed the hard schooling in Anglo-American loyalty taught by Winston Churchill and Harold Macmillan.

The offenders are not always, or even mainly, cabinet members. Early in 1965 one of Mr. Wilson's advisers told him that the Prime Minister and his cabinet need not worry about American support for the pound because Britain had an effective weapon to keep the Yanks in line. Britain could inform the United States indirectly that if she did not receive the help she needed, the government would throw the $4,000,000,000 worth of American securities, which it holds, onto the New York stock market.* I do not know Mr. Wilson's answer. But I submit that this is an odd way to run an alliance.

The second respect in which Britain fails the alliance is the reluctance of British leaders openly to criticize American

* Private information.

96

policies. Goodness knows, American administrations have never suffered from inhibitions on this score where Britain was concerned. But in Britain, and, most remarkably, since Suez, there has been a belief that it was better, where the Americans were concerned, to proceed by indirection, by subtle suggestion rather than by forthright statements.

There were many occasions during the Eisenhower regime when a stiffer line in London might have helped the two governments avoid mistakes. For example, British leaders, particularly Mr. Macmillan, were generally more aware of the role that General de Gaulle's ambitions for France would play in precipitating the current Atlantic crisis than were most Americans in power during the late Fifties. Yet the tendency in London was to soft-pedal warnings about what De Gaulle might do to NATO and to the equilibrium of the West.

The first great French blow to the development of a wider Atlantic community was directed against Britain, in the form of General de Gaulle's veto of the United Kingdom's application to join the Common Market. Harold Macmillan's government never renewed wholeheartedly its effort to enter Europe, partly because the glee on the part of some Tories at De Gaulle's veto reflected the continuing divisions in the party over Europe, and partly because the government soon moved into a period of crisis that began with the Profumo affair and ended with Macmillan's illness and resignation in the autumn of 1963.

The Labour government numbered a few, a very few, pro-Europeans in its ranks when it took office in 1964. But the mood of the party, set by its Prime Minister and leader, was anti-Common Market. Labour's Britain, it was soon made clear, was willing to cooperate on specific projects with France or any other individual member of EEC. But the new

97

administration, while declaring its interest in participation in the planning of European political unity, made no substantive gesture toward joining the Common Market. Indeed, when Prime Minister Wilson visited General de Gaulle in April he confined his observations on EEC to a pious hope that the gap between the Community and EFTA would be narrowed. It was clear that Mr. Wilson had no interest in entering Europe, and, as a result, the two governments were able to do business in a modest way.

They will explore cooperation in the research, development, and production of sophisticated military and civilian aircraft—the Concorde supersonic airliner is an Anglo-French enterprise—and of advanced computer systems. Both governments realize that, with the costs of such hardware rocketing and with national markets very limited, they must combine to get the planes and computers they want. There is in both capitals a conviction that it is only through such combination that American and West German competition can be met.

The Tories, in opposition, took the initiative. Sir Alec Douglas-Home, the party leader, early in 1965 emphasized a fact that many Britons would like to forget. The country, he said, must "think in terms of industrial cooperation and coordination that is continental and beyond. When it comes to the production of the highly sophisticated machines which will be increasingly in demand—machines requiring heavy expenditure in research and development—their production must be organized on a scale comparable to that of the United States and markets must be complementary. Recent experience in the aircraft industry has underlined the truth of this conception and the same will be true of development in the fields of space and rocketry, telecommunications, computers, and the development of electronics."

At that time, because they were out of government, the

Tories, Sir Alec pointed out, could not foresee the circumstances or the conditions under which Britain and her EFTA partners could take the initiative. Meanwhile he promised Britain must do its utmost to bring "ourselves and our partners and The Six closer together."

"Every country will gain from closer economic union and the maximum political collaboration," Sir Alec emphasized, "and if I am right in saying that the Europe of the future will be one of the great constellations of power—economic, military, and political—then Britain must not shirk her role of helping to shape its destiny."

Sir Alec thus took up where Harold Macmillan left off, and with a great deal more emphasis than his predecessor had ever employed. The Tories' leader had substantial support from his closest associates. Edward Heath, Reginald Maudling, Iain Macleod, Duncan Sandys, Peter Thorneycroft are all convinced "Europeans." Back-bench Parliamentary opposition has dwindled.

Here the Conservatives were doing more than challenging the Labour party's "Little Englandism." They were in fact challenging the familiar opposition to change that inhibits the rationalization of the British economic structure. Opposition to a new approach to Europe reflects the strength in Britain of two concepts that have little validity in the world today.

The first is the Commonwealth. The vision of a globe-girdling Commonwealth, including such varied members as Canada and India in a single family, attracts many in the United Kingdom. But the true Commonwealth in the minds and hearts of most Britons was that first established on the foundations of the white "Dominions," Canada, Australia, New Zealand, and South Africa. For political, as well as economic, reasons this was a real family, as its record in two world wars attests.

99

Now Britain is the center of a tenuous Commonwealth in which Nigeria jostles Canada, and New Zealand, theoretically at least, is equated with Ghana. Certain economic benefits still accrue to the United Kingdom. But does anyone suggest that Britain's export interests in the Commonwealth will be more important in the long run than those in Europe? With Australia, New Zealand, and Canada moving slowly but surely into the dollar area, can it be argued that Britain's old position as the financial center of the Commonwealth is intact?

The harsh fact is that the common interests of the Commonwealth in Britain have diminished as Britain's power has diminished. No amount of high-flown talk by politicians can change that. Nor can it be doubted that Britain's devotion to the Commonwealth's interests, which so influenced France's veto in 1963, was misplaced in view of the subsequent evolution of the economies and policies of Commonwealth members.

The second fading international idea, to which I have referred before, is the "special relationship" with the United States. This, too, has suffered from the reduction of British power. The effect of this relationship on the average Briton is more psychological than material. Until the mass of Britons rid themselves of the idea that the "special relationship" insures them, and the governments they elect, a unique role in the Atlantic community, they will be inhibited from taking the step that must be taken—a new effort to enter Europe.

After the Labour government's fifteen percent surcharge on imports, it should have been clear that the rather tenuous European Free Trade Area would not recover from the blow. It had never been a full-blooded rival of the European Economic Community. It owed its origin to the British; most of its members depended upon and believed in British interest in their economic welfare. Mr. Wilson burnt Britain's bridge to half of Europe. It will be up to his successors to build a new bridge to The Six, that is, the Common Market.

Can this be done? Probably not while General de Gaulle rules in the Elysée. Should it be attempted, in the sense that the ground work is begun now? Certainly. It seems impossible to complete European unity, to maintain an Atlantic community of political and economic interest, and, from the British standpoint, most important, to revive the British economy without British membership in Europe. Given the United Kingdom's proximity to Europe, the growing intercourse between British and continental industry, the general identity of political aims between, say, the Netherlands and Britain, it appears that only the British can keep themselves out of Europe.

The road will not be easy. The British must be prepared to suffer the snubs and occasional insults of General de Gaulle, his ministers, and his successor. They will find, however, that much as the General likes to represent himself as the spokesman for The Six, he has many enemies on the issue of British entry.

The British government that knocks on Europe's door will have to do a great deal of explanatory spade work. This was not done adequately in 1961 and 1962. Nor was the opposition to entry within the Tory party, now reduced, adequately answered by Macmillan and his ministers. The government of the day also must show a more open mind about Europe, a greater willingness to accept what has been done in the Community than the Macmillan government ever did. Above all, the British will have to view with greater realism their ties with the Commonwealth and the "special relationship" with the United States. The whole process will require intelligent political perseverance. Europe is the great test of Britain in the second half of this century.

All this will demand a change in British political attitudes as drastic as those the situation demands in the economic field. These changes cannot be evolutionary. They must be rapid and thorough. What I deeply fear is that the new Britain that has arisen since 1950 will be unable to make further drastic changes.

Britain has undergone almost a quarter of a century of social and political change. This is evident. But the rate, or the desire for basic change, has slowed down at the very time when it is most necessary. Early in 1965 most Britons I met in a tour across southern England and Wales seemed certain that the most radical changes had been made. Of course, Harold Wilson might do something about education. And someone ought to stop those people from making so much money on land speculation. And it was a crying shame that the unions had too much power. And why didn't we get rid of, or build up, Britain's nuclear forces.

The people of Britain seemed to be lapsing into a period in which they were prepared to abandon the direction of their destinies to others. They were not willing to renew the campaign for a leap into Europe. On the whole they appeared more favorable to a comfortable economic absorption into the United States economy. This is a two-way street. Although the Americanization of British economy has been attacked by Labour politicians for many years—General de Gaulle, too, has made great play in France with this bogey man—there is in Britain's case a considerable amount of British investment in the United States. Most Americans don't know about it. And those who do forbear to complain, seeing it merely as a welcome aspect of transatlantic interdependence.

102

British direct investment in the United States in 1964 was somewhere in the neighborhood of $2,500,000,000. This was concentrated mainly in industry, oil, finance, and insurance. Indirect investment, government holdings, investment trusts, unit trusts, pension funds, and private and company portfolios was estimated at about $3,780,000,000.* Since the time when the British were on their uppers just after the war, their investment in the United States has risen by over one hundred and fifty percent.

There has been, as everyone knows, a great expansion of American investment in Britain in the same period. To this proliferation of economic ties must be added the evident social fact that the two countries today are much more like each other than they were in 1914 or 1939 or 1950.

This is not primarily the result of an Americanization of Britain in the sense that the British are imitating our society or want to be like the United States. Rather, it reflects the tendency of great industrial nations to evolve the same sort of societies, in which the mass of the people wear the same sort of clothes, drive the same sort of cars, see the same movies and often the same television programs. This is not an Anglo-American phenomenon. The traveler in Western Europe will notice how much alike, outwardly at least, are the people of Lyons, Frankfurt, and Turin. National individuality in dress, in amusements and, slowly, in food is one of the casualties of European prosperity.

Here is another Anglo-American paradox. In their ways of life the average American and the average Briton today are closer than they have ever been. But, at the same time, the drastic change in the power relationship between the two countries insures a growing difference in their outlook on world affairs. This would have occurred whatever the out-

* *The Sunday Times* of London.

come of the 1964 election in Britain, and the divergence will continue, as long as Britain wishes to remain independent, under any sort of government.

As long as Britain wishes to remain independent . . . For those who witnessed the startling renaissance of British vigor and enterprise in 1940 (industrial as well as military, it is worth remembering), references to Britain as the fifty-first state in the union have always appeared ludicrous. But are they quite so ludicrous in the mid-Sixties? Britain's future role, I believe, is as part of a European union, federation or confederation. Yet it must be recognized that the stagnation of her economy and the consequent loss of military power and political influence abroad must impel many Britons toward an easy way out.

One easy way is increasing dependence upon the United States, a gradual movement into the American economic sphere. The interdependence of the two economies is already established. The rocketing costs of modern armaments may lead an impoverished Britain to rely more and more upon American weapons for defense and the abandonment of independence in the key area of nuclear arms. This process, in fact, was well advanced long before Harold Wilson went to Downing Street.

As a highly political people, the British are quite capable of displaying all the outward signs of independence while, behind this façade, they become increasingly dependent upon the American power. After all, the Canadians, who yield to no one in displays of brash nationalism, are daily becoming more and more a part of a vast economic, political, and social bloc that reaches north from the Rio Grande to the Arctic and is centered on Washington and New York. The Australians and New Zealanders, other peoples of firm national convictions, are moving at a slower pace toward inclusion in an

104

undeclared American group. In time, why not Britain? There is nothing in the recent histories of the two countries to make the question irrelevant. Except, perhaps, that Britain's refusal to rationalize her economic situation makes her a bad risk for further economic integration with the United States.

The other easy way out, often discussed in the early Sixties when Britain was "havering," as the Scots say, about entering Europe, was the United Kingdom's gradual assumption of a role somewhat akin to that of Sweden. The idea attracted many "Little Englanders" among the Socialists who saw it as a means of opting out of embarrassing and expensive national commitments overseas and of achieving neutrality in the great power struggle.

Historically the idea is not as fanciful as it may appear at first sight. The Swedes were once a great military power and political influence in Europe, capable of taking on and defeating the Russians and the Prussians. But since the Napoleonic era they have withdrawn into a prosperous and jealously guarded neutrality. Why, the Little Englanders asked, should not Britain follow the same course?

It is impossible, however, to believe that the genius of the British people will allow them to take either of these easy ways out of their present dilemma. Geography and history have placed them at the heart of the Atlantic community. It is in our American interest, and in the interest of that community, that they continue to play a full role in its political and economic progress. But how? With what?

Five years ago, ten years ago the questions would have been easy to answer superficially. A few references to the Battle of Britain and El Alamein, a quotation from Shakespeare, would have reassured the doubters. It is the measure of Britain's present plight that those who believe most in her must ask these questions.

The key question is "how." This deals not so much with the British ability to play a role worthy of their past, but with what stimulus is necessary to induce them to play it.

The strong vein of nationalism common to the older European nations, and tapped so successfully by General de Gaulle in France, exists in Britain. The British have a reputation and a record for political stability. But this does not preclude the presence of ambitious extremists on both the left and the right. It is easy to envisage the rise of a Tory figure, deeply involved in the mores and ambitions of the middle class, who might lead a sort of British Gaullism. The primary conditions would have to be present: the further impoverishment of that class by a decline in Britain's political and economic position in the world, reflected in a growing tendency to depend either on the United States or Europe or to lapse into Little England.

We might then see a brief, because it would lack a true base, burst of British energy. The Trades Unions would be cajoled or, in the last resort, dragooned into acceptance of government economic policy. Economic planning, sternly implemented, might be introduced on a more lavish scale than anything the Attlee or Wilson governments have attempted. The appeal to "the meteor flag of England" would be emphasized. The outward symbols of democracy would be observed, but Britain could lapse into an authoritarianism ill-attuned to her fundamental political nature.

This is a more likely solution than the establishment of a left-wing Labour nationalism. The Labour party may well be the voice of the majority of the British working class. But it has never successfully generated or used the innate patriotism of that class or any other in Britain. In times of stress the British turn, instinctively, to someone who seems to represent the ruling classes. I say "seems" because when Winston Churchill led Britain in 1940, it was assumed by many in America that he embodied aristocratic leadership. In fact Churchill was then, and for many years afterwards, a maverick from the Establishment. The prewar rulers thought they could use him at a particularly desperate moment in British history. In the event, he grew too big for them. But a British leader, even in the changing society of the Sixties, must have something of Churchill's background, above all, his blind, unwavering, noble devotion to his country and its history.

But none of this answers the second question: "With what." The parlous state of the United Kingdom's economy since the end of World War II has given the impression that the British are poorer than they are. This impression has been deepened by the natural tendency of the Briton to see the country going to the dogs, to praise any nation but his own, and to lead the uninitiated to believe he is not being particularly interested in doing better.

Britain has a great reservoir of scientific and technical skill and an adept and, when moved, energetic labor force. Her industrial and financial resources, although far less than they were in the great days of the Victorian era, remain very great. Here we should note the very strong demand on the part of many disparate elements in British society for a more energetic use of these resources. But it is discouraging to note that these people—the young investment banker in the city, the white-coat worker in electronics, the eager young civil servant, the strident critic on the local newspaper—have no common ground at present.

I do not mean by this that they are Labour or Tory or Liberal. I mean that in the years since the war there has been a gradual and only half-realized rejection of the common British interest. Those who are the most violent for change unfortunately are those least likely to combine with others of the same outlook on a truly national basis. Perhaps this is because for nearly fifteen years the idea of the communal interest, of patriotism, if you will, has been held up to ridicule by a generation of adroit novelists, playwrights, and publicists.

Britain needs change, rapid change. But as long as those who see the need for it, and who have the youth and energy to work for it, are so deeply divided I see little hope that they can bring it about. On one hand we have a country in desperate need of change. On the other we have a society boasting a very high quota of intelligent, restless, energetic people who, united, could meet the need. Nothing Germany or France has done in the last fifteen years cannot be done or surpassed by Britain. But what is the spark, where is the challenge that will release their energies?

"I wish we 'ad a Churchill," a man said in a pub on Chandos Street. I knew what he meant, but I also knew that his wasn't the answer. There must be a consensus among Britons now, as there was in 1940, before there is a basis for leadership. And that consensus must begin with the national recognition that Britain cannot go on as she is. It is because so many Britons believe she can, that the country is in her present plight.

No one can blink the attractions of life in Britain, that is, in her more favored sections, as it has been lived since the mid-Fifties. There have been social problems, the influx of colored immigrants from the West Indies and Africa and India and Pakistan, for example. There have been, as we have seen, recurrent crises over the balance of payments or the trade gap. There has been a steady lowering of moral standards, and so there has been in the United States or in any other Western power you care to mention.

But on the whole Mr. and Mrs. John Bull have never, in

Mr. Macmillan's much misinterpreted phrase, had it so good. To them there is no urgent need for change, no special virtue in enterprise, no attraction in novelty. Indeed, to the couple, there is so much that is novel in their own rise to affluence that they are sated with change. What they do not realize is that innovation in Britain is slow compared to that in other countries, that the rather gradual changes they consider revolutionary have been accepted for years in rival industrial economies.

Complacency is a sad situation for any society. It is grievous to see a great people so sunk in it that they cannot make more than superficial changes. And yet, my bet is on Mr. and Mrs. Bull. Ten years ago, seeking the single resource that encouraged an optimistic view of their future, I chose that indefinable element, character. It is there still, behind the tawdry trappings of a newly affluent society. It better be— they will need it.

## Chapter V

# GERMANY ON THE BOIL

Reunification vs. the Ties with the West • The Danger
of National Independence • Herr Strauss in the Wings •
France and Germany: the Unhappy Alliance • The
Coming Moment of Truth

The national political developments in Western Europe
that have helped bring about the Atlantic crisis vary in character from country to country. In France the challenge to
transatlantic cooperation arises largely from the ideas, authority, and influence of Charles de Gaulle. In Britain the
socio-economic structure is the root of the problem.

But in the Federal Republic of Germany the problem, in
the largest sense, is political. What is important to Germany's
allies in the Atlantic community is not primarily which of the
major parties, the Christian Democratic Union/Christian
Socialist Union or the Social Democratic Party, rules, but the
direction of German political development on two great and
connected problems in the next five years. These problems,
which affect every German, and—let us not forget it—every
American, are the reunification of Germany and Germany's
future attitude toward the great blocs of East and West. This
is a period of the utmost importance to Germany.

For seventeen years, ever since General Lucius D. Clay

110

decided to introduce a credible currency into what was then the American Zone of Occupation, West Germany has been virtually a political and military dependency of the United States. At the outset she was also an economic dependency. But "the German miracle" of the early Fifties enabled Bonn to operate on the strongest economic base in Europe.

There was naturally a great deal of opposition abroad to this political and military relationship. When the iron imperatives of the cold war began to ease after Stalin's death, criticism of American coddling of the Germans developed. On the west, the British, the Dutch, the Danes, the Norwegians were all strongly opposed, as peoples if not invariably as governments, to the American policy. On the east, the U.S.S.R. and the East European states were ferociously critical. The reasoning behind the attacks by the Communist governments on American policy was obvious. American support for the Federal Republic helped block Soviet military and political ambitions in Central Europe.

However, in the nervous atmosphere of the early Fifties, Americans tended to overlook the powerful Germanophobia of Eastern Europe. In those days Soviet opposition to any United States policy was enough to secure its support by American public opinion. When it was suggested that Russian and satellite opposition to the American policy of building up Germany had a good bit to do with German aggression in two world wars and the behavior of the German forces in the second, this was dismissed as the vaporings of fellow travelers. Soviet propagandists, naturally, exploited American policy in West Germany, creating the picture of American and German generals planning a new war that would devastate Eastern Europe anew.

Those who argued that some attention should be paid to the feelings of the Poles, Czechs, Hungarians, and others never got a real hearing. The German-American alliance, born in the exigencies of the Czechoslovak Putsch and nourished by the hard and anxious years in Europe that followed the outbreak of the Korean War, prospered. It was militarily rational. It was anti-Communist, and, therefore, it must be right. It suited the mood of the times.

But the German-American alliance, which is now the military heart of NATO, and NATO itself, and all the other combinations that have arisen, the Common Market and the French-German Treaty of Cooperation, have not been able to solve the central German issue. This is German reunification. The question has been with us now for twenty years. It is the colossus among Europe's political issues because it affects the future of the entire continent.

The important secondary issue raised by General de Gaulle —whether Germany's interests lie with a European Europe or with an Atlantic community—cannot be resolved until there is a solution to German unity. Until there is at least a framework on which Germany can be reunited, it is not much good talking about European Union or an Atlantic community because a viable European Union and a true Atlantic community presuppose the membership of a united Germany.

The question is big. It deals with the future of eighty-odd million of the most industrious, inventive, and virile Europeans. The question is dynamite. For both the Germans and their neighbors it has a high emotional content. And, until the two Germanies come together, as the rest of Europe must come together, there will be no sure peace for the old continent. The issue affects Scots and Basques, Texans and Danes as surely as it affects Pomeranians and Swabians.

The question is urgent; just how urgent few Americans realize. Here is another difference in the European and American approaches to Europe. To many in Washington the issue of German reunification is one that can be considered leisurely in long consultations among the ambassadors of the four interested powers, the United States, the United Kingdom, France, and West Germany.

Europeans see it differently. In West Germany what the leading parties say and, if possible, do about reunification will have a profound effect upon the elections. But the urgency is not confined to the Federal Republic. In Brussels, The Hague, Paris, London, and the capitals of the East European states the belief is spreading that something must be done soon about German unity. In this atmosphere of urgency new proposals, like De Gaulle's, and old ones, like Polish Foreign Minister Adam Rapacki's, are being examined for clues that will solve the mystery of how Germany is to be reunited in peace and without disturbing the stability of Europe.

The argument that reunification is essential to European peace has invited virulent criticism for the last twenty years. At its crudest, such criticism, equally vehement in Warsaw or London, is focused on the terrible memories of the past. It can be summarized in the question: why in God's name unite the Germans? Look what they've done, twice, in this century when they *were* united.

An entire generation in the West sympathizes with this argument. It spent a great deal of valuable time at the receiving end of German military aggression. The Germans *did* start the war. The Germans *did* act with terrifying brutality, not only toward the Russians and Poles but toward Americans, Britons, and French. Authoritarianism lets loose the worst in the Germans, and any development that encourages it, such as a national crusade for unity, should be a proper target for the severest warnings of which the great powers are capable.

The crux of the matter is that the *division* of Germany may be the motive for the development of a new authoritarianism. This is the immediate danger. The dangers of a united Germany are understood in the West and in the East. But it is foolish to carry the argument too far. It is un-Christian and politically absurd to continue a vendetta from 1945 to 1965, especially when the hatred it generates obscures the wisdom of positive action. The West can forgive without forgetting.

Nothing so betrays the poverty of thinking on foreign policy among many members of the British Labour party as their unwavering hostility and distrust where Germany is concerned. This is accompanied, in the case of many Labour M.P.'s, by a fatuous willingness to see East Germany as a socialist paradise free from the militarism they profess to see in the Federal Republic. It was Winston Churchill, the father of victory over the Third Reich, who first offered the hand of friendship to Germany, not the university professors and civil servants of the Labour party who played, with some honorable exceptions, a rather minor role in the great conflict.

Another, and more subtle, argument against support for reunification is that the present division of Germany keeps Europe in balance. Any attempt to disturb this balance by uniting Germany would invite a great crisis in European affairs. This is a counsel of weakness. It overlooks the existence of a crisis. Germany's division, the desire of millions of Germans for unity, the division of Berlin are a crisis. Even in periods of détente between the Soviet Union and the United States, the division of Germany must be recognized as a danger to peace, an incitement to dangerous adventure by Germans of East or West.

This continuing crisis in Germany will affect the future development of West German politics and policies. As long as Germany is divided, West German politicians, unscrupulous or otherwise, will have at hand a highly explosive national issue. Other members of the Atlantic community, understandably, fear the advent in the Federal Republic of a government whose bias is toward nationalist independence rather than internationalist interdependence. In the former they see the taint of authoritarianism. The other Western powers may fear this development. Nevertheless they acknowledge two facts: as long as Germany is divided the danger exists, and, much as the governments of West and East Europe would deplore a revival of authoritarian nationalism, there is plainly little they can do to prevent it.

This sort of government, once in power in West Germany, could arouse mass emotional support for reunification and, independently, make the first approach to Moscow. The complacent agree that it "could" but ask whether in fact it "would." The Germans of the Sixties, they point out, are less sensitive to the call of unity than the Germans of 1945–1950.

To a degree this is true. Millions of Germans from the East, including Czechoslovakia and Poland as well as East Germany, have settled in the Federal Republic. Inevitably the memories of the homeland fade. The exiles' grievances against the East German Communists and their Russian masters are now ten, fifteen years old. At the moment, there is no overwhelming national demand for unity, although it is important to note that no German political party omits a reunification plank from its platform.

The danger lies in how an authoritarian, nationalist government would use the latent desire for unity. Modern mass propaganda could turn a popular issue into a crusade overnight, a crusade in which popular emotion overcame rational argument. Such a crusade would be very difficult to restrain in Germany; it would be impossible to prevent from abroad.

Suppose a nationalist government in Bonn opened negotiations on unity with the U.S.S.R., offering withdrawal from NATO as a guarantee that a united Germany would be neutral. Who will stop the Germans from negotiating? Would any single European government, would NATO use force to prevent reunification? Of course not. The reaction would be oral. We would hear a great deal of talk about the German danger and, in the circumstances, rightly so. A chorus of "I told you so" would arise in every Western capital where there were those who, from the start, opposed the policy of German conciliation. We also would hear a good deal, as we did in the early Thirties, about Germany's legitimate aspirations to unity and about how the reunification of the country would contribute to European stability.

The dangers of bilateral, that is, German and Russian, reunification are obvious. All of Germany might well be lost to the development of political union in Western Europe and in the Atlantic community as a consequence of the price paid for unity. A united Germany, theoretically neutral, would hold the political balance in Europe, courted by East and West. Who would keep her neutral? Who would prevent her making her own nuclear weapons?

The West would not be dealing with the Germany of 1945–1950, helpless and occupied. Or even the Germany of the Fifties, painfully working her way to international respectability and prosperity. West Germany today is a powerful, modern state with the strongest conventional armed forces—and the strongest industrial economy—on the continent. It is located at the heart of the conflict between East and West. Already many of its politicians have embraced the concept of independence of the United States first advanced by General de Gaulle.

In the circumstances, the Atlantic powers, principally the

United States, the United Kingdom, and France, with the cooperation of the Federal Republic must seek German reunification through negotiations with the Soviet Union. The alternative, a Russian-German deal, is too dangerous. The West must find a means of reuniting Germany, certainly based on self-determination, that will not disrupt the Atlantic community or invite new Soviet political progress in Central Europe.

A start should be made now. The postwar organization of Western Europe already is under serious strain. Two or three years hence it may not be strong enough to support the joint diplomatic effort of negotiating with the Soviets on so vital an issue. Should Western Europe disintegrate into a loose confederation of rival nationalisms, as De Gaulle evidently intends, Germany will deal with her future on her own. Little in the General's own program for German unity offers much solace to the anxious Germans who understand the urgency of the problem. Here is what he said on February 4, 1965, at his news conference:

"What must be done will not be done, one day, except by the understanding and combined action of the peoples who have always been, who are, and who will remain principally concerned by the fate of the German neighbor—in short, the European peoples. For those peoples to envisage first examining together, then settling in common, and last guaranteeing conjointly the solution to a question which is essentially that of their continent—this is the only way that can make reappear, this is the only link that can maintain, a Europe in the state of equilibrium, peace, and cooperation from one end to the other of the territory which nature has given it.

"Certainly, the success of such a vast and difficult undertaking implies many conditions. Russia must evolve in such a way that it sees its future, not through totalitarian constraint imposed on its own land and on others, but through progress accomplished in common by free men and peoples. The nations which it has satellized must be able to play their role in a renewed Europe. It must be recognized, first of all by Germany, that any settlement of which it would be the subject would necessarily imply a settlement of its frontiers and of its armament in agreement with all its neighbors, those on the East and those on the West. The six nations which, let us hope, are in the process of establishing the economic community of Western Europe, must succeed in organizing themselves in the political domain as well as in that of defense, in order to make a new equilibrium possible on our continent. Europe, the mother of modern civilization, must establish herself from the Atlantic to the Urals in harmony and cooperation with a view to the development of her vast resources and so as to play, in conjunction with America, her daughter, the role which falls to her in the progress of two billion men who desperately need it. What a role Germany could play in this world ambition of the rejuvenated old continent!" *

The concept, like many of those put forward by the General, is superficially attractive. But on rereading, it quite plainly is not a program for reuniting Germany but for delaying reunification. The conditions laid down by the General are so complex, the situations he foresees will take so long to evolve, that in effect he was telling the world that nothing can be done about reunification now.

Naturally, the Soviet Union welcomed the General's words. Any proposal that excludes American influence from Europe, especially on an issue as important as German reunification, is certain of applause from Moscow. The Russians interpreted De Gaulle's words as another French movement away from

* Official French government translation.

the Western alliance and toward an understanding with the East. They have their own diplomatic strategy on unity and nothing would suit them better than the absence of the United States from negotiations.

By excluding the United States from talks on negotiations, De Gaulle's proposal strengthened a Soviet position that was already strong. The Soviet Union holds the key to German unity. Unless the political, military, and economic power of the United States is used to support any Western approach to the Russians on reunification, the approach will fail. If the United States does not use its power, then those Germans who would trade unity for the abandonment of their country's ties with the West, NATO in particular, will be encouraged.

Even with Western Europe still reasonably cooperative politically, the difficulties facing Germany on the path to reunification are formidable. There is national support in Germany for unity. Some of this, clearly, represents blind, vengeful nationalism at its worst. But most of it reflects the deep, patriotic feelings of millions of Germans who want their country reunited, whose friends and families live on the other side of the Iron Curtain and who are desperately worried about their fate. Yet these Germans face abroad the same psychological problem as the nationalists. Indeed, it is because of what rampant German nationalism did under the Kaiser and Hitler that the opposition to unity is so strong among the European states.

Poland, Czechoslovakia, Austria, and other East European states see the recreation of a single German state as an immediate economic and political danger. Their concern, now, about a German military menace is less pronounced. The East Europeans hope that the nuclear strength of the Soviet Union will suffice to deter any reestablishment of German

119

militarism. But memories are long. Many still remember that it was the Soviets who, in the Thirties, helped the Germans train the Reichswehr that became the foundation of Hitler's armies, which, of course, were turned finally against Russia.

Opposition to German unity is equally strong, although perhaps more disguised, in the West. In theory the British, French, and American governments support it. But it would be a bold diplomat who asserted that this support would continue if reunification suddenly became possible. Diplomats and politicians throughout Western Europe understand latent public opinion on this issue, no matter what they may say in speeches. The spectacle of the reunification of eighty million hardy, vigorous, and industrious Germans in the center of Europe would send a tremor of apprehension through Europe from Norway to Greece.

These, then, are the dimensions of the central German problem; how is unity to be achieved, through multilateral negotiation or independently by Germany? The second, and related, problem is how the Western powers are to bind Germany to them so that she will not move on her own. What can be done now to strengthen Germany's ties with the Atlantic community? The problem is one of tactics rather than strategy. The West, including General de Gaulle, agrees that the ties should be strengthened. The question is how this is to be done. And exactly which ties are involved?

The first and most familiar means is through the establishment of European political unity based on the six powers of the Common Market. Ever since the establishment of the European Economic Community, political leaders of the six nations have looked to the day when economic union would be followed by political union. The German, French, Italian, and Belgian governments have all made proposals to this end. The Council of Europe, legislative committees, academic groups, private organizations have produced a flood of suggestions and studies dealing with the question.

As in the case of German reunification, the process is bound to be a long one. For the reasons mentioned above, it is to be fervently hoped that by the time the Germans approach unity, West Germany, the most prosperous and powerful part of the country, will be bound as tightly as possible to the Atlantic community.

The principal stumbling block, today and for some time to come, is French policy. Although this is the policy of General de Gaulle at the moment, there is little reason to doubt that it will also be the policy of his immediate successors. It is a negative policy based quite openly on unremitting opposition to any program for political union that envisages the establishment of supranational organizations. In other words, no federal government, no true United States of Europe. The best that Europe can hope for as long as De Gaulle and his heirs are in control in France, and in a position to block progress toward federalism, is the development of a European confederation of national states.

Such a confederation would not include the supranational political organizations or the treaty commitments indispensable if Federal Germany is to be bound irrevocably to membership in a West European Union. It lacks the necessary degree of unity. Nor is it the sort of Europe that can build the political equality with the United States within an Atlantic community that is essential to greater cooperation in the Western world. As long as Europe persists in substituting narrow nationalism for federation, she cannot generate the true European spirit that alone will enable the continent to develop political unity. Beyond that, it is highly questionable whether a Europe built on The Six, that is, a Europe that excludes Britain, Norway, Denmark, Sweden, Switzerland, and Austria, can really represent the continent.

But the gravest demerit of Gaullist policy in this respect is the weakness of the ties that would bind Germany to her partners. It is highly doubtful that a Federal government inspired by the national emotion of unity would be deterred from negotiating with the Soviets by the rather tenuous links to its allies envisaged in De Gaulle's Europe of Fatherlands. This would be especially true if De Gaulle succeeded in convincing the Germans that his idea of a European Europe could work only if Bonn severed her political and military ties with the United States.

This choice between membership in a European Europe and membership in an Atlantic community, through NATO, already has been offered the Germans by the General on more than one occasion. It is a choice that will be offered again. Each offer will deepen the dilemma of those Germans who believe in European unity but who believe equally that their most prudent political and military policy is to maintain their ties with the United States at their present level of intimacy. Like reunification, this is not exclusively a German dilemma. The choice Germany makes will influence the whole political development of the West, and it will certainly affect directly America's hopes for retaining a united Germany as part of the Atlantic world.

There is a latent danger of a revival of authoritarian nationalism in Germany. But the danger is less than it was five or ten years ago. There have been profound changes in the mood of the Germans in the last twenty years. If these changes continue, and if there is no single national issue on which German passions focus, the West and East can be reasonably certain that the old overbearing attitude toward

Germany's neighbors will be replaced by a cooperative European attitude.

Already years of prosperity and political stability have brought about some outward changes in the German character. Ten years ago the German tourist abroad was noted for his surly boisterousness. At home, the Germans were famous for the willingness with which they tried, from cabinet minister to taxi driver, to play one European off against another. In discussing the war the Germans professed an ignorance about the Hitlerian atrocities, which few foreigners believed, and retained a defiant belief that the war and the ruin it brought them and others could not have been the fault of Germany. Slowly these attitudes are disappearing.

Whatever Europe's feelings about the past, the German record in postwar cooperation is impressive. The movement toward European unity started as a national policy in West Germany and France. The Germans have honored their commitments to NATO and, under prodding, to EEC. The German government and German finance have carried out a program of investment in underdeveloped countries of Africa and Asia. The Germans are trying hard to be good Europeans. In view of this, they are understandably sensitive to what they consider the unjust prolongation of foreign hostility arising from the Hitler era.

Germanophobia in a newspaper editorial or a political speech raises German tempers. A section of the British press and of the Labour party is especially virulent. Britain's attempt to enter EEC would have won more enthusiastic support in Germany had it not been for the tendency of some British newspapers and politicians to think of Germany in terms of 1940 or, at best, of 1945.

German politicians have demonstrated a commendable coolness under the pressure exerted by De Gaulle and an ability to rise above his calculated slights. The contemporary German leaders keep their tempers even when accused by their French ally of being American satellites. They are willing to put up with this because they understand that the new friendship between France and Germany must be the starting point for any future political union.

The Federal Republic of Germany now has twelve army divisions, a total of 400,000 men, two air force groups whose main weapons are fighter and fighter-bomber planes, and a growing navy. All the West German forces are committed to NATO. Germany, certainly from the standpoint of ground forces, and, possibly, on a basis of all-around strength and efficiency, thus has the most powerful conventional forces in Europe. Fifteen years ago when the first, furtive moves were being made toward German rearmament, opponents of this measure argued that to rearm the Germans was to reinsure another bid by Germany for European hegemony.

As we know, nothing like this has happened. Nor is there any sign that it will happen. There are, of course, material reasons why it has not occurred. The West German forces are so interlocked with those of their NATO allies, the dependence of Germany on American nuclear support and arms supply is so great, that it would be almost impossible for Germany under the present political regime to take the sort of independent action that was the bogey man of the postwar years.

Nor has there been a revival of fascism in Germany, although many have tried, especially in the immediate postwar years. Credit must go to the leaders of the Federal Republic, principally Chancellor Adenauer, and to the Allied High Commissioners, notably the late Sir Ivone Kirkpatrick, who combined to eliminate neo-Nazi elements, such as the Naumann circle, whenever and wherever they appeared.

The romanticists are tempted to believe that Germany has learned her lesson. Perhaps the answer is simpler than that. Nations change, and Germany has changed more rapidly than most. Once the great outsider, Germany now is safely and honorably within the West's system of alliances. Once friendless, she now has powerful friends in every Western capital. Although still feared in Eastern Europe, she finds that even there attitudes are changing and that Krupps, a name synonymous with the German war machine in two world wars, is welcomed to Poland to help in building Polish industry.

Certainly there is a fascist fringe in Germany, as there is in France and Italy and Britain. Clearly there are many Germans who, for a variety of reasons, do not believe democracy is a workable system of government. Too many of the war criminals went unpunished, too much that was done between 1933 and 1945 has been glossed over by Germans and their friends.

But the proof of fifteen years of change is there. Bonn has remained faithful to the concept of European interdependence. The United States has no more loyal ally in NATO. Perhaps this is because the Germans, who know the Russians better, are less ready to believe in the existence of a true détente with the Soviet Union than the French or the British. The umbilical cord that binds the Bundeswehr to the Pentagon remains uncut.

Except for the death of Ernest Reuter, the Mayor of Berlin who was the ablest Social Democrat of his day in Germany, the Federal Republic has been lucky in its leaders. Dr. Ludwig Erhard became the Republic's second chancellor, replacing Dr. Adenauer. With the widening of West Germany's interests beyond Europe, he has had to deal with problems that did not arise during his predecessor's long period of rule.

Dr. Erhard's touch is surer on economic policy than on foreign affairs, where he and his government are prone to the old German inability to understand foreigners. But on the central question of the Federal Republic's international priorities, the Chancellor has shown good judgement.

The present Chancellor does not have the bravura of many political leaders in Germany. He is stolid and rather pensive. His nickname is "rubber lion." But he exudes common sense and his quiet demeanor is no handicap to his country. Europe has had enough of dashing national leaders in Germany.

The Chancellor, although he looks, and usually is, amiable, can be tough. The French at first misjudged him because he accepted without violent protests some of De Gaulle's brutally rude remarks about the new government's Atlanticism, meaning its fidelity to the American connection. However, when De Gaulle tried to bully Erhard into breaking this tie, he got nowhere.

Chancellor Erhard suffered at the outset of his rule from the presence of Dr. Adenauer. Although retired from the chancellorship, *der Alte* remained a power in the government party and a willing critic of his successor. Through "leaks" to newspapermen and whispers to old party friends, Dr. Adenauer sought to keep German policy on the lines he had laid down during his long chancellorship. He, too, failed because, like De Gaulle, he failed to realize that there was more lion than rubber in the makeup of his successor.

Dr. Adenauer and, to some measure, modern Germany are the products of the cold war, and it is understandable that the old man sees contemporary politics against its background. His hero was John Foster Dulles. The death of Mr. Dulles, the election of "that young man," as Dr. Adenauer called John F. Kennedy, and the building of the Berlin Wall created a situation that demonstrated the difficulties of dealing with the unity question when allied with the hypersensitive West Germans.

During the Berlin crisis of 1961–1962 the Kennedy Administration saw that the division of Germany was the central factor in the crisis. Consequently it tried to find some means of broadening the contacts between the Federal Republic and East Germany, principally in areas of technical cooperation such as the operation of railroads and canals. The Administration also planned the establishment of an International Access Authority, which would safeguard access to Berlin across East Germany. The East Germans serving on this authority would be equal in status to West German officials.

The American proposals also envisaged the establishment of a number of commissions, composed of representatives from both Germanies, to deal with technical problems. The basic idea was to broaden the contacts between the two sections of Germany in the belief that the superior economic position and political freedom of the West would exert an irresistible attraction through these contacts. Dr. Adenauer and his cabinet, however, were deeply troubled by this approach to reunification. They thought it would weaken the Western position in Berlin and bolster, rather than reduce, the prestige of the Communist republic in the East.

The proposals made little headway. French objections reinforced West German opposition. Bonn thoughtfully leaked the least attractive sections of the plan to reporters. The most important by-product of the proposal was the new Franco-German friendship that flowered as a result. The then Chancellor, Dr. Adenauer, had been an architect of the new Europe and an admirer of De Gaulle. But the General's help in this instance won the old man's passionate gratitude.

The affair has a lesson for those who in the future must come to grips with the German problem. This lesson is that

West German governments, while agitating for unity at every opportunity, will be very wary in the negotiating stage. The Federal Republic, of course, must play an important role in any negotiations. But precisely because it has more to lose than any other interested party, Bonn will proceed with the utmost caution.

Consequently the most obvious starting point for any new diplomatic approach to Moscow on reunification should follow the pattern already tacitly approved by the Federal government: the establishment of technical committees, composed of East and West German members, to deal with mutual problems. Once these committees are showing some evidence of real cooperation on an all-German basis, it should be possible to name other committees to examine the means of settling the various issues linked to reunification: the division of Berlin, access to the western half of the city, the levels of forces and armaments in a united country. The committees would not negotiate these matters. But they should be empowered to submit their findings to the four powers entrusted with Germany's reunification, the Soviet Union, the United States, Britain, and France, and to the governments of East and West Germany.

The work of such committees is not likely to prosper, however, unless, at the same time, the cooperation between the two Germanies impresses upon the East Germans the advantages of working toward a united country. This impression could be created by their contacts with the greater prosperity and more liberal politics of the Federal Republic.

There does not appear, however, to be much chance that the original Western proposals for unity, the election of an all-German constituent assembly, the drafting of a constitution, and the holding of free elections, have the slightest chance of acceptance by Russia or East Germany. It is possible, however, that, after a period of economic and political contact through the joint committees, East Germany might be prepared to enter a customs union with West Germany, with both governments remaining independent. As the political and economic contacts multiplied and a general German cultural pattern developed, it would be possible for both sections to talk in less emotional and more substantive terms about eventual unity. The obvious next step would be a loose confederation.

The Western powers, particularly the United States, must realize that there is no shortcut to unity. The process outlined above might require ten years of effort by both sides. The essential is to make a start now.

The development of economic and, to some extent, political independence in Eastern Europe prompts one final word of caution. East Germany, as will be pointed out later, is no longer the starved ugly duckling of the East European Communist states. The continued development of the East German economy and further rises in living standards will influence popular opinion in favor of the regime. Twenty years of police-state rule have either eliminated the regime's strongest opponents or driven them into West Germany, where they are now settled and thriving. Consequently, the Western powers, including the Federal Republic, must consider the possibility that East Germany will *not* be powerfully attracted to union with West Germany. It is possible that ten years from now there may be two Germanies, both prosperous, competing against each other.

West Germany is fortunate that both its present leader, Dr. Erhard, and his Social-Democratic rival, Willi Brandt, are more flexible in their approach to reunification than Dr. Adenauer. The ex-Chancellor sees the Russians biding their time, counting on an American withdrawal from Europe and the revival of French and Italian Communism to spark a massive takeover of Western Europe. All this *der Alte* imparts in his harsh voice to anyone, German or foreigner, willing to listen. His difficulty is that he is an old man in a young man's country.

One young man especially has been singled out for the enmity of Dr. Adenauer and also of General de Gaulle—Dr. Gerhard Schroeder, the Federal foreign minister. Dr. Schroeder is of the new breed of German politicians, as is Erhard to a certain extent. He has no serious connection with the Nazi past or with the civil service that ran Germany under the empire, the Third Reich, and the Weimar Republic. He is international in outlook, which makes him an easy target for the nationalists. Schroeder, because of his supposed liking for Britain, is often drawn by cartoonists wearing a kilt and a Tam o'Shanter. He spent some time at Edinburgh University.

The foreign minister, like his chief, is sensitive to the importance of the American connection. This has brought him the enmity of the Gaullists in his own party as well as that of the General himself, Adenauer, and French foreign minister Maurice Couve de Murville. Their candidate for the next foreign minister is Franz Josef Strauss.

Dr. Erhard and his government face an election in the autumn of 1965. Their immediate preoccupation has been to keep peace within the party at a moment when political thought in Germany is being torn by the conflict between the Gaullist ideas of Europe and the American connection. In the spring of the year many Christian Democrats believed that the task of holding the party together was paramount. If this could be done, beating the Social Democrats, if not easy, was certainly probable.

The Christian Democratic party is closely allied with its Bavarian offshoot, the Christian Socialist Union, which con-

130

trols about fifty of the coalition's two hundred and fifty seats in the Bundestag. The chairman of this party is Franz Josef Strauss, one of the most significant figures in German politics. Strauss, once Minister of Defense, was ousted by Adenauer because of a scandal uncovered by *Der Spiegel,* the weekly news magazine that is the most powerful and liveliest publication in the Federal Republic. Strauss has a great capacity for survival. By late 1964 he was well on the road to political rehabilitation, using German Gaullism as his vehicle. He is bitterly anti-Communist, a strong supporter of German independence in defense, and gifted at playing upon the emotional appeal of reunification.

This butcher's son from the Schwabing students' quarter of Munich is now forty-nine, at the height of his powers. He is a powerful man physically, so much so that the first impulse is to dismiss him as just another strong man without the brains to do more than pose and gesticulate. This is an underestimate. Strauss is a highly intelligent, well-educated man with the true politician's instinct for the jugular. His failing is that the presence of an audience brings out the worst in him.

The writer of a letter to *Der Spiegel* complained that Strauss "appeals like Hitler to the inner pig-dog in the German—the pig-dog which springs to life at the sound of phrases like 'our justifiable, vital national interests' or 'we are a great nation' or 'political rape committed against us.'" There is a good deal of the demagogue in Strauss, as there is in many politicians. He has the gift of rousing an audience and employs it, cynically. He is very quick to call his critics Communists, and he thinks, more often and more obviously than is good for his career, solely in terms of personal power.

None of this would be particularly disturbing if Strauss were an Italian or a Dane. But he is a political element in

Germany, and even in the prosperous, stable Germany of Dr. Erhard, Strauss the demagogue could be dangerous. For there is always in the background the issue of reunification to be used by any ambitious politician with a trick of arousing national emotions.

The Bavarian's policies are fairly obvious. He believes in a European defense as does De Gaulle. His enemies say that to Strauss a European defense is a means of getting nuclear arms for the Federal Republic. Strauss' version is that he seeks a Europe that would be the "second great power in the West" with its nuclear power under the control of a European government. Here he parts company with De Gaulle, who is dead set against any supranationalism. Like the French General Staff, and some German military men, Strauss rejects the idea of a controlled defense to Soviet aggression, one that would employ nuclear weapons by stages. He is an advocate of immediate nuclear bombing of the Soviet Union at the moment of Russian aggression.

How strong is Strauss politically? German businessmen, who want above all the continuation of the present economic prosperity and political stability, dismiss him as a noisy clown. The civil servants, whose influence grows yearly, detest him as the sort of politician most likely to disrupt their neat, administrative patterns.

Strauss, one of his admirers once remarked gloomily, is a man without an hour. There was, he thought, no place for Franz Josef in the sensible, safe Federal Republic. Perhaps so, but to be sure we would have to know more about the subsurface currents in Germany that would rise to the top in a national emergency. What can be said now is that Strauss has very little appeal to the business community, very powerful in Germany, or to the mass of socialist workers and youth. Strauss does appeal to the unreconstructed exiles from East

Germany, Poland, and Czechoslovakia, to the "Gaullists" in his own party who want greater independence of the United States, and to those Germans in whom the admiration for firm, totalitarian government continues undimmed despite sixteen years of democracy.

At the moment this is not enough. But Germany, having swung one way, toward democracy and stability in the great change since 1945, is capable of swinging the other. This is an element in the crisis in the Atlantic world. The United States should not be ashamed to use its influence against Strauss and for those in Germany who have been its loyal friends.

One interesting sidelight on America's influence in Germany developed in the last American election. Like the majority of German politicians, Strauss is a poor judge of politics abroad. He thought, for example, that Senator Goldwater had a good chance in the Presidential election of 1964 and warned his supporters against taking an anti-Goldwater line. The Senator's crushing defeat deflated Strauss because it seemed to show Germans that their great ally across the Atlantic had rejected the sort of extremism that Strauss preaches. This is unlikely to stop him for long.

Nowhere is Strauss more hated than in the Social Democratic Party. And the Social Democrats are now a power in West German politics. After years in the wilderness they have started to gain, winning elections in the states until they now control the majority of state or land governments, and assuming new authority as the opposition in Bonn.

One reason is the arrival of a popular Socialist leader, Willi Brandt, the Mayor of Berlin. Brandt is popular not solely with the Social Democrats but also with the uncommitted voters who, in Germany as in Britain, represent the decisive element in the electorate.

133

Brandt is a big, voluble, direct person. As Mayor of Berlin he commands the Federal Republic's outpost against Communism and reaps the political benefit. He is a good speaker in the rather bombastic style that seems natural to German politicians. By experience and interest he is far more international in his outlook than many of his party and, indeed, many politicians of the C.D.U./C.S.U.

He became the party's leading politician and potential chancellor at about the time when the Social Democrats were changing their image in Germany. This was necessary for political survival. For as long as their opponents could charge that the S.P.D. were Marxist and hence next door to Communism, as they did, the German electorate's uncommitted center found them unattractive. The Socialists naturally had a bedrock of solid old-line party members. But these were never numerous enough to win a national election.

So the S.P.D. quietly divested itself of some of its Marxist trappings. The party's anti-Communism, which since the days of Reuter and Schumacher had always been a powerful element, was given full play. The voters were informed that the Socialists, if elected, had no desire to disturb the course of German economic progress, although they did promise to improve housing, education, and public services.

All this—the advent of Brandt, the alteration of the outer face of German Socialism—took place when Germany was emerging from the Adenauer era. Millions of Germans, of every party, rightly recognized *der Alte* as the maker of modern Germany and the guarantor of peace and stability. Voting against him seemed almost an act of bad faith in the Germany he had created. Dr. Erhard has many admirable qualities. But he does not arouse intense personal enthusiasm. He is identified with "the German miracle," the tremendous economic boom of the Fifties, and this has endeared him to the business community. However, the Chancellor lacks his predecessor's grip on the patriotic loyalty of Germans. They will vote for him for reasons of logic rather than of emotion. This can be a rather flimsy political foundation among the most emotional of Europeans.

The Social Democrats by early in 1965 were in a good position to win the autumn elections. If they do not win they may come so close to victory that they and the C.D.U./C.S.U. will form what Germans call "the great coalition," something like the national governments in Britain in the Thirties. The Free Democrats, now in the government coalition, may find themselves squeezed out of office by the Socialist upsurge.

Whatever the outcome, it is certain that the next two or three years will be trying ones for German democracy. This is not only because of the existence of major problems, unification and the choice between De Gaulle's Europe and America, but because in the last five years there has been a growing dissatisfaction with the manner in which the Bundestag, the German House of Representatives, has carried out its duties.

Herbert Wehner of the Social Democrats recently called it "a self-castrated parliament." Members from all parties have protested against the manner in which this, the highest legislative authority, is bypassed by the executive branch and told as little as possible by the government. There is a belief that policy is made by the ministers on the advice of senior civil servants with little regard to the views of the people's representatives.

Rudolf Augstein, publisher of *Der Spiegel* and the gadfly of German politicians of every party, is convinced that Chancellor Erhard's moderate approach to problems at home and abroad, an approach that Brandt probably would follow in office, is sapping the life of German politics and the vitality out of democracy. To Augstein, Germany has been moving away from democracy "back to the administrative state of the Prussian Kaisers, back to the rule of the civil servants whose mission it is to serve and defend the Obrigkeit, the Establishment. To the sterile system in which order becomes a political end in itself."

Complaints similar to those made by Wehner and Augstein can be heard, of course, about government in London or Paris. They are more important in Germany because, like the demagoguery of Strauss, they appear in a country where democracy is still rather new and where it faces tremendous national issues. It is not enough to say that German democracy works; it must be seen to work on the most important matters before the electorate.

This affects all Germans, not only those living in the Federal Republic. For years the West Germans and their allies have counted on the political and economic attraction of the Federal Republic to induce finally a movement by the East Germans toward reunification in freedom. With the rest of Eastern Europe, but not the German Democratic, that is, Communist, Republic moving toward a greater independence of the Soviet Union, there is now at least the possibility that the East Germans, finding themselves isolated in their servitude to Russia, may take the first, tentative steps toward negotiations on unity.

This is not likely to happen, however, if the Communists among them are able to assert that the democracy of Bonn is a sham and that the Federal Republic's present chancellor, who by then may be Franz Josef Strauss, is simply another authoritarian leader. Are such considerations irrelevant? In a country with Germany's history and problems, every possible contingency must be examined.

The Federal Republic's economic attraction to East Europe

is acknowledged. The German miracle has gone on longer and produced a greater change in the country than France's prosperity or Britain's boom in the Fifties.

By the end of 1964 the total of goods and services produced in West Germany was four times the gross national product when the Federal Republic was established in 1949. Economic growth last year was 6.5 percent, or 4.5 percent when price rises are taken into account. Foreign trade rose by 10 percent in 1964, to more than $30,000,000,000. Bonn, too, seems to have held inflation in check. The cost of living rose by 2.9 percent in 1964, the least of any major industrial nation. But this was more than balanced by an increase of 7.5 percent in gross wages and salaries during the year.

This Germany, this fat, calm, complacent burgher, troubled only occasionally by inner spasms and sinister memories, is America's chief responsibility in Europe. For to a considerable measure the Federal Republic of Germany is a creation of our republic at the zenith of America's postwar power. James W. Byrnes, George C. Marshall, Harry S. Truman, Lucius D. Clay, John J. McCloy were its godfathers. Representing unchallenged military and political power within the Western alliance, these coaxed and bullied other allies into approving the formation of the new German state. They had help—Ernest Bevin in Britain, Robert Schuman in France, Konrad Adenauer in Germany. But it was American statesmanship or, some might say, folly that established West Germany.

More than that; it was American nuclear power, beginning with the anxious years after the outbreak of the Korean War and lasting until the present, that has protected the German democracy against the Russians and their allies across the Elbe.

Now, in this crisis between America and Europe, is the time to strike the balance. Where were we right? Where did we go wrong?

For twenty years Uncle Sam has been "Mr. Steadfast" in Berlin. Allies, from time to time, have hinted at compromise. Neutrals have advocated a less forthright defense of West Berlin. The United States has never flinched from the challenge, never grown weary of the burden. When allies or enemies question the Republic's right to leadership in the West, Berlin should be the first answer.

The United States was right, too, in seeking to weld the infant German state to Western Europe. France, Italy, and the others were receptive in varying degrees. Anthony Eden, a foreign minister of genius, found the means of rearming Germany within the Western alliance. But none of this would have availed had it not been for the constant support by the United States of West Germany's integration first in NATO and later in EEC.

This high statesmanship was accompanied on America's part by an eye on the main chance. Germany, America's creation, has been a good customer. The cynic would say, and the cynic would be right, that German rearmament has meant good business for American manufacturers of aircraft, tanks, and other weapons. Such a mixture of lofty political purpose and commercial advantage has been practiced by other great nations in the past.

Where America went wrong, and it is hard to see how in the harsh circumstances of the cold war this could have been avoided, was in pushing Germany too fast, too far. The Germans in recent years have shown more restraint than most expected in their role of favorite child. But the effect on other European powers, chiefly Germany's neighbors, has not been entirely to America's advantage.

An alliance between America, with her nuclear might, and Germany, with her history of aggression, has been a godsend to the Communist propagandists. This was anticipated. What no administration bargained for was the resentment aroused all over Europe by this favored treatment of the pariah among continental nations.

A prosperous, democratic West Germany became, under the circumstances, a power to be feared rather than one exercising an attraction on East Germany and the other states of Communist Europe. This situation existed from 1949 until about 1956 when, without any real assistance from the United States, the East European states began their halting, intermittent progress toward independence of the Soviet Union.

America did not build a bridge to Eastern Europe. She built a fortress in Central Europe. Only the relaxation of Soviet rule in the East has enabled the former captive peoples to reach out toward the West. The United States, then, is experiencing the situation known to many fathers of families. The boy has grown, shows intelligence, still is dutiful. But he is changing. How long will he remain tractable? How far does paternal authority extend? Father does not know. He can only guess on the basis of the son's relation to his equals and contemporaries.

The French-German relationship is decisive to the future of European unity. For seven years the formidable personality of Charles de Gaulle and his ministers' adroit use of France's economic protection and diplomatic influence have obscured the fact that, in this relationship, Germany is by far the stronger partner. The French-German Treaty of Cooperation in 1963 in effect was a singularly successful, although certainly temporary, instrument for renaming a rivalry an alliance.

France is Europe's farm. West Germany is Europe's factory. Europe can buy its bread elsewhere. It needs German industry far more than it needs French agriculture. When the days comes, if it ever does, when all the tariff barriers are eliminated among EEC partners and French industry is exposed to direct competition with German, those weaknesses in the French industrial structure, so ingeniously disguised by her leaders, will become apparent. Germany will then move from a leading role in the European economy to *the* leading role.

This process will have little to do with national policies. The Germans in the economic sphere have the big battalions. In a united Europe or even in De Gaulle's confederation of fatherlands, Germany is bound to become the paramount economic power. She is already the foremost military power in terms of conventional forces. The combination of these two will give West Germany in the future a political influence far beyond that of any continental power.

Visitors to France frequently remark that the French-German Treaty has not entirely eliminated the distrust and fear of Frenchmen for Germans. Nor has it, on the other side of the frontier, eliminated the distrust and contempt in which many Germans hold the French. However, there has been a great effort on both sides to heal the wounds and forget the past. The results are difficult to assess. There are moments when, in a town in the Pas de Calais or in the Rhineland, the visitor is struck by the sameness of life and bewildered by the existence of any enmity between the two peoples. And there are moments when a derisive story, a muffled curse, a contemptuous comment illuminates the survival of the old hatred.

We are moving out of a period in which every effort was made by both countries to emphasize the closeness of their relationship and the importance of cooperation, into one in which France is trumpeting the benefits of nationalism and independence. Will Germany, faced with such overwhelming problems, choose a similar policy for their solution?

If there is an answer, it lies in the recent developments in the German attitude toward the Soviet Union and the East European nations.

West German governments were distinguished for the fervor of their anti-Communism for the first decade after the foundation of the Federal Republic. This was not wholly attributable to the desire to stand in well with American governments, although that was a factor. Here it might be noted that the genuine liberals in the Adenauer government were deeply worried by the advent of Senator McCarthy. In 1952 one of them said somberly, "We've seen it all happen here; an aging president"—Hindenburg—"and a ruthless, ambitious politician"—Hitler. This comparison with the Eisenhower-McCarthy relationship was not confined to Bonn.

Another cause for anti-Communism was the sufferings of the East Germans, first under Soviet military occupation and later under the rule, in some ways harsher, of the Communist regime. This was superimposed upon the old hatred of Russia and the recent memories of the looting, raping, and burning by the Soviet armies in 1945.

It was an era during which the Germans conveniently forgot what their own forces had done during the war and when gentlemanly diplomats from the Ivy League colleges considered it rather rude to raise such matters. The Federal Republic, having been created as a bastion of the West, outdid the rest of Western Europe in its anti-Communism.

But even while Dr. Adenauer ruled in Bonn, issuing his denunciations of Moscow on the hour, German business was doing well in Eastern Europe. For many years the trade between West Germany and that area dwarfed that of other Western powers. One of the least elevating aspects of German political life in that period was the contrast between the good Doctor's denunciation of those British or French or Italians who might dare to trade with Germany's enemies, and the mounting figures of West German trade with the East.

In recent years Bonn has been franker, and no less successful, in its relations with East Europe. The Hallstein doctrine still forbids West Germany to establish diplomatic relations with any of the countries that recognize the German Democratic Republic. But the Hallstein doctrine says nothing about the trade missions that the Germans have been busily installing all over Eastern Europe.

The Germans are aware of the political changes in the area. They want to take advantage of them. They believe, as does General de Gaulle, that the isolation of East Germany among the increasingly prosperous states of Eastern Europe will force that half of Germany to turn westward toward help and unity. Where they differ with De Gaulle is their belief that this should not be a long-term process but something that should be attempted now. This difference over timing is an almost certain cause for future difficulties within the French-German alliance.

The United States, Western policy toward Russia, and the establishment of NATO and of EEC dominated the developing years of the Federal Republic. Now her people and rulers find their economic interests attracted by the East. There is as yet no tug of war between East and West in German policy-making. But there will be. How Germany meets this situation will be a major part of the continuing Atlantic crisis.

By political outlook and economic connection the Federal Republic is now a West European rather than a Central European state. It seems highly unlikely that these links with the West could be broken by Germany under ordinary conditions. If there is a break, it will come as a result of the Federal Republic's disillusionment with the policies of the West, especially the policies of EEC.

The new generation of Germans now coming forward do not look upon EEC and the plans for political unity as inconvenient restrictions on Bonn's freedom of action, as many Gaullists do. These plans and Germany's place in NATO are the proofs that Germany is now an equal in Europe, that she has largely outlived her past, and that her one-time enemies are prepared to work with her toward a closer cooperation.

Consequently the German view of the Europe of the future is not as restrictive as the French. Bonn was not dismayed early this year when the Conservative party in Britain re-emphasized its desire to lead the United Kingdom into Europe once it was restored to office. The Germans are not afraid of British economic competition within EEC, and they retain a high and perhaps misplaced opinion of British political competence. Finally, the entry of America's closest ally into the Common Market would not be displeasing to the Germans, who do not share General de Gaulle's distrust of the United States' leadership of the West.

The Germans' own bitter experiences have left them less convinced than the General that the nation-state is the supreme achievement of political development. They are more receptive, especially in the industrial centers and in the northern ports, to the idea of an Atlantic community than the French.

The priorities of power play their part in this German attitude. It is the Atlantic community, led by the United States in NATO, that offers Germany the best protection against the East, just as it is the support of the Atlantic community, again led by the United States, that appears to them to promise the best chance of negotiating a reunification of their country.

The German government has not been impressed by General de Gaulle's somewhat mystical conception of a European nuclear defense. Even if it were, it would be impolitic to say so, for the Federal Republic is denied the so-called A-B-C weapons, atomic, bacteriological, and chemical, by the treaty that permitted her rearmament.

The Germans also are good judges of the possible at this point in their history. They see no point in spending vast sums to help the French build their nuclear force when that force has little chance of playing any real role in global nuclear strategy. Nor are they anxious to give France the prestige of being the self-styled protector of the European community. Their reliance is on the United States.

These German attitudes toward EEC and the Atlantic community could change if De Gaulle makes it impossible for the Federal Republic to receive what it wants from the United States, military protection and political support. The real danger is not that De Gaulle will divert German interest from the Atlantic community to Europe. It is that his policies will alienate Germany from both EEC and NATO and prompt her to seek her own national solutions for her problems. The result of Germany's disillusionment with the dreams of the postwar years could be a swing away from Western Europe. The alternative to a revival of German nationalism is Germany's inclusion in a united Europe and a leading role for that Europe in the Atlantic community.

When all the evidence of Bonn's present interest in the Western alliance is taken into account, when the pro-Western outlook of her leading statesmen is considered, the Federal Republic still must be considered the least certain element politically of Western Europe's big four. Geographically, Britain, Italy, and France are part of the West; they have nowhere else to go. Germany has. To her east lies the Central Europe she once dominated, that other Germany, which Russia might surrender for the transfer of German allegiance from NATO to her own interests.

This is the reason why Germany's behavior in the next few years will be important to the entire alliance. It is impossible to think of a united Western Europe without Germany. German industry makes credible the concept of Europe as an industrial power rivaling the United States. German participation in West Europe's planning for the harmonization of industry and agriculture in EEC gives weight to these plans. German participation in the defense of Western Europe provides more men and conventional weapons than any other continental power.

Thus if Europe is to be truly united, it must include Germany. And if the Atlantic community is to include a powerful Europe cooperating with a powerful America, not only in the defense of freedom but in the development of Africa, Asia, and Latin America, that community and that Europe must have Germany as a leading partner.

The mistrust of Germany felt by a whole generation of Europeans and a sizable proportion of Americans makes such conclusions unpalatable. But from the standpoint of power politics, they are inescapable. We in the West can lose Germany if we ignore the importance to the Germans of reunification or if we try to delay or sabotage its achievement.

The answer, so often heard, that it's "up to the Germans to prove their loyalty" is too easy. That loyalty now is strong.

But it will be subjected in the coming years to heavy strain at a time when the postwar pattern of German politics is changing, when, in fact, the policies that brought the Federal Republic to life are being challenged. It is up to the Germans. But it is also up to us.

## Chapter VI

# ITALY, THE NEGLECTED ALLY

Boom and Near Bust • Africa Starts South of Rome •
Christian Democracy and the Challenge from the Left
• The Political Realists of NATO

The Western world is accustomed to thinking of a United
Europe and of the Atlantic community in terms of the continental countries that look out onto the Atlantic, principally
Germany, France, and Britain. But to have any validity the
concept of European cooperation must include Italy. The
Italian Republic's presence in EEC and in NATO fulfills the
condition that any economic, political, or defensive grouping
cannot really represent Europe unless, on the south, it is
firmly anchored in the Mediterranean.

The toe and heel of Italy point to Africa and the Middle
East, where Europe and the entire Atlantic community are
now competing for influence with the Communist powers.
The east coast of the Italian peninsula looks out on Yugoslavia. Italy's northeastern frontier is a window on Austria
and the East European Communist states. Finally, Italy is at
the center of the great inland sea, influencing, and influenced
by, Spain and Portugal on the west and Greece on the east.
Geographically she is indispensable to the construction of a
united Europe.

Italy's claim to a voice in the councils of Europe is unassailable. Historically the unity of Western Europe *began* in Italy, in Rome. It was Rome that first imposed a political unity upon western Europe. The Empire was based on the Mediterranean but at its height the roads ran straight and the legions marched to Gaul and Britain and the Rhine. Rome gave the peoples of the Empire unity and law and order, but, more important, it introduced to Spaniards, Britons, Gauls, and Greeks the idea of a single political system, administered under uniform laws by a civil service devoted to upholding these laws. As Dr. René Albrecht-Carrié says, "Here is precisely where the great legacy of Rome is to be found, unity, order and law are what Rome gave the world and for that reason one is justified in saying that Europe is Roman." *

The idea of a single allegiance survived the fall of Rome in the form of allegiance, in this case a religious one, to the Pope at Rome. But the concept of a single temporal authority remained in men's memories and, whatever its weaknesses, the idea of a Holy Roman Empire attracted men as an example of what could be, of a Europe free from feudal and later national wars.

Italy's direct connection with the first attempt to unite Europe is an important historical element in the development of European unity. But Italy means far more than that in the present crisis of affairs within the Western world. From a politico-military standpoint Italy's membership in the Atlantic alliance is vital. There can be no claim to a politically united Europe unless it includes a democratic Italy. There can be no pretense of a Western defensive position in Europe unless that position stretches across the Alps into Italy. Finally, unless Rome, the center of world Catholicism, is part of

* *One Europe: The Historical Background of European Integration.*

148

European unity, that unity's appeal to Catholics throughout the world will be sharply reduced.

The state of Italy today, however, contributes directly to the crisis in Atlantic affairs. Politically, Italy is less stable than Britain, France or Germany. The Italian Communist Party is the largest in Europe. Roughly one quarter of Italians vote Communist. The country must meet and solve complex socio-economic problems before it can achieve a stability comparable to that of Italy's neighbors in the north. Compared with Spain and Greece, two Mediterranean neighbors, Italy's economy is flourishing, although the last half of 1964 and early 1965 saw a slowdown. Within NATO, Italy has been a good ally. But being a good ally depends to a great extent on a healthy economic and political condition. Can Italy expect to achieve this condition in the coming critical years?

When the dimensions of the Italian economic miracle are considered, there is a strong temptation to believe that the Italians can achieve anything. Their miracle was the last of the great upsurges of economic energy among EEC partners, preceded by that in Germany in the early Fifties and by that in France in the late Fifties and early Sixties. Italy, however, started her expansion on a smaller industrial base than Germany or France and in a country handicapped by a grievous division between the bustling northern industrial area and the stagnant, agricultural south. Yet, by 1961, Italy was able to record a dazzling increase of 8.3 percent in gross national product over the figures for the preceding year. Up until 1962, the Italians were able to combine their expansion with stability in prices and wages.

In that year the danger signals flew. Italian labor, customarily the worst paid in Western Europe, demanded and received sizable wage increases. This inaugurated a tremendous increase in internal consumption, with the usual results. Consumption outstripped production. Prices rose. Exports fell because purchasers at home were buying the production intended for sales abroad. European producers, scenting a new market in Italy, flooded the Italian market with their goods. Profit margins declined. And, consequently, so did investment in the expansion of productive capacity. By the end of 1963, the situation had grown so dangerous that the Bank of Italy had to impose credit controls, including a prohibition on further borrowing abroad by commercial banks. A turnover tax was levied on certain luxury goods. Tax reliefs were granted for reinvested earnings.

These measures did not suffice. By early 1964 it was apparent that other measures of economic restraint were necessary. These included a purchase tax on new automobiles, increased taxes on gasoline, controls on installment buying, and an amendment of the tax on dividends to promote the flow of funds into the capital market. Other restrictions were imposed on credit terms for the import of cars and of household goods. The measures were taken just in time. The growth rate of the gross national product had dropped alarmingly from 8.3 percent in 1961 to 6.3 percent in 1962, 4.8 percent in 1963, and 2.5 percent in 1964. Meanwhile, unemployment rose to about 2.5 percent of a labor force of twenty million.

There are grounds for optimism. There was a shift of nearly $2,000,000,000 in the balance of payments from the deficit of 1963 to a credit balance in 1964. Exports rose by 19.1 percent and imports fell by 2.3 percent. There was a substantial increase in Italy's chief "invisible" export, tourism, based partly on substantially lower prices in Italy than in France. Capital began to return to Italy for investment.

Recovery, however, was not complete. The left-center coalition that rules Italy finally approved, after long deliberation, a five-year development program early this year. This program is intended to end violent fluctuations in economic climate and to insure a steady growth rate during its lifetime. But, having approved the plan, the government failed to insure its survival, a failure that is bound to plague Italian politics for the next few years. The cabinet apparently just could not decide whether parliament should be asked to pass a law making the program binding on future governments and other authorities concerned with it, or whether parliament should limit its approval to ad hoc measures intended to implement the plan. Premier Aldo Moro's government thus left unanswered the fundamental dispute over whether the five-year plan should be coercive or persuasive in character.

The inability of the government to take the really important measures necessary for Italy's economic health is a source of weakness in Rome, as, indeed, it is in London. The Italian planners, moreover, seem far too impressed by the boom of the last decade, assuming, for example, an annual economic growth rate of 5 percent between 1965 and 1969. They were probably justified in believing that economic growth would spurt ahead of the 1964 figure of about 2.5 percent, but other Europeans studying the Italian economy saw no reason to believe that Italy would "automatically" achieve the 5 percent figure.

It is essential for Italy that the plan work. Can it? Some think it can be implemented only if the government has the courage to apply a tough policy on wages. But the unions, most of them dominated by Communists, are unlikely to accept such a policy. Labor claims that management should have taken advantage of the economic miracle to introduce the technological changes that would have insured a steady increase in productivity. They demand more wage rises, which, they say, will increase consumer buying. To this management answers that any further increases in wages will lead inevitably to unemployment.

The five-year plan apparently has fallen into the middle of the three-cornered argument among the employers, the unions, and the government's economic planners. The unions demand a rise in wages. The employers want increased profits so that these can be reinvested in industry. The government through the Bank of Italy is slightly on the side of the employers. Others seek increased investment in public works as the only sure method of avoiding an even more serious recession.

This is one of the many areas where the solution of Italy's economic problems is dependent on the advent of a more resolute government. Germany's problems in the largest sense are political. Italy's are both economic and political and so closely interwoven that it is difficult to say where one ends and the other begins. Nowhere is this more true than in Italy's handling of her greatest social and economic problem: the revival of her south or *mezzogiorno*, literally "midday." The struggle to revive the south and to give it something approaching equality with the bustling, dynamic north is one of the most exciting developments in Europe.

The Italians say that Africa begins south of Rome. The south is poor; it has been poor since the Middle Ages. But the southern half of the Italian boot plus the islands of Sicily and Sardinia amounts to 41 percent of Italy's territory, and 38 percent of her people live there. Yet the *mezzogiorno* produces only 24 percent of the national income, and average incomes there are only a little more than half what they are in the industrial north.

The problem has historical roots. Italy was unified a century ago by northerners, most of whom had little knowledge of the south and no interest in its problems. Cavour, for example, never ventured south of Florence. The south, jolted out of semifeudalism by unification, in turn resented the northerners and the tax system they imposed. The system was borrowed from that of the Kingdom of Piedmont in the north, and the conviction grew in the south that the benefits of unity, and of the new taxes, went to the north rather than to the south.

This situation has changed slowly since 1950, when the drive to revive the south began. Now it is the prosperous north that is paying for the national effort to end poverty and backwardness in the south. The Cassa per il Mezzogiorno, the government corporation handling the development of the south, was established in 1950. Since then it has spent an average of $280,000,000 each year on highways, water and sewage systems, power plants, and aid to private industry. For every dollar the Cassa has spent, private industry estimates it has spent ten.

For the moment the old disparity between northern affluence and southern poverty is almost as great as ever. In the north the extraordinary expansion of industry has proceeded at a rate far greater than anything to be expected in the south. The south needs time for the great investment to show results. And, in view of hundreds of years of slow decay, fifteen years of improvement are not enough, perhaps one hundred years will not be enough, to redress the balance.

The disparity between the two areas is important to Italy and to the Atlantic world. The former can never play a full role in the latter until the south has been modernized and Italy is united, economically and socially as well as politically. Political union, as in the United States between 1875 and 1900, means little to the south unless it can stand on its own feet as an economic partner with the north.

Southern Italy has benefited greatly from the money

poured into the area by the Cassa per il Mezzogiorno. Yet the visitor to Italy south of Rome still feels, as he feels in southern Spain, that he is not in Europe. There is an African quality to the atmosphere. All Italy is Mediterranean. But this is the Mediterranean world of Sicily, another Italian problem, or Tunisia or western Algeria—poor, bleak, hot and barren.

Despite the plans for development, much of southern Italy lives as it has since malaria drove the people out of the coastal plains up to the mountain villages. The hills themselves are bare and the scanty grain crops sweated from their poor soil demand an inordinate amount of labor. Any other people but the Italians would have left the inhospitable land centuries ago. But, although to the traveler's eye things are very much the same on the surface, clearly something is stirring among these people. If the development program has given them anything, it is a conviction that they are no longer alone, that there is hope. This, itself, may be more important to the future of Italy than all the assistance projects and all the billions of lire sponsored by Rome.

Land reform in the early Fifties was the first step toward the salvation of the south. Some peasants, once they had acquired their own farms, tiny by American standards, were able to triple or quadruple their yearly incomes. Land reform could not stop simply with the redistribution of the lands expropriated from the latifundia, the great feudal estates. To be economically viable, the new farms had to have roads, electric power, and water, which meant dams and irrigation canals. Southern Italy, finally, was given the framework of a modern economy.

Meanwhile, some of the prosperity of the north has splashed down into the south. The road south from Rome takes the visitor past new factories that, as often as not, are the offshoots of the great companies of the north. These, while welcome, are not the most important part of the program for the south, where the goal is to create a vigorous, indigenous economy.

The principal development areas are at Valle del Pescara, Bari, Brindisi, and Taranto on the east coast and the Caserta-Naples-Salerno strip on the west coast. In Sicily the main targets are Palermo, Catania, and Syracuse and in Sardinia, Cagliari. Scattered across the map of southern Italy and the two ailing islands are smaller local development areas. It is a great work, and one finds in the Italian officials directing it a sense of enthusiastic purpose unusual in European bureaucrats.

The results are self-evident. More automobiles, that unfailing standard of the expanding economy today, are noticeable throughout the south. Food is more varied. The peasants are breaking away from the old tyranny of the employers. The south is moving, slowly but still moving, into modern times.

One problem that has not been solved is emigration. The south, if it is to benefit from the planning, needs to keep its labor. But 2,750,000 people left the south between 1951 and 1963, with 300,000 going in the latter year. This was unparalleled even in a land accustomed for centuries to sending its sons and daughters all over the world. Most of the emigrants went to man the expanding industries of the Italian north, to Switzerland, and to the countries of the European Common Market experiencing a labor shortage.

If the south is to recover completely, it will have to have an industrial base of its own. That will involve movement, if not emigration. Workers will have to move out of the hills to the coastal plains and river valleys where industry can be established. But only the major industries have the resources

155

to build in the south. Here IRI (Institute for Industrial Reconstruction) and ENI (the National Hydrocarbon Board), Montecatini and Shell are the pioneers. The smaller firms are wary of entering an almost alien world where they may expect the obstruction of local bureaucrats, the hostility of local landowners, and the isolation of their factories from supplies of raw material and spare parts.

When the major industrial companies move south, they show what can be done. At Taranto IRI has built Italy's, and probably Europe's, most modern steel plant at a cost of $550,000,000. The same sort of plant could have been built in the north for a good deal less. But this would not have helped the *mezzogiorno* or the ancient, decaying city of Taranto. Now the plant turns out steel at a rate of 2,500,000 tons a year. A two-mile conveyor belt carries ore from the harbor to the blast furnaces, and two of the world's largest basic-oxygen furnaces turn out the steel. The success of the IRI plant, opened in November 1964, has attracted other industry. Royal Dutch Shell is building a refinery that will employ more than three hundred workers. A brewery, a cement factory, and a metal-working plant are all working at maximum production, and it is estimated that more than twenty smaller plants will be built.

Similar progress has begun all through the south. Monteshell has built a petro-chemical plant employing 4,500 people at Brindisi. Like the IRI plant at Taranto, the success of this pilot industry has encouraged others. Bari now has a shoe factory employing 2,000 workers and the promise that ten more plants will be erected in the vicinity. Italy's largest oil refinery has been built at Augusta on Sicily's east coast, and a new petro-chemical plant has been built at Gela. Sardinia is developing rapidly with the coming of petro-chemical plants, paper mills, oil refineries.

The advent of these industries has been complemented by the improvement of public utilities in the *mezzogiorno*. The Cassa boasts that since 1950 work has been begun and in many cases completed on 5,000 miles of irrigation canals, 4,560 miles of new roads, 8,560 miles of improved roads, 2,063 power stations, and eight dams.

The test is what smaller companies will do in the south. The Italians recognize that secondary industries are needed if a solidly based industrial society is to develop. The government has done what it can to encourage small industries. In the development areas new industrial sites are guaranteed road, water, and power facilities. Companies investing up to $14,000,000 get tax remissions and cheap credit. These inducements have been productive in the Taranto area and at Bari and Ferradina. Business has been encouraged by the growth of a market for light industrial products. Success in the end will depend on the ability of new enterprises to attract local labor forces. The experience at Taranto thus far is that the southerner is hard-working, quick to learn, and eager for overtime work. What are lacking thus far are trained senior workers, the non-commissioned officers of industry, the foremen who can make a production line hum, who have the experience to take responsibility.

Despite this progress it is questionable whether the *mezzogiorno* is progressing fast enough. EEC, after studying the problem, has proposed the location of ten large industrial units each with twenty or more auxiliary units in the Bari-Brindisi-Taranto area. These would employ another 10,000 workers and their establishment would require an investment of more than $200,000,000.

The program is in a sensitive state of development. Inflation and the weaknesses of the central government threaten progress. But the foreigner, even if he touches the south only peripherally, notes the changes. If Praia a Mare is an example, the development will continue. Here is a village that fifteen years ago had a population of about 800, fifteen motor vehicles, and water for one hour a day. By 1965 the population had risen to over 3,000. There are four small industrial plants employing 1,200, four hotels to attract tourists to the coast, and more than 500 automobiles. All this is due to energetic private enterprise from the north taking advantage of the loans and grants in aid offered by the Cassa. One derelict part of Italy's south has been brought into the twentieth century.

The south is Italy's biggest problem. But the very concentration of Italy's problem in one area often diverts attention from others that also affect the entire country. When Italians, either in or out of official life, are asked to list these, they almost invariably place the bureaucracy at or close to the top. Some civil servants are bold enough to admit this charge. They concede that the administration of the country suffers from sloth, ignorance, and lack of interest. The citizen will agree, and will add corruption to these failings.

The point of conflict between the people and the civil service is that the latter, imposed a century ago, is unable to deal with the demands of a rapidly changing society. The highly centralized Italian bureaucracy, like the tax system it administered, was borrowed from Piedmont, which, in turn, borrowed it from France. Whatever its virtues then, it is today clearly incapable of handling the problems of modern Italy. For example, when land reform was approved, the officials of the Ministry of Agriculture, it soon became clear, were unable to implement the program. Consequently a new department, staffed by more flexible and vigorous minds, had to be established to do the job.

The demand for change comes from both the public and

the civil servants. Other circumstances enforce it. If the five-year plan is to work, it must be administered by a modern bureaucracy. If the south is to prosper, then the centralization that is so dominant a feature of the civil service will have to give way to localization. Reform, too, must aim at halting the present duplication of government effort, reflected in the absurd situation in which a government department, plainly unable to do a modern job in a modern Italy, is paralleled by another organization established to do the job the regular department cannot do.

One interesting point: roughly eighty percent of the posts in the higher ranks of the civil service are filled by southerners. This is natural enough; government service was a road of escape for the bright young man in the stagnant south. But this did not make the service any more popular elsewhere in Italy. And the unpopularity of the civil service generally has retarded the growth of a true political feeling in Italy. One is Italian and that is enough. What the state does is something to be endured, not to be altered by one's own efforts.

In this Italy of expansion (Rome, for example, has almost doubled in population since the war) education is another pervasive problem. It is also a problem in Britain, Germany, and France, and its dimensions in all four cases are the same: how is the nation to superimpose advanced scientific and technical education on systems that remain basically classical? In Italy, however, the protests against the archaic character of the educational system and the demands for its modernization, both in facilities and in teaching, are perhaps stronger than anywhere else.

Theoretically, Italian education is compulsory and free for children aged six to fifteen. Actually, Italy is short of 200,000 classrooms, especially in the south. The development of sub-

159

urbs in the north has created a demand for new school buildings. A conservative estimate is that there are 800,000 children between six and fifteen not attending any school. All this in a country where illiteracy remains a national problem, with eight percent of the population over the age of six unable to read or write. In education, as in the day-to-day business of administering an increasingly modern country, the civil service has failed. The educational system, like the bureaucracy that sponsored it, is cast along lines laid down in 1860. Like the bureaucracy, it is totally unsuited to the needs of modern Italy.

This is a varied, and beautiful, land. One can fly in a day from the iron triangle of the north anchored on Milan, Turin, and Genoa, to the stark, gray-brown valleys of the south. It still contains the most appalling contrasts between rich and poor. The population finds room for local magnates in the south clinging desperately and dangerously to the vestiges of feudalism, and great industrial pioneers in the north like Count Carlo Faina of Montecatini. This is an Italy in which the big industrialists are more liberal in outlook than some left-wing politicians and more alive to the advantages of long-term planning than many government officials.

One situation is unique in Italy: the effect that television is having on a population that for centuries was largely excluded from what most Americans consider the amenities of life. Television now covers the whole peninsula. The television bosses in London and Paris and New York never tire of extolling their medium as a great educational tool. But it is in Italy that this is most true. In Italy education by television means not simply education by lessons, but education in what the modern world is like. The Italians are not only intelligent; they are quick. The models, offered them by television, portraying what life in the modern world can be like, have contributed to the present ferment in the south and, in fact, in backward areas all over the country. Italians want to be like the people they see on the screen; if this entails leaving the village or taking on new work in the village, then they do.

Italy, partly because of geography and partly because of history, has always been a less unified political and social state than France or Britain. This situation is changing, and television should get some of the credit. It has encouraged the growth of the idea that, although a man may be born a Calabrian or a Sicilian or a Roman, he is primarily an Italian, and has emphasized that he is part of a large country that has a political entity, whose overall good may ultimately be more important than the good of Calabria or Sicily or Rome. At the same time television is breaking down some of the barriers of language (the dialects are bowing to standard Italian) and of custom. The southerner is being taught to think of himself as a person who should have the same opportunities as the northerner. He no longer believes that man is ordained to live on pasta alone. He knows that there is a new world in the making and he wants his share.

Italy's postwar economic development has pushed her well ahead of other Mediterranean countries such as Spain and Greece but left her still behind France, Germany, and Britain, the three countries she approximates in population. During the same period she has gone through a wide range of political situations ranging from stability to something approaching chaos. Italian politics have a turbulent character that often leads the foreigner to think that chaos is just around the corner. But the postwar Italian has been able to keep chaos there. The Anglo-Saxon, moreover, too often confuses the explosiveness of Italian politics with revolution. In reality he is encountering an intelligent, skeptical people who, if they refuse to make a fetish out of party politics, as do some more stolid northern Europeans, maintain, against all the pressures of conformity, a gallant individuality.

The curse of pre-Fascist politics in Italy was that they were not really concerned with principles and programs but with the maneuvers and stratagems necessary to keep various combinations of parties in office. In that era some parties like the Socialists refused to abide by the rules of parliamentary government, thus helping Mussolini walk into power. Since the fall of Fascism, Italian politicians—except the Communists, who pursue their own devious game—have been far more interested in policy than in tactics, although, naturally, they have had to use the latter when necessary. The effort to modernize the south, begun by the predominantly Christian Democratic governments of the early Fifties, is by any standards and in any country a great public program. Italy, Americans may reflect, moved earlier to cure its Appalachia than did the United States.

The Catholic social democracy's claim to international political value lies also in the manner by which it established tranquillity in Italy. It was, and is, like all great political parties, a coalition; it combines factions united only by their hatred of Communism and by their Catholicism. The former, especially in the immediate postwar years, gripped the party to a startling degree. This was natural; Communism was there, ready and waiting. But it has left the Christian Democrats with a tendency toward blindness in their approach to the world scene. At dinner an Italian senator berated two Americans for the United States' support of the nuclear test ban treaty. His argument told a great deal about the fear in which the Italian conservative lives. By merely signing an accord with the Soviet Union, he charged, the United States had encouraged the great mass of Italians to believe that the Soviet danger was over and that the Communists in Italy were, as they have claimed to be, merely another Italian party seeking a better life for Italy's people.

The Christian Democrats' absolute majority vanished in the 1953 election. Since then they have been forced to cooperate with other parties, and this has led to a revival of the off-stage bargaining and outside influence that emasculated parliamentary government in Italy immediately after World War I. And since the Christian Democrats themselves were an alliance of factions, similar adjustments went on within the party. Compromise, of course, is a large element in the politics of any country. But in Italy in recent years it, rather than policy, has seemed to become the object of politics.

The basic fear of the left fostered among the Christian Democrats a strong opposition to the inclusion of the Socialists in a government coalition. The Socialists, despite their own fear of the Communists, also have been reluctant to join with the Christian Democrats largely because they feared that as a result they would lose some of their more militant Marxist followers to the Communists.

Two factors helped establish the left-center coalition. One was a familiar factor in all European calculations, from the decline of NATO to the willingness of General de Gaulle to defy the United States: the easing of the threat to Western Europe of militant Soviet Communism.

The second factor was the change within the Christian Democrats themselves. Prosperity, and the reduction of the Communist danger, combined with the recognition that Italy urgently needed widespread social and economic reform. It was evident that these aims could not be achieved by the Christian Democrats alone. The party, in many respects, developed exactly as did the Conservative Party in Britain after the election debacle of 1945. It moved away from the right to the center, then slightly to the left of center. Since it rightly received credit for much of Italy's economic advance in the late Fifties, this gradual political movement was accomplished without a serious loss of popular support to the right-wing parties.

At the same time the Socialists had to change their political base. Like all on the left, they were mesmerized by that hard-dying cliché, the solidarity of the working-class movement. Cooperation with a party of the bourgeois, many felt, meant selling out the revolution. But Italy was changing. "The revolution is already here," a Socialist said in London in 1962. "Italy is a new country, France is a new country; what has happened is that we in the West have revolutionized our lives. It is the Russians who are out of date." Such thinking affected other left-wing parties besides the Italian Socialists. The movement away from working-class solidarity owed much, too, to the savage repression of the Hungarian revolution by the Russians. So, in December 1963, the left-wing or Nenni Italian Socialists took the plunge and entered an Italian government.

The difference between theory and practice in politics is one of that art's first lessons. In Italy, theoretically, a coalition of center and left should have been competent and powerful enough to deal with major problems. Unfortunately for the coalition, the first major problem was one that set all its antipathies on edge. It was economic and it arose from the recession.

From the center and from the right the remedies were clear: higher taxation, wage restraint, greater productivity. Naturally the Socialist members of the government could not see the solution that way. But as things grew worse in Italy, some of their leaders became convinced that some restric-

164

tions, which they carefully emphasized must fall on the rich as well as the poor, had to be introduced. Their effect, when introduced, was to shake the confidence of many Socialists in the wisdom of joining hands with the Christian Democrats. For the restrictions seemed to fall most heavily on the working people who were benefiting most from the new prosperity and who had voted Socialist. The party leaders naturally feared that these voters would be enticed away by Communism, which had always attacked the left-center coalition as a feeble sham.

The Communists are not the Socialists' only problem, although they are easily the most important. A splinter party, the Socialist Party of Proletarian Unity, woos left-wing Socialists with promises of a militant Marxist, but non-Communist, front. The uneasiness among the Nenni Socialists over their movement into the government and the inability of the left-center government to solve some of Italy's most pressing problems have created a situation the Communists can exploit.

The Communist strength in Italy is one striking difference between that country and its partners in EEC, among whom Communist strength is negligible. In the national elections in April 1963 the Communists got 7,763,864 votes, or 25.3 percent of the total, and elected 166 deputies to the national assembly. The Communist vote increased by one million. Only the Christian Democrats did better. They got 11,763,418 votes, or 38.3 percent of the total, and elected 260 deputies. The two branches of Italian socialism together polled fewer votes than the Communists. The left wing, led by Pietro Nenni, received 4,251,966 votes (13.8 percent) and elected 87 deputies. The right wing, headed by Giuseppe Saragat, got 1,874,379 (6.1 percent) and elected 33 deputies.

There is a rather dangerous tendency in Western Europe, however, to discount the importance of the large Communist vote in Italy. They are not "real" Communists, Americans are told, the voting strength is merely a protest vote against present conditions. Such assurances are rather empty. The stronger the Communist party becomes in Italy, the weaker will be that country's ties with NATO and the Atlantic community. Nothing in the political development of Italy since the 1963 elections shows any reduction of the party's strength. It is well organized. It has a strong appeal to the voter who feels he has not received his proper share in prosperity and, indeed, to the voter who feels he wants more. The Communists, in Italy as elsewhere, appear to know exactly what they want.

The present situation provides the political and economic atmosphere for a Communist move forward. The Socialists, as we have seen, are part of a government preaching, and enforcing, a measure of austerity on the worker. Unemployment is rising. The Communists dominate the unions. They have working agreements with the left-wing Socialists at local levels. Communist power and influence in Italy are modified to some extent by an odd irresolution about how these should be used at this juncture. The elders of the party oppose participation in parliamentary democracy. But the new leaders apparently are more inclined to use the powerful party bloc in the Chamber of Deputies to support a government that would benefit the party's program.

No one, certainly not the Communist leaders, claims that the one Italian in four who votes for the party is a party member. But this should not divert the other Western powers from recognizing the threat to the stability of the West posed by Italian Communism. This is a situation that could develop disastrously for American policy in Europe. Like reunification in West Germany, the problem is always there, always dangerous. One figure to keep in mind: the combined

Communist and left-wing Socialist vote is just under forty percent of the total.

But if Communism is a danger, fascism is not. There are, of course, some hundreds of thousands of Italians who yearn for the old days or who believe that an authoritarian government offers Italy the only means of solving her problems. But these voters and the minor parties that represent them have little effect on the course of national politics.

The left-center coalition in power has one signal advantage: there is no clear alternative to it in Italian politics. The coalition's goals of stability and progress suit the mass of its supporters. But almost since it took office, the government has had to deal with the ugly facts of the economic recession. It had to do too much too urgently to be able to construct a sound long-term program for the future; in a country changing as rapidly and as basically as Italy, this was dangerous.

By April 1965, however, there was a visible improvement in political stability. Amintore Fanfani, the most dynamic of the Christian Democrat leaders, returned to the cabinet as Foreign Minister. This and other changes broadened the base of Premier Moro's government by extending it to cover both the conservative wing of the Christian Democrats and the left wing of their Socialist collaborators.

Meanwhile, the Christian Democrats, aware of the poor impression made by their continual squabbling, made efforts to unite. The party executive was reformed to include representatives of all the warring factions. Conciliation was in the air, and the partners in the coalition, the Christian Democrats, Socialists, Social Democrats, and Republicans, met to draw up a program for united action. Its first point was an agreement on the measures to meet the economic situation. This situation showed some slight improvement during the first months of 1965. The balance of payments position improved, and retail prices, although they continued to rise, did not accelerate as they had in 1964. The politicians knew, of course, that this improvement was the result of restrictive measures that had reduced production and increased unemployment.

The outlook for Italy is fairly good. The coalition seems to have found its feet. It has weathered the first economic crisis. It has strengthened itself to meet political and economic challenges in the future. It is moving toward a long-term program. Generally, politics are more stable than they were a year ago.

Of course, problems remain. They touch the Atlantic crisis at two points. The first is the internal political struggle against Italian Communism, which, despite twenty years of democratic rule, still shows remarkable vigor. Any setback for the party is a gain for democracy not only in Italy, but throughout the Atlantic community. The second point is the attitude of a government, many of whose members are convinced Socialists, toward a Europe whose two chief powers, France and Germany, are ruled by right-of-center governments. In EEC the Italians have shown a remarkable flexibility in getting along with the French and Germans. But continued cooperation may place new strains upon the coalition.

From the outset Italy has been one of the foremost supporters of Europe's political and economic unity. The leaders of Italy, and millions of Italians, appear to have learned the lesson of 1939–1945 that nationalism in the complex, interdependent modern world does not pay. The lesson, in fact, seems to have sunk home more deeply in Italy than in France or Germany.

Both NATO and EEC have meant much to Italians. The

Atlantic alliance has provided the protection that a militarily weak power like Italy could not provide for herself. In this respect, Italian governments have been closer to those of the Benelux countries and NATO's two northern members, Denmark and Norway, than they have to Paris. In the North Atlantic Council Italy has upheld the principle of integration, which General de Gaulle's representatives have attacked, and Italy welcomes unashamedly the protection offered by the United States Sixth Fleet in the Mediterranean.

Because of the vigor and organization of the Italian Communist Party and the size of the Communist vote, non-Communist Italians seem less disposed to take it for granted that the Soviet danger is dead. The reduction of pressure from the East has had some influence on internal politics. But nationally, Italy remains more alive to the possibility of a resumption of Russian military and political pressure than many of her European allies.

Italy ended the war in appalling condition, psychologically as well as economically. Her economic recovery came later than that in Britain, France, or Germany. But her psychological recovery was hastened by membership in NATO and in the European Economic Community. To Italian leaders, EEC offered participation in building Europe's future and an honorable break with the past. Consequently Italian governments have been strong supporters of any move that would appear to strengthen the Common Market. But they have not subscribed to the view, popular in Paris, that EEC should or could be led by any one power or that Europe's political unity should be fashioned along lines laid down by General de Gaulle. The Italians, like the Germans, value their connections with the Atlantic world through NATO. They also find it difficult to accept the General's belief that

Britain's entry into Europe would weaken the basic structure of EEC.

Most Italians of any political influence believe that Britain's Tory governments made a mistake in not applying earlier for membership. They feel that when Britain did take the plunge, the Macmillan government overestimated the strength of its position. But having made these points, they go on to emphasize that Europe needs Britain as Britain needs Europe and that no true European unity can be built without British participation. But, they always end, Britain must move quickly. The world, as all Italians know, often to their cost, is changing rapidly.

Italians like still less suggestions that the new Europe should exclude the United States. When they discuss this, the strain of mordant realism that lies beneath the attractive gaiety gets full play.

"De Gaulle talks nonsense," an Italian said in Naples. He gestured toward the American carrier in the bay. "Will we build that? Will France? The Americans protected us in bad times. Clearly we owe them something for it. We Europeans should understand the world. It is all one, now. Very small. You cannot separate Europe from America and we don't want to."

In Italy, as in some of the smaller nations of northwestern Europe, there is another aspect of the desire for the continuation of the American presence in Europe. This is the tendency to see the United States not only as the protector of Western Europe against the Russians but as an arbiter of European rivalries in the future. The Italians' trust in Germany's continued stability is a good deal less than complete. Repeatedly the Italians tell foreigners: we know those Germans, we were their allies, that's when one learns to know people. The American involvement in Europe to them is an assurance that the continent will never again be torn asunder by nationalism. Like most intelligent people the Italians know that Europe cannot survive another civil war.

As an advocate of European unity, Italy is particularly fitted to be its missionary in the Mediterranean world. Without any desire for colonies, the Italians now appear to the North African countries, Tunisia, Algeria, and Morocco, as representatives of much that is best in contemporary Europe. The same is true of Italian influence in Spain and Portugal, two other Catholic nations. Here, again, the Italian conviction that a united Europe will benefit the entire Mediterranean area is important. What the Italians are saying is that unity is not only for the great and the strong but also for the relatively underdeveloped countries of the south. A stable Italy may yet be the bridge across which the new concept of Atlantic unity will reach the other Mediterranean nations.

## Chapter VII

# RUSSIA'S TROUBLES,
# THE SATELLITES' CHANCE

European Communism after Stalin   •   "Liberalization"
and Its Extent   •   The Satellites Move Toward National
Identity   •   Russia's Troubles and Her Allies' Chance   •
The Rumanian Example   •   East-West Trade: the Advantages and the Dangers

The developments in the Soviet Union since the death of
Stalin have influenced political and military policies in the
Atlantic community, and in Western Europe particularly.
More recently the halting but definite progress of the countries of Eastern Europe toward greater economic independence and the beginnings of cultural and political independence have affected Western Europe's thinking about its future
economic development and the political prospects for the
continent as a whole. Significantly, for the first time since the
war, West Europeans now speak of Europe as including the
Communist states that lie between NATO's eastern frontier
and the borders of European Russia. Should the present
trends continue in these states, the next ten years could be
the period in which all Europe, not solely the countries west
of the Elbe, regains her identity as an undivided geographical area. The process in East Europe has been evolutionary.

But its effect on European thinking has been little short of revolutionary.

For almost twenty years politicians and public opinion have used the general term "Russia and her satellites" to describe this area for purposes of international discussion. It is symptomatic of the changes that this description is no longer applicable except in the widest context.

At the outset the description was apt. The years between 1945 and 1949 (the year the Soviet blockade of West Berlin was frustrated by the United States, Britain, and France) was the period in which the U.S.S.R. consolidated its hold on the newly overrun satellite states: Poland, East Germany, Czechoslovakia, Rumania, Hungary, Albania, and Bulgaria. Yugoslavia, freed by her own exertions, was spared the perils of "liberation" by the Red Army, and, although Communism was triumphant, it soon developed powerful national aspirations and loyalties.

Elsewhere, however, native Communists, most of them trained in Moscow, held office with Soviet advisers at their elbows. Stalin, dominant in Russia, was equally dominant in the satellite capitals. Moscow directed policy on almost every level, and the presence of the Red Army guaranteed its implementation by the Kremlin's puppets. Such opposition as had survived the war was liquidated. The Soviet propaganda machine exhorted the satellite peoples to follow the Red flag, ceaselessly warning them of the dangers of aggression by the Americans with their atom bomb. The bomb and the supposedly power-maddened American generals in fact played a very important propaganda role in enforcing the unity of the "peace-loving" peoples of East Europe.

The span of Soviet domination in those years appeared long, infinitely so. The peoples of East Europe had no long tradition of democratic government. On the contrary, since

173

the dissolution of the pre-World War I empires, they had been exploited by weak and often corrupt regimes. Some maintained the trappings of parliamentary rule, while others, as in Rumania and Hungary, lapsed into outright dictatorship. These war-weary peoples submitted without significant overt resistance to the new yoke, which, for the masses, could be no worse than the Nazi yoke of the war years. The ambitious young saw the Communist party as the road to advancement. The civil services took their orders from the new masters. The rich and the middle class, ruined by Communist looting, lived in silence and in fear.

Such was the satellite bloc in those immediate postwar years. The Russians, it is true, were but little better off than their new vassals in terms of material wealth, but psychologically they were in an infinitely stronger position. They had won. At what cost only they knew, but, having won, they intended that this danger of invasion could never come upon them again. East Europe was therefore of decisive military importance to Mother Russia. In those days, 1946 and 1947, all its states were to the Soviet leaders buffers to resist and contain future attacks.

Almost before the ink was dry on the various signatures that brought a kind of peace to Europe, the Soviet government and its propagandists began to stress the dangers to Russia and her satellites of an alliance between the United States and Western Germany, then in a pitiable state. Some light-headed European commentators later cited this propaganda as a singular example of Russian prescience. It was nothing of the kind. Stalin's aggressive policy in Eastern Europe, the rape of Czechoslovakia, the blockade of Berlin, the pressure on Greece were the source of first NATO and later West Germany's inclusion in that alliance. The West was reacting to a real and evident danger.

On the whole the United States acted with restraint. I know from private sources that at that time, 1950, Winston Churchill believed that the Truman Administration would have been justified in threatening Stalin with the use of the atomic bomb. This was not done. Nor were other measures, less extreme but probably equally restraining in their effect, ever employed. In Europe today, now that the danger is temporarily over, there are wiseacres who regard the cold war as something evolved by imaginations in Washington. It is well in this to remember the succession of desperate crises that hurried Europe into a defensive alliance.

This, then, was East Europe in the late Forties and early Fifties. An all-powerful Soviet Union with its semicircle of satellite states all armed and trained by the Russian military services was at the summit of affairs. Stalin's writ ran from the Elbe to Moscow, from Stettin to the Adriatic. The prospect of change seemed remote indeed. Both Stalin and the West reckoned without the march of events. No single policy, no one act of state changed the satellites into what they are today. They evolved under the pressure of happenings, often remote, and that evolution has not ended.

What is the Russian empire in Eastern Europe now? It is an increasingly loose alliance of states held together by a common ideology, over the interpretation of which there is the most savage argument, and by a common fear of the Western powers, which, although still strong, yearly becomes less important in the calculations of the governments. The economic unity that the Soviets strove to implant is weakening. For the present, all these countries are moving, at different rates of speed, toward the reestablishment of their national identities. There is an analogy, for example, in the present Rumanian attitude toward Russian leadership and that of General de Gaulle's France toward American leadership, although it is important not to follow this too far.

The "whys" of contemporary affairs are infinitely more interesting than the "who, what, when, and where," and nowhere in Europe is this more interesting than in the lands east of the Elbe. The starting point was the death of Stalin. Although this seminal event occurred twelve years ago, its effect in Europe still has not been fully understood in the United States. Perhaps this is because of the stridency of that section of opinion-makers who ceaselessly proclaim that Communism never changes. It does change. The change may not always be to the advantage of the American Republic. But change it does.

The effect of Stalin's death on Eastern Europe was twofold. First it meant the passing of the tyrant who had imposed upon Eastern Europe the rule of the police state similar to that suffered by his Russian subjects. Police-state rule was nothing particularly new to Poles, Czechs, or Bulgarians; they had endured it under other masters. But this time it was police-state rule of an unsurpassed extent and brutality. Moreover, in most cases it was imposed by an alien and traditionally hostile power. Russia's control of East Europe did not perceptibly weaken with Stalin's death. But it did occasion a certain loss of direction among the Soviet military, police, and political pro-consuls in the satellites.

"For eight years," a Hungarian recalled, "we had become accustomed to thinking of the Russians as unshakable automatons, unmoved by argument or appeal. Suddenly in that spring of 1953 we found them less assured, clearly worried, operating, it seemed to us, with one eye on what was happening in Moscow. Small things, the failure to finish a 'trial,' the unexplained absence of an officer of the security services made us realize that the certainties of Soviet rule had been

176

undermined. There was no sudden relaxation of control. Instead there was an obvious uncertainty about the source of authority. I do not think they ever recovered. They tried, of course, to reassert their old mastery in 1956 and that led to the revolution."

Secondly, the death of Stalin and the elevation to leadership of first Malenkov, then Khrushchev and Bulganin, and finally Khrushchev alone led to the weakening of Moscow's authority in the ideological field. It was as though an authoritative medieval pope had been followed not by one but by a succession of popes, all prepared to alter doctrine to suit their interests. The chief casualty was that impression of monolithic infallibility that, in Stalin's day, had made ideological control of Eastern Europe as easy as, and much less expensive than, military and political control.

Stalin, of course, had been challenged in his lifetime by Marshal Tito. Pope Pius XII, I understand from private sources, thought this the most significant event of the postwar period—and he was right. It encouraged in all the Communist parties of the world a tendency to question the doctrine of Lenin as interpreted by Stalin. When Stalin's successors, less awful than the Georgian tyrant, began their own interpretations, there already existed a body of skepticism, if not of dissent.

In the Communist world of East Europe between 1945 and Stalin's death in 1953, power went to those native Communists who most faithfully mirrored the wishes of the terrible Georgian. When he died, these leaders immediately lost some of their own authority, although the full effect of his death upon the satellites was not felt until well into the Fifties. Communist leadership is conspiracy leadership; that is, men conspire for power instead of being elected to it. The death of Stalin encouraged those Communists in the satellite governments who were both hungry for power and intelligent enough to anticipate the changes in Soviet policies. They were little less servile to Khrushchev at the outset than they had been to Stalin. But in time events in Russia and in international Communism made such servility less necessary.

So in the Fifties both Soviet political and ideological control of the satellites began perceptibly to weaken. The East Germans, the Poles, and finally and most tragically the Hungarians, all took action against the Soviet Union's domination. They were encouraged by the easing of Russian controls and by what, for want of a better word, we must call the liberalization of Soviet society. Again, it is wise to be prudent. "Liberalization" in the Soviet Union has quite a different meaning from liberalization in America or Britain or France. The principal effect was within the Communist party itself rather than on the millions living under its rule.

For example, an American returned to Moscow in the late Fifties anxious to learn the fate of Serge Zhukov, which is not his name. He had known Serge in London during the war; he had watched his face one day in that dark summer of 1941 when the BBC announced, quoting the Nazi communiqué, the overrunning by the Germans of the Ukrainian town where his parents and two younger brothers still lived. There developed between the two men a friendship born, as they so often are in war, out of shared dangers and anxieties. The American saw the Russian after the war in Moscow and other capitals. Then suddenly Serge disappeared. Russian diplomats, queried at parties in Geneva or London or Bonn, changed the subject. The American, returning to Moscow in a period of tension arising from the Berlin situation, asked again for his friend. The first Russian he asked said, "Certainly, I know where he is; he's working for me. Here's his telephone number."

This, in itself, was extraordinary. In Stalin's day party members and officials just did not have telephone numbers, as far as the Western foreigners and enemies were concerned. There was a pleasant reunion the next day. Serge offered the American lunch at a hotel where every contact between an official and a foreigner would be noted. He had, he said, spent four years in a labor camp in Siberia, sent there by Stalin on the grounds that he was "too friendly" with the Americans and the British.

"Now I am back in what you call circulation," said Serge. "I am as good a Communist as ever and we are going to change things. This party is not Stalin's or any one man's; it is the party of people like me. We are going to have more to say about what it does and what it thinks with each year. And no one ever again will be able to rule the party or Russia as *he* did. Russia deserves better than that."

There are other Serges. Their determination to keep the party and the country free of personal rule, in the Stalin sense, clearly had a great deal to do with the eventual ousting of Khrushchev. One of the most interesting aspects of the Russian attitude toward Khrushchev in those days and later was that there was sometimes a hint that he would not be there forever. And there were also even stronger hints that serious Soviet diplomats considered that Nikita lacked the gravitas proper to the ruler of All the Russias.

Evidently there is the growth in Russia now of a tendency to judge the ruler, Malenkov, Khrushchev, or Kosygin, on standards of intellect and ability that no official or party member would ever have dared apply to Stalin. This dawn of political criticism may be a more important aspect in the evolution of Russia than any amount of social liberalization. It is also a terribly sensitive development. The Russian, official or worker, party member or skeptic, is above all a patriot. It

179

requires no extraordinary knowledge to foresee that in a moment of international crisis—and it is our burden that we live in times when such a crisis can arise overnight at any one of a dozen flash points—the Russians, whatever they thought of Comrade X or Comrade Y, would rally to him as they did to Stalin in 1941 to the defense of Mother Russia. Western policy, more by chance than design, has not provoked this formidable psychological unity of a patriotic people. But it is in the interests of the West to promote liberalization where it really counts, in the party and among the officials. It is precisely there that the new mood has had its greatest effect on Eastern Europe.

There is very little evidence that the liberalization of Russian culture has influenced East Europe in its movement toward identity. The Russians have, for nearly twenty years, tried to sell their contemporary culture to the nations east of the Elbe, without any great success. One reason clearly is that the Soviets had so little to offer. What the East Europeans knew and liked of Russian culture antedated the establishment of Soviet political hegemony on the satellites.

A German left-wing socialist once said that he was sure that the Soviet policy for East Germany was the right one; it must have been for him because he subsequently became a big man in the Socialist Unity Party, the "cover" group for the Communists, in Magdeburg. But he could not stomach its culture. To him and to many thousands elsewhere in East Europe, Russian culture was represented by Tolstoy, Turgenev, Dostoievsky, Pushkin, Chekov. They regarded the widely exploited writings of the Stalinist period, the novels of Fadayev or Simonov, for example, as party trash. When, under Khrushchev, writers began to tackle the themes of life under the Stalinist tyranny, they were not particularly impressed. They read the books. They noted that they could be written and published. But they thought little of them. They were applying the standard of literary quality, probably the last thing Khrushchev expected.

The development of East Europe probably owes more to two other factors—economic opportunity and the great ideological and political schism between China and Russia—than to cultural liberalization.

The economic opportunity arose when it became apparent that even the inefficiency of Communist bureaucracies could not entirely prevent the efforts of patriotic Czechs or Rumanians or Poles to improve their national economies. At the same time the realization dawned on Eastern Europe that the Soviet Union, despite immense natural resources and rising production, especially in heavy industry, was far from being an example or a mentor for Communist economies elsewhere. The failure of successive Soviet governments to deal with the day-to-day problems of the Russian economy, particularly in agriculture, encouraged among the East European governments the sensible idea that if their nations were to prosper, they had better strike out on their own.

For the last five years Russia's allies and the West have been treated to a bewildering range of statistics about the Soviet economy. The situation may not be quite as grim as it was described by a distinguished Western economist—"one more bad harvest and Russia is flat on her back"—but it nevertheless was and is bad enough to make East European governments aware of the dangers of relying too heavily on the Soviet economy as the mainspring of their development. The reshuffle of resources to attain this or that end, the drop in the grain crop, the failure of the virgin-lands scheme, the sudden and never explained slaughter of pigs in 1963, the continued unevenness of quality in industrial production, all these have been red lights to Russia's allies.

Some of these allies have been planning their economies on a revival of Russian progress. But those who do so are prey to widespread doubts. For example, industrial energy, which means oil, is of the utmost importance to most of these allies. They have been proceeding in their planning on the assumption that Russia's great Tataria field, exploited unrestrictedly since the end of the war, would, through the pipelines running west to Poland and Hungary, provide sufficient energy for industrial development.

The first setback was the slowness in completing the pipeline. The Russians manufactured pipe, but a very high percentage of it proved to be far below the quality necessary. Pipe had to be bought abroad, in Italy and Britain. But there was an even more important threat to Russia's position as the source of oil-energy for Eastern Europe—the future of the Tataria field itself.

This year two thousand Soviet geological prospecting teams have taken the field to find new oil fields. The Russians have been doing this, although not in such large numbers, for the last ten years. They have been impelled to do so first by the knowledge that their own energy requirements were growing with inexorable rapidity and later because they were aware that the Tataria field, rich as it is, would not last forever. The Soviets have made two strikes, one above the Arctic circle in Siberia, the other in central Asia. Neither is as rich as the Tataria field. Distance from industrial centers and transport difficulties have reduced the importance of the Siberian strike; that in central Asia may prove more workable.

When in the spring of 1965 the Kosygin-Brezhnev regime once again concentrated the government on the improvement of agriculture, the states of East Europe drew the obvious conclusions. One was that agriculture was in an even sorrier state than the Soviets had admitted. The other, shared by some Western observers, was that the scale of the Soviet program was so great that it effectively removed from immediate consideration any serious Russian involvement in events abroad. This has been interpreted as meaning that the agricultural crisis is so urgent and the means of dealing with it so demanding on the general economy, that the Kremlin is not now prepared for aggressive foreign policies like the attempt to penetrate the Middle East in 1956–1958 or the challenge over Berlin in 1961–1962. The Russians, in other words, cannot risk war or even a prolonged crisis while they are preoccupied with the farm crisis. This may be a dangerous oversimplification of the Soviet situation, but it has gained wide credence.

Against this background of inefficiency and uncertainty in Soviet industry and agriculture and of doubts about Russia's future ability to make the most of her great natural resources, the loss of authority by the Council for Mutual Economic Aid (COMENCON) is understandable. COMENCON was devised by the Soviets as a means of integrating the economies of East Europe with Russia's through a supranational planning board. Although some countries, notably the more advanced ones like Czechoslovakia, received some advantages, none got very much out of the system. It was seen, although few Communist leaders had the hardihood to say so in public, as a means of preventing individual states from developing independent integrated economies, of leaving them dependent on the U.S.S.R. for essential resources and markets.

By the late Fifties, Russia's economic prestige and influence in East Europe had declined sharply. And this was exactly the period when Moscow's position as the only true spokesman for international Communism was first challenged by Mao Tse Tung and the Chinese Communists. Here was a challenge far more serious than that issued by Marshal Tito a decade before because it came from the largest and most revolutionary of Communist powers. The doctrinal complexities of the schism need not concern us here except for one point. The quarrel began over the interpretation of Communism, that is, on an ideological front. But it soon moved into the political field, embracing such shamefully capitalist and imperialist concepts as spheres of influence and manifest destiny. These terms, of course, were not used by the agitated comrades in Moscow and Peking, but they were what the two parties were talking about a good deal of the time.

The effect of the quarrel on the Communist states in Europe was far more profound than that of the Tito breakaway. They were now less dependent upon the Soviets economically. Incidents in East Berlin and the rebellion in Hungary had fostered doubt and spread disillusion even among those native Communists who had been the stoutest in their repudiation of the Yugoslav heresy.

Albania, the smallest and weakest of the satellites, distinguished itself by becoming Peking's most violent partisan among the European parties. The Polish, Hungarian, and Rumanian parties, although supporting the Soviet Union in the dispute, were by no means enthusiastic about the entire Russian position. The Bulgarians were warmer and the East Germans warmest of all. The explanation for the latter was simply that proximity to the West, the presence of twenty Soviet divisions, and a leading role in the cold war in Central Europe had made the East Germans the most biddable of Russia's vassals.

As the dispute with China continued, the Russians found that they could no longer rely completely on ideological subservience from East Europe. As in so many other things, the governments, parties, and peoples were beginning to think for themselves. With the exception of Albania, the East European Communist regimes were repelled by that part of Peking's policy that emphasized support for wars of liberation, that is, guerrilla and other conflicts against the West. Although they protested their loyalty to the sacred tenets of Marxism, it was quite clear that this loyalty could not and would not be pressed to the point of giving more than oral support to "liberation movements" like the Vietcong in South Vietnam.

East Europe, in this respect, was almost as concentrated on its own affairs as the states of West Europe. Internal stability and economic progress were competing successfully with world revolution as national aspirations.

One other condition helped sap Soviet authority: the gradual reduction in East Europe, as in West Europe, of the fear of war. The process has not developed as far in the East, largely because of the incessant drumfire of Russian propaganda about West Germany's "plans" to launch a war of revenge. Such propaganda falls on fertile soil, although it is reasonable to assume that its effect will decrease as West Germany expands her economic and political ties with the East, as she is now doing.

The propaganda also has to contend with the plain facts of life in Central Europe, which is where the line is drawn between East and West. Since the Cuban showdown of 1962 the area has been quiet. There has been nothing in NATO's activity to be characterized as "hostile demonstrations" against the peace-loving democracies. Nor, on the Eastern side, has there been any activity reflecting aggressive intentions. It is quite correct, as SHAPE often reminds the West, that the Soviet capacity for aggression remains unimpaired. But, aside from Marshal Malinovsky's periodic boasts that he can lick any man in the house, the Russians have been remarkably temperate in East Germany recently.

When the Russians do go off the reservation, as they did early in April 1965, their object is not to challenge the Western allies of yesteryear, the United States, Britain, and France, but to impress upon West Germany their support for East Germany and its claim to West Berlin. This is in keeping with the present Soviet tactics of building up the supposed independence and sovereignty of the German Democratic Republic with the aim of making it a more credible rival to the Federal Republic in the continuing crisis over Germany.

So we have three causes—economic, political, and ideological—as well as military for the change in East Europe. The change has affected the various countries in different ways. But there is one aspect of it that touches all the governments and parties. This is the gradual rise to positions of authority of the industrial managers at the expense of the party hacks who have run the economies and the countries for so long.

The importance of this development cannot be minimized, especially in its relation to East Europe's attitude toward West Europe. The men who are coming to the fore now are not blinded by Communist dogma, although many of them are Communists, to the extent that they will reject an advantageous deal with the capitalists to enter their country. They are more pragmatic, they have little patience with the weird blend of ideology and economics that governed their predecessors' thinking, and they increasingly consider their countries not as dependencies of the great Sino-Soviet land mass but as individual parts of Europe.

This development in the industrial personnel at the top is reflected, too, in the higher ranks of government in East Europe. During 1964 and early 1965 a steady stream of visitors from the East flowed through the Elysée Palace and the Foreign Ministry in Paris. The French, always sensitive to the nuances of leadership, found new ideas and, occasionally, new Communist types among them. All the visitors were naturally careful to emphasize their devotion to Communism in an alien and, to them, intrinsically hostile land. But in their private discussions they proved flexible in their outlook and self-assured. They were anxious, too, to show that they were no longer tied to Moscow's apron strings in the field of economics and culture. And there were the hints, the veiled allusions to a growing political self-assertion that were not mentioned publicly.

Of all the East European states, Rumania is the most interesting to examine. In their quiet way the Rumanians have moved faster and more decisively recently than most of the other nations. This was unexpected. The country's history is not famous for stalwart independence; indeed it is not many years since George V's taunt—"Rumania isn't a nation, it's a profession"—was common currency in Europe.

The economic starting point for Rumania was her possession of resources that have never been efficiently exploited in the past. She has oil, minerals, agriculture, and lumber. She is the only East European country that is self-supporting in grain. These comparative riches were the basis for the rapid expansion of the Rumanian economy and for the Communist government's insistence on its right to direct the country's economy. In April 1964, the Rumanian Communist party issued one of the most remarkable documents of postwar party history in Eastern Europe. It said in part: "The planned management of the national economy is one of the fundamental, essential and inalienable attributes of the sovereignty of the socialist state." In other words, Rumania wanted no more interference by COMENCON in the running of Rumania's economy.

This assertion of economic independence has been accompanied by a degree of independence on ideological matters.

The Rumanians support the Russians in their dispute with the Chinese to the extent that they, like most of the European Communist parties, deplore the Chinese conviction that the capitalist enemy must eventually be destroyed by war. But Rumania does not approve of Russia's tactics in the debate with China; it was particularly opposed to the idea of a world conference at which, presumably, the Chinese were to be arraigned. The Rumanians also were apparently affronted by the ebullient personality of Khrushchev; their leaders find the less showy Kosygin more to their taste.

The Rumanians meanwhile have been developing their economy to the point of achieving considerable freedom in their dealings with the West. Rumania wanted a steel plant, although iron ore is one raw material that the country does not have in abundance. But imitation is a powerful factor in Communist, as in capitalist, policy-making. Both the Poles and Czechs had steel plants; the Rumanians thought they should have one. But the plant will include ultramodern equipment from Britain and France as well as two rolling mills from the U.S.S.R. Production is scheduled to begin in 1966, with a target of 2,000,000 tons of steel annually by the end of the decade.

The Soviets find themselves in the unusual position of competing for orders in a Communist country. They were successful in one coup early this year. The Rumanians signed a contract, probably worth about $100,000,000, to buy turbines and generators for their share of the giant Iron Gates power dam on the Danube.

One interesting sign of Rumania's independence is that the government saw no objection to admitting more than one hundred and fifty British and French technicians to install the equipment bought in their countries. Such defiance of Communist xenophobia is becoming more customary throughout

East Europe. So is the inclination to look beyond Communist frontiers for raw materials as well as equipment. The Rumanians are largely dependent on imports of iron ore from Russia. But they are seeking other ore supplies in North Africa, India, and Brazil and simultaneously raising their own production.

If steel production is one means of passing into the industrial economy "club," automobiles and trucks are the universal signs of an expanding economy. Here again the Rumanians are depending more on their own work than on Russian models. The main concern, now, is trucks. Production is expected to be three and a half times as great by 1970 as it is today, and Rumania is one Communist country in which production bears a fairly close relation to the planned figures. Meanwhile cars are being imported and there are plans for producing a Rumanian automobile, although this is unlikely to appear until the economy's growing appetite for trucks is appeased.

The present economic plan ends this year. Under it the annual growth rate for industrial production was set at thirteen percent, but the Rumanians claim it has averaged around fifteen percent, far ahead of the figures among Rumania's neighbors. As in most East European countries at this stage of their economic expansion, the main emphasis is on heavy industry, petro-chemical as well as steel. But in the last two years the output of consumer goods has risen, and there has been a solid increase in the construction of housing. The cushion for industrial expansion is the favorable situation of Rumania's agriculture. There has been a sharp rise in investment in the nation's collectivized farms, but in Rumania, as elsewhere in Eastern Europe and in the Soviet Union, there is a shortage of machinery, fertilizers, and technical assistance.

Rumania's indifference to COMENCON also is evident in the manner in which she has been expanding her trade with capitalist countries. But it is well to remember that she also has maintained and widened her commercial contacts with her neighbors. However, trade with non-Communist countries is rising faster than that with members of the Eastern bloc; commerce with Western Europe has more than tripled in volume in the last five years. Rumania has been more successful than most of her neighbors in selling to the West because of the care taken to install the best equipment, regardless of its origin, in the new factories. The quality of Rumanian products is fairly high. The government has also gone to the West for what it needed, unashamedly shopping among the capitalist economies.

A trade treaty was signed with France in February 1965, and Rumania is buying and selling in Britain, West Germany, and Italy. Rumania leads the other East European governments in the boldness of its trade policy. She has made it known she is prepared to spend a billion dollars on imports, ninety percent of them from the capitalist West, in the next five years of her economic plan.

The death early in 1965 of Rumania's president and Communist party leader, Gheorghe Gheorhiu-Dej, did not divert the country from its policy of liberalization and independence. The trend toward establishing a Rumanian national identity within the Communist world of East Europe continued; Rumania was an ally, not a vassal, of the Soviet Union, free to trade where she liked and to emphasize her own Rumanian brand of Communism.

This involved what some have called the de-Russianization of Rumanian society. One step in this direction was the closing of the Institute for Rumanian-Soviet studies in Bucharest. Another was the attention paid by the Rumanian security police to Soviet diplomats, who, to their indignation, are now tailed exactly as though they were capitalist lackeys. As David Binder has pointed out, the principal aspects of the policy have been the establishment of full equality, mutual respect for national sovereignty, and parity in economic relations with Rumania's giant neighbor. To do this the Rumanian government has had to widen the base of its support among the people.

Nicolae Ceausescu, the new Communist party secretary, has done this by bringing in peasants and intellectuals. In the last three years party membership has grown from 900,000 to 1,400,000, an increase of forty-four percent that has made it the largest party in the Balkans.

The liberalization of the regime has continued. More than 10,000 political prisoners have been released in the last two years, the restrictions on internal travel have been lifted, the system of forced internal exile has been abolished, and there has been a slight but obvious relaxation of police control. Travel by Westerners has been encouraged, and a reform of the strict penal code has been begun. Finally, the Rumanian press has been allowed, after years of dreary confinement to party and government statements and propaganda stories, to print considerable amounts of foreign news. The Soviet press service TASS, long the chief source of news from abroad, has been replaced by Agence France Press as the principal supplier of such news.

The Rumanians, and the Poles, Hungarians, and Czechs, have seen the value of multilateral trading even though, in theory, the government is committed to bilateral trade deals. East Europe, if its economic condition improves, will be on a shopping spree in the West, and there seems to be very little that Russia can do about it. She has troubles of her own, as East European diplomats point out.

Finally, Rumania also provides an excellent example of the trend in leadership that is general in the former satellites. Managers, engineers, and technicians now moving to the top are doing so in many cases regardless of party regularity or class origins. Class distinctions are being discarded to the extent that a working-class background no longer is the only possible one for the ambitious young man or woman seeking higher education and a well-paid career.

To give balance to the picture of East Europe, however, it must be kept in mind that, although countries like Rumania, Poland, Czechoslovakia, and Hungary are all changing at various rates of speed, there has been almost no change, politically or ideologically, in East Germany, the German Democratic Republic. The state of affairs in this country is of extraordinary importance to the Atlantic world because it is part of the German nation whose reunification remains that world's most perplexing problem and which the United States, Britain, and France are pledged to seek.

East Germany's problem has been to win recognition as a national state without in any way relaxing the Socialist Unity Party's, that is, the Communists', iron grip on the country. The country is next door to the Federal Republic's booming economy. Twenty of the Soviet Union's twenty-six divisions in East Europe are stationed there. It is of the utmost importance, politically and militarily, to the Soviet Union and to international Communism.

Nevertheless, it became apparent by 1963 that something had to be done to change the image of East Germany in the eyes of the world from that of a garrisoned concentration camp. The country had to shed its isolation and its propaganda role as the principal enemy of West Germany and establish a position as a viable East European state. This was difficult because the 17,000,000 East Germans, despite their mastery of industrial technique and their record as workers, were living in an economy that for years had been plagued by bad harvests and shortages of raw materials and impeded by rigid and unimaginative management from East Berlin.

The first step, which appears to have been moderately successful, was to raise production, national income, and the standard of living. Published statistics in East Germany are unreliable, as they are in nearly all Communist countries, but it seems probable that the national income did rise by about 4.5 percent in 1964. Foreign trade increased by about a billion dollars. Western intelligence services noted a reduction in the complaints about shortages of food and consumer goods. The East Germans, citing their own statistics, claimed that the country had become the world's seventh-ranking industrial power.

The second step was to use this improvement as a basis for winning recognition in Europe and abroad, thus defeating the purpose of the Hallstein doctrine, which was intended to make East Germany a pariah among the nations. This doctrine provided that the Federal Republic would refuse to have diplomatic relations with any country that recognized Walter Ulbricht's East German regime. Bonn's fidelity to the doctrine has been watered down in recent years. The Soviet Union was exempted from it from the start, and West Germany has established commercial relations with other Communist bloc nations in the East, which, of course, recognize the German Democratic Republic.

Ulbricht's first success over the Hallstein doctrine outside Europe was his reception by the United Arab Republic, an independent non-Communist country. The reception was all the warmer because of Ulbricht's promise of $100,000,000 in economic aid for the U.A.R. Yet the East Germans had proved their point; they had become in the eyes of the leading Arab nation a national entity, capable of providing assistance and accepted as an independent state and not as a vassal.

West Germany's political hostility to the German Democratic Republic, incidentally, does not prevent her doing business with the Communist state. The total value of trade between the two countries in 1963 was $576,175,000, an increase of nineteen percent over the previous year. The elastic and official West German attitude, which is difficult to reconcile with Bonn's attacks on the Ulbricht regime's illegality, is that this trade should be regarded as an internal affair strengthening ties between the two parts of a divided country and not as a question of foreign support for a German Communist government. West Germany has moved that far from the iron certainties of anti-Communism of the early Fifties.

Trade with the Communist bloc by Western countries is the great emollient of the cold war. It has increased each year since the middle of the last decade, and in the competition for orders, the West Europeans, the British, French, and Italians, first, have flouted the old rule, long upheld by the United States, that credit terms should be limited to five years.

The question today therefore is not whether there will be changes in East Europe. It is how far they will go and where will they stop. Before governments in the West begin following General de Gaulle and talking of a Europe that extends from the Atlantic to the Urals, they would be prudent to recognize certain limiting factors on the other side that argue against any dramatic political change in East Europe.

For example, there has been no armed rebellion against a Communist regime in the bloc since the tragic Hungarian failure in 1956. Nor are there any indications in those countries that are changing most rapidly, Rumania, for example, of a desire to overthrow Communism by armed action or to develop another form of government not based on the Communist ideology. The simplest reason is that Hungary taught potential rebels that the Soviet Union would use force to crush any rebellion and that the United States would not risk a war with the Soviet Union to go to their aid.

A more sophisticated argument, popular with the non-Communist left in Europe, is that as Communism evolves in East Europe, many of its harshest aspects and most serious weaknesses will disappear. The Hungarians are no longer hungry, the Czechs are moving into a sort of bourgeois Communism, the Rumanians are expanding; so runs the argument. Communism, the left says happily, is moving gradually into a new phase where it will presently become indistinguishable from left-wing social democracy.

Both these arguments discount one of the most powerful factors in maintaining a static political situation in East Europe, a situation that leaves the power in the hands of the Communist parties. This situation is the pervasive and powerful influence of propaganda throughout East Europe. The West is well aware of the more flamboyant aspects of this propaganda: the articles, posters, television and radio programs, the interminable speeches that paint the United States and most of its allies as imperialists aching for a nuclear fight.

There, is, however, a continuing propaganda campaign of a positive nature through the Communist bloc. Its aim is to maintain among the nations the impression that the Communist system is the only system that enables them to avoid the horrors of capitalism, usually equated with the slavery of the masses. This campaign is somewhat more sophisticated than that directed against the imperialists. It will admit shortcomings on occasion and deplore difficulties. But these, the propagandists insist, are only transient problems to be conquered by the coming victory of Communism. The basic theme never deviates: Communism is the only system.

The American or the Briton marvels that any people can swallow such stuff. But the Westerner forgets the essential ingredient in the success of Communist propaganda in countries where the party is in control: quite simply, there is no standard of comparison. The introduction of a sprinkling of Western newspapers, a few broadcasts, a smattering of Western technicians cannot compensate for the absence of any real knowledge of the West against which Communist propaganda could be judged.

Some shafts of light do penetrate from the West. But they are few and far between and often of doubtful value. The impact of a few hundred Western jazz records on Soviet or East European society is unlikely to alter fundamental political beliefs. Nor is the apparent eagerness of the young people in the East to imitate the West in styles of clothing or dancing likely to lead to serious ideological change. After all, Western societies periodically indulge themselves in a craze for Russian ballet or theater or books without damaging the foundations of political belief. Too much is made of similar cultural crazes in the Communist bloc.

It has been noted that an increasingly high percentage of the men coming to the fore in management in East Europe are not orthodox Communists and that a greater flexibility has been remarked among some of the Communist political leaders. The prudent, however, will remember that this "new class," like the old, owes its jobs, its comparative affluence to the Communist system. The party may seem at times to be dated, interfering, and shortsighted. But the system and its members are the products of the party, and to revise the party in any of its essentials is to revise the system to which they owe everything. This is why Communist states like Rumania or Poland may take issue with Moscow on party questions, may even proclaim their economic independence, but invariably fall short of any serious attack upon the basic principles of the ideology. The number of people in positions of authority, from secret police chiefs to the heads of collective farms, who would stand to gain from a change in the system is minute. The number who would lose is limitless.

Another important point is that for thirty years the peoples of East Europe have lived in constant turmoil. A few, the Czechs and the Poles, have some memory of a form of democratic government. But for most the period has been one of constant instability lit by the fires of the most terrible of all wars. Fascism was succeeded by chaos, which in turn gave way to Communism. To the men and women in their forties, now moving toward control, the present system, with all its faults, provides at least stability. Naturally, they are envious of the West. They wish they could have some of the good things of life. They are irked by party supervision, not as onerous as it once was, but still there. They are moved by national motives. This is all true. But it should not be equated as a desire to abolish Communism and embrace democracy, especially when they are told, day after day, that democracy is a hazardous life in which they would be prey to economic upheavals, unemployment, and rapacious bosses.

The position of the Soviet Union in this situation has altered as conditions in East Europe have altered. Earlier we have seen the reasons for this change. But even if the fear of war is not as great as it was, the Soviet Union still enjoys the role of the chief protector of the East and, through the Warsaw Pact, remains the military director of the governments concerned. Russia cannot pose as the guarantor of liberty, about which East Europe knows depressingly little, but it can say that under its military protection stability has flourished, standards of living have risen, and full employment has continued. Man may not live by bread alone, but there are few signs that the peoples of East Europe are yet prepared to take a chance and try something else.

The present chapter has stressed the progress made by Rumania's economy. But it is evident that the other East European countries are not doing so well and that their dependence on the Soviet Union continues, although, of course, it is less than it was. The rundown on East Europe's economies as presented by the Soviet journal *International Life* in March 1965 was revealing and gloomy. The Russians, quite clearly, were reminding their allies that the earthly paradise was still some distance away.

Two Soviet economists, A. Alexsyev and L. Ivanova, said frankly that a general economic recession had set the bloc back five years in the campaign to overtake the capitalist economies in the West. COMENCON had forecast that the Communist bloc powers would be producing fifty percent of the world's industrial goods by the end of 1965. Instead, *International Life* noted, they are producing only forty percent and will not reach the 1965 target until 1970. The aggregate growth rate in the COMENCON nations fell from 13.3 percent in the period 1951–1955 to 8.6 percent in 1963. The most reliable Western estimate available to the writer is that the growth rate dipped below 8 percent in 1964. The survey blamed the recession on difficulties that have been familiar to students of East Europe since the establishment of the Communist regimes: errors in planning, shortages of raw material and fuel, poor cooperation among COMENCON members, and, inevitably, failures in agriculture.

*International Life*'s survey made the following points about individual national economies:

*Hungary:* "A certain lowering of the tempo of production

in connection with the preparation and achievement of progressive changes in the structure of its industry, including a reorientation on the advanced branches of chemistry and instrument-making."

*Czechoslovakia:* "The negative effects of the desire for an excessively wide assortment of industrial goods production."

*East Germany:* "The insufficient growth of the accumulation fund in the period 1958–1961."

*Bulgaria:* "The consequences of a strained raw-material situation are being felt."

*Poland:* "Unfavorable results of the agricultural year and difficulties in the field of foreign trade with capitalist countries."

Significantly, Rumania was not mentioned among the laggards. But the article's insistence on the value of cooperation through COMENCON was an oblique criticism of Rumania's resistance to cooperation and desire for independence.

COMENCON, *International Life* pointed out, had recommended that each nation should specialize in building various types of machine. But the survey found East Germany building ninety-two percent of all types of machinery built in the world and Czechoslovakia seventy percent.

"The course of development of the world socialist community is not a task filled with roses," the article concluded. "It is a complicated, contradictory process involving different tendencies, complex problems and often sharp contradictions."

East Europe, to repeat, is changing. The reasons for the change are apparent. Too much, and too little, can be made of them. The prudent will keep in mind that the Soviet Union, through the possession of nuclear weapons, ideological primacy, and the greatest productive capacity in the bloc, remains in the driver's seat. The essential question is whether the Russians can ever haul in the reins and check East Europe's move toward economic independence and political flexibility.

Personalities enter here. Kosygin and Brezhnev, the diumvirate that replaced Khrushchev, gave the initial impression of being rather cautious leaders, more aware of the grave problems facing the Soviet Union in China, Southeast Asia, and East Europe. Their initial moves, especially those of the quiet Kosygin, were less abrasive, less aggressive than those Khrushchev would have made in similar circumstances. There were no shocks, no surprises in the first five months.

This development, acceptable to the West, must be seen against the historical background. Russia has, throughout her history, thrown up men of demonic energy and ruthless ability, from Ivan the Terrible through Peter the Great to Lenin and Stalin. Is this line dead? It is perfectly possible that a leader of this type will arise tomorrow and seek to reestablish the Soviet Union's complete leadership of East Europe.

On balance, the tide has flowed against Russia in world affairs since 1960. This is as true in Europe as it is in Asia. But Russian nationalism endures. It must be served in peace just as it, instead of Communism, has to be mobilized in times of national crisis. It is quite easy to see any Western move toward German reunification being used as a focus for that nationalism and as a reason for restoring the old hegemony in the East. In the spring of 1965, many people in authority in West Europe feared that the chapter that began with Khrushchev's withdrawal had not yet ended.

What does this situation in the East mean to the West, to the divided West of 1965 torn by its own internal crisis? One warning is already clear, the West cannot be too confident that the developments in East Europe will increase or even that they will continue at anything like their present rate. These developments are sensitive to events in the West.

One of the most serious weaknesses in the West's position is that at this juncture, when the Soviet empire is showing signs of dissolution, there is no agreed policy, indeed no common attitude, toward the countries of the Communist bloc. Nor is there agreement on the key question: does the West, in establishing commercial ties and extending long-term credits to East Europe, help its potential enemies?

France has adopted the most adventurous policy toward Russia and East Europe and by doing so has attracted the flattering attention of both the Soviet Union and her former satellites. Her reasons are both political and economic. France, to both East and West, symbolizes independence of American leadership. But her policy toward the East represents far more than De Gaulle's desire to demonstrate that independence. He is convinced that Europe's great problems, including primarily German reunification, must be settled by all Europeans. Because the General thinks primarily in political terms, it must be assumed that this is the most important consideration to him.

Understandably, the General's proposal to include Germany's neighbors in the negotiation of her unity, frontiers, and arms levels was welcomed enthusiastically in East Europe. Fear of the Germans, exacerbated by Communist propaganda, has made German unity *the* issue in that area. The same propaganda emphasized that the prospects of a peaceful settlement were remote as long as the United States, always identified as the supporter of the new German militarism, played a major role in any settlement. What could be better suited to Communist plans for Europe than a cozy little conference with Russia and her allies on one side of the table and France and the smaller countries of Western Europe on the other.

France's economic needs are also a factor. East Europe needs French help in building industrial plants, and this is an area where French order books are less full than they have been in the recent past. The bulk of French trade is with her partners in EEC, but there is little demand for this specialized activity in the Community's industrialized members. To France, trade with the East means the sale of petro-chemical and other chemical plants, as well as machine tools and finished products.

The West German attitude toward trade with the East, although shadowed by fears that it will be turned to advantage by the East Germans, is unashamedly avid. German industry has a long history of Eastern trade; under both the Empire and the Third Reich it tended to look on the Balkan countries as close to being an economic fief. Politically, Bonn is less interested in developments east of the Elbe than Paris. West German governments are and have been less independent of the United States than others; neither the Federal Republic nor Washington is convinced that De Gaulle's idea of an all-European solution to reunification will work.

Britain, more than ever desperate for overseas trade, is now competing with Germany and France for the largest share of the trade with East Europe. Under the Tories, the restraint exercised by Washington had some influence on London until the twilight of Conservative power. The major British trade pact with the Soviet Union was signed in 1964, however, and since then British business has been prospecting in East Europe with new vigor. A Labour government, some of whose members are less anti-Communist than the Tories, is likely to encourage this trend. But whoever rules in Downing Street, the bars are down and the British are in on the hunt.

Oddly enough, they suffer from one disadvantage in dealing with East European governments. The United States and the United Kingdom are so closely linked in Communist minds that British businessmen intent on doing no more than earning an honest pound find themselves regarded as secret agents of the CIA or of British intelligence, sometimes both.

The United States' rearguard action against the expansion of trade with East Europe and especially against the grant of long-term credits had clearly failed by the end of 1964. To those who watched the action as it was fought at NATO conferences and in the NATO Parliamentarians' conference, it was clear that a great deal of hard thinking had been done in Washington on what was an irrelevant issue in the circumstances.

Bright young economists were ready with chapter and verse to prove how Western exports to East Europe would allow the governments there and in the U.S.S.R. to divert industrial resources to armaments. No one doubted their statistics; indeed, some of the larger governments had made their own reckonings. What they did doubt was their relevancy. America's allies had made up their minds to trade with the East, and trade they will. With the exception of West Germany, they have never matched America's virulent anti-Communism and they are no longer frightened of Soviet military or political aggression. Here is another facet of the Atlantic crisis.

Is the West taking a risk in expanding trade with the East? If we are certain that the developments of the last five years will continue both in the Soviet Union and the countries of the Communist bloc, then the risk, while there, is not great. But it is painfully evident that we cannot be certain. New rulers with new policies may arise in the Soviet Union. The Atlantic alliance, which has been a formidable barrier to Communist ambitions in the past, is weak, perhaps dying, torn apart by the conflicts that have arisen as a result of its success.

The West is no longer united. There is the weakness. If it were, if NATO had the unity and the authority of a decade ago, then the dangers of expanding trade with the Communist bloc would be minimal. But until the powers of the Atlantic community can reestablish some unity in dealing with the issues that divide East and West in Europe, we run a grave risk of helping our enemies—and Kosygin is just as much an enemy of capitalism as Khrushchev—with little real benefit to ourselves.

Nor should the United States and its allies be deluded by the change in East Europe into discounting the assistance given by its governments to antidemocratic forces outside Europe. The Rumanians, the Czechs, or the Poles certainly are disinclined now to become involved directly in international Communist adventures. But so-called "liberation" movements in Algeria, Zanzibar, Cuba, Malaysia, and Vietnam all have been equipped with arms and other supplies from East Europe. In the coming struggle to control the political direction of Latin America, Africa, and the Middle East, and in the continuing struggle in Asia, from Vietnam to Afghanistan, these East European nations will play an important role in Communism's undeclared war against the West.

The growing disarray of NATO has been of the greatest political and economic benefit to the Communist bloc. And because the West is in disarray, it has been unable to take advantage of what has happened within the bloc. Can the situation be retrieved? Only if European unity extends into the political field and that unity is then welded into a larger Atlantic community.

The examination in succeeding chapters of where we stand now in relation to these goals demonstrates that success is distant unless there is a revival on both sides of the Atlantic of the enlightened statesmanship that brought NATO into being and laid the foundations of EEC. Of such statesmanship, there is now no sign. Instead we have conflicting national ambitions and temporizing statesmanship. The Russians are not the only ones in trouble.

## Chapter VIII

## EUROPEAN RETHINK

Progress Toward Economic Unity  •  The General and
Political Union  •  Dr. Hallstein's Views  •  The United
Kingdom Thinks Again  •  Europe's Views of the Anglo-
American Alliance

Both the dreamers and the doers in Europe always have
agreed that political unity among the six members of EEC
can develop only when a solid base of industrial and agricultural unity has been established. Progress toward this goal
has been steady and, considering the problems, remarkably
rapid in the last two years. The Six now are within measur-
able distance of achieving their economic base. Consequently,
political unity is moving out of the realm of theory into substantive discussion.

July 1, 1967, is now the target date for the establishment
of the industrial common market. From that date, if all goes
well, customs duties among the six members will be eliminated and they will be protected by an external tariff. The
date is a good deal earlier than that envisaged by even the
most optimistic two years ago, and testifies to the gradual
acceptance throughout the Community of the need to end
internal tariffs.

The 1967 date also is the target for the establishment of a

common farm system. July 1 was chosen arbitrarily because that is the day the agreement on grain prices will go into effect. The Community's officials and the various national governments hope by then to agree on prices for other farm products. The importance of the accord on grain prices cannot be discounted. It took EEC successfully into a sensitive area of national policies, one that involves the future of some fifteen million Europeans living on farms.

Progress in these areas has been accompanied by the tightening of EEC's internal machinery. From the beginning of 1966, the three existing bases for European unity—the High Authority of the European Coal and Steel Community, Euratom, and the various commissions of the European Economic Community—will be merged into one High Authority that will direct every aspect of EEC from Brussels.

Henceforth there will be a single body to deal with the Council of Ministers, representing the six governments and their individual policies, and to establish policies of The Six on such outstanding and delicate issues as the energy problem. Among other things, energy means oil. And oil is high politics, involving not only the interests of EEC but also of the Middle East, South America, and the United States.

The new High Commission's greatest test, however, will be the fusion of the treaties under which the three communities, then merged, had been operating. These are the Treaty of Rome, which established EEC and Euratom, and the Treaty of Paris, which set up the European Coal and Steel Community. The conclusion of a new treaty, governing all three communities, will take integration in Europe a step further. Perhaps the step will be one that General de Gaulle, with his known dislike for integration of supranationalism, will prove unwilling to take.

Except for government experts and scholars, few in the

207

United States or Britain appear to have realized just how far this recent progress has taken Europe down the road to economic and political unity. For example, the competition of the agricultural community will give Brussels a considerable measure of authority over the agricultures of the six members. Dr. Sicco Mansholt, a vice president of the European Commission, the governing body of EEC, will come very close to being a European Minister of Agriculture. The Agricultural Commission eventually will have around a billion dollars at its disposal in the agricultural fund. Ultimately some of this money will be used to finance structural changes in European agriculture; that is, the officials in Brussels will be paying for improvements in what has heretofore been a jealously guarded field of individual governmental activity.

French opposition developed almost immediately. An agricultural fund sounded to Paris like a European budget. The fact that it would be under the partial control of the European Parliament added the element of supranationalism De Gaulle detests. The General's unwavering opposition to federalism and supranationalism is a basic element in the coming struggle for Europe's political future. Many problems must be solved. What kind of political system will develop to control the unified executive of the European Community? Will the European Parliament achieve international authority or will De Gaulle win out and keep power in the national governments? And if the Parliament does get real power, where will it meet? The progress made thus far encourages the belief that the answers will be found. But they are as likely to be found as a result of evolving situations in Europe as through protracted negotiation. It is already apparent, however, that the merger of the three communities into a single European Commission of fourteen members, instead of three commissions of twenty-three members, will introduce a new center of power in Europe, whether the General likes it or not.

The agreement on grain prices was rightly welcomed as a great forward step. But agreement has yet to be reached on milk and butter and on meat, eggs and poultry, fruit, vegetables and cheese. As the Commission sees the future, each main group of farm products will have its own market organization and a price system. There will be a single target price set to provide a fair return for the efficient producer, a support price, from five to ten percent lower than the target price, below which prices of the markets of The Six will not be allowed to fall, and a variable import levy insuring that farm products from outside EEC are not offered on its markets at prices below the target price.

The system is a highly complicated one. Organizing and administrating it will demand skill and tact for, to repeat, the EEC officials here are entering an economic area that traditionally is very sensitive politically. In both France and West Germany the farmers are a vocal, protected, and politically powerful minority. Yet it is exactly because the Commission has established a bridgehead in the area, long a stronghold of European protectionism, that there is reason for cautious optimism about political unity.

Until early this year there was a shortage of detailed plans for political unity, possibly because the governments involved have been skeptical about progress in the agricultural common market, possibly because of the political repercussions on electorates. In this field, as in many others, France acted first and got very little in return. The Fouchet Plan, bearing the name of De Gaulle's present Minister of Education and the unmistakable imprint of the General's political views, was presented in April 1962.

The Fouchet Plan proposed a loose confederation of sovereign states whose leaders and ministers would confer at stated intervals on European and international issues with the object of exchanging information and, perhaps, of aligning national policies. This was *l'Europe des Patries*, the Europe of separate nations, or fatherlands, and it fell far short of the dreams of the federalists, who believe in the creation of a supranational government in the Europe of The Six.

The plan was the subject of prolonged and intense negotiation among the governments of The Six. Discussion focused on three central issues: the relationship between a politically united Europe and NATO, the relationship of a European political organization with EEC, that is, with the economic side of unity, and the future of a united Europe, including, primarily, its development into a more integrated unit that eventually would move toward federalism.

Led by West Germany, most of the governments involved demanded that there be clearly defined links between a united Europe and the Atlantic alliance. The French, whose hostility to NATO was developing rapidly even then, resisted, but a compromise solution was worked out.

In the discussion over the political community's relations with EEC, the majority of the governments emphasized that they did not want altered the European Commission's prerogatives in economic affairs, which were established by the Treaty of Rome. Again a compromise was worked out.

The negotiations broke down over the issue of the future development of unity once the Europe of the Fatherlands was established. The smaller members of The Six, traditionally the strongest supporters of federalism, sought guarantees that progress toward political unity would not end with the implementation of the Fouchet Plan. These guarantees were refused by France. The negotiations broke down.

General de Gaulle relegated the Fouchet Plan to that well-stocked attic where he keeps spare policies and discredited plans against the day when they will be dusted off and again presented to his allies with blare of trumpets and roll of drums. But the plan remains the most definite approach thus far to political unity. Chancellor Erhard's proposals in 1964 dealt largely with questions of procedure now rather than the long-term development of unity. Its reception among The Six was cool.

Greater interest has been aroused by the suggestions of Paul-Henri Spaak, Belgium's Foreign Minister. He began with the realistic assumption that a compromise between the Europe envisaged by the Fouchet Plan and a federalist or supranational Europe is out of the question at the moment. But he felt that the basic form of cooperation suggested by the Fouchet Plan, the regular meetings of ministers, should be retained and put into operation.

As a link between the ministers and EEC, Spaak proposed the establishment of a Committee of Three chosen from EEC. The Committee's task would be to prepare for meetings of ministers, to carry out any decisions taken, and to draft, in the light of EEC's experience, "a definite treaty providing for a united Europe." * By establishing the Committee, Spaak believed that the governments of The Six would have to recognize that there is a Community viewpoint, which may oppose a national viewpoint or even a national policy, and that the solution of differences between the two viewpoints may be found in discussions between the Committee and ministers of the country or countries concerned.

Progress toward political unity often reminds one of a long-distance race in which first one and then another runner takes the lead. In the spring of 1965, an Italian proposal was in the lead. Its main point was a meeting of the heads of gov-

* *Foreign Affairs,* January 1965.

211

ernment of the six EEC members once the ground had been thoroughly prepared by their foreign ministers. At this meeting, the Italians proposed, the six leaders would draft a declaration laying down the general lines to be followed in the achievement of political unity. Then would come a three-year period in which policies would be brought together through yearly meetings of the heads of government and by conferences every three months among the foreign ministers. The talks would be prepared by a commission representing the governments concerned. But the main point, Italian ministers insisted, is the necessity of a meeting of heads of government.

Once again General de Gaulle slammed on the brakes. Maurice Couve de Murville, his foreign minister, was sent to Rome to inform the Italian government, which was feeling quite proud of itself for restarting the movement toward unity, that a meeting of the foreign ministers on May 10 was unacceptable to France. Couve de Murville made it clear that France's interest in progress toward political unity did not extend beyond its own Fouchet Plan.

De Gaulle's sudden use of the brakes shook up his fellow passengers. Manfred Klaiber, West Germany's ambassador, hurried around to the Elysée Palace to express his government's concern, only to be told that the General agreed in principle with the Italian proposal and that Chancellor Erhard should not worry; De Gaulle's promise to proceed on European unity in 1965 still held good.

But after a French cabinet meeting it was clear that the promise would be redeemed only on certain conditions: a favorable outcome to the bargaining among The Six on agricultural prices, favorable, naturally, to France. The Cabinet's statement carefully avoided mentioning "unity" in connection with political development. Instead it talked of "a close political cooperation" among the partners in EEC. The distinction was understood by those federalists who think in terms of unity rather than in terms of cooperation under the Fouchet Plan.

The affair is worth describing in detail because it demonstrates the lengths to which De Gaulle will go to block anything that even appears to take political leadership among The Six away from France. Less than three months earlier, the General had promised Chancellor Erhard—unconditionally, according to the Germans—that he would support the movement toward political unity in 1965. But two years before the meeting with Erhard, the General, by agreeing to the French-German Treaty of Cooperation, had given French support to European unity. The Treaty's preamble mentions as one of the joint goals of the two governments "the unification of Europe as initiated by the creation of the European communities. . . ."

It is impossible to see France's stand on the Italian proposal and her opposition to an EEC budget in any other light but sustained rejection of any terms for European political development but her own. In this situation the efforts of other European statesmen in the future are likely to encounter the same implacable opposition. Spaak's suggestion is an ingenious plan to bridge the gap between the confederate and federal concepts of European unity. The Italian proposal with its emphasis on the individual roles to be played by the governments leans more toward the Fouchet Plan. But the idea of federalism remains alive with its supranational aspects intact. It is the older if, for the time being, less popular concept of European unity.

Professor Walter Hallstein, President of the Commission of EEC, in a speech at the University of Kiel, illuminated the task.

"We are trying to replace one political prejudice that has for centuries past swayed human beings in Europe, that has made the political map of Europe what it is today—the national prejudice—by a better attitude, a European attitude; provided you do not take it as a piece of cynicism, I would even say: by a better, a European, prejudice."

European unification "is a matter of politics," Professor Hallstein reminded his audience. And it is national politics or, as he would say, national prejudices, that will affect its course.

Walter Hallstein, now sixty-four, is one of the most remarkable of the new group of international servants to develop in the service of European unity. A distinguished professor of law, he became State Secretary of the German Foreign Ministry, that is, its professional head, in 1951 after leading the German delegation to the Schuman Plan Conference in 1960. He became President of the Commission of EEC in 1958. Professor Hallstein is a quietly affable man with little of the rigid legalistic approach that might be expected from his background. His speech at Kiel was remarkable for the light it cast on the workings of what might be called the European mind.

"The reasons why European unity is useful, necessary, inevitable are quickly enumerated," he said. "They are mainly psychological; on the one hand, a new feeling of spaciousness that makes people see things—including public affairs—on a bigger scale, whether it is the fight against poverty or the danger of atomic war or Communism or the economy and its organization and so on; on the other hand, the extent to which national sentiment has suffered, its weakness as a result of the dreadful misuse to which it was put in the orgiastic adventure of the Second World War. We now have a vision of a world in which powers of continental scale shape

214

politics, and there is room for Europeans in this world only if they will decide to club together."

Describing the Commission he heads, Professor Hallstein called it "the Community organ par excellence" whose members appointed by agreement among the six governments "receive no instructions from them." They can be dismissed only by the European Parliament "to which they alone are responsible." The Commission, as EEC's executive arm, now rules an administration of some three thousand people from the member countries; roughly one quarter Italian, one quarter German, one quarter French, and one quarter from the Netherlands, Belgium, and Luxembourg.

"The Council of Ministers is a federal organ," Professor Hallstein emphasized. "The member states act in and through it. Their representatives do not, however, simply represent their national interests; their duty is rather to serve the Community as a whole. The Council is the actual legislator of the Community. The Commission's legislative powers are secondary, although in the course of time they have been somewhat extended, especially as regards agricultural policy, and will tend to develop further.

"The voting rules in the Council are such as to make it impossible for one state to dictate to the others or wield supreme power. This will be evident after January 1, 1966, when voting by qualified majority becomes the rule. The three big countries—France, Germany, and Italy—each have four votes, Belgium and the Netherlands two each, and Luxembourg one. In all matters that have to be passed by qualified majority, and for which the Treaty [of Rome] requires a proposal from the Commission, twelve votes are needed; this means that the majority of the 'Big Three' is effective only when they support the line put forward by the Commission. Otherwise the twelve votes must be drawn from at least four member states. To put it the other way round, a proposal from the Commission cannot be rejected simply by one member state or by the Benelux countries together, a veto can be exercised only by a combination of two or more countries. To amend a proposal put forward by the Commission, on the other hand, unanimity is required."

Professor Hallstein, like many dedicated Europeans, puts great emphasis on the European Parliament because through it "the European citizen, the man in the street, is to take part in the great political process of integration, for it is a fundamental, democratic conviction of our peoples that he ought to do so."

The Parliament's members are chosen from the six national parliaments, and under the Treaty of Rome its functions are purely advisory at this stage of European political development.

"The real problem" as Professor Hallstein described it, is that as the parliament "has no substantive power of decision," its role "of dramatizing and popularizing the great decisions —which makes it a decisive factor in forming public opinion —cannot be played with full effect. The danger is not that the Community's progress will be halted by this, but that the Community may become too remote to be understood."

The Professor emphasized that in methods, procedures, and aims, reunification "is from A to Z a work of peace." He pointed out that under EEC's "common discipline" states often at war in the past now find war impossible. Presenting a united front to the world The Six strengthen the movement toward peace by demonstrating that old enemies can cooperate.

Past peace settlements in Professor Hallstein's eyes were "the confirmation of the right of the victor" but EEC is replacing this "barbaric principle by peaceful, rational balance."

He asked, "Is it not one of the greatest wonders of our age that the real victor of the Second World War, the United States of America, is itself working for this change and giving up the right of the victor?"

When the idea of European political unity first reappeared in Europe after the end of World War II, its advocates thought largely in terms of a United States of Europe. The war had set their minds against nationalism. The mounting pressure from the Soviet Union convinced them that only a federal union of West European states could survive.

The United States encouraged the idea through its officials and diplomats, then ubiquitous and omnipotent in Europe. The dream of the United States of Europe, they assured their pleased clients, was by no means unreasonable. These Americans could not foresee, of course, that their efforts to rebuild economic and political stability would result in the revival of nationalism, although anyone with a nodding acquaintance with European history should have recognized that this was a potential result. Where they were more at fault was in giving the European partisans of a United States of Europe the idea that the process of federation would be a relatively easy one. In this they overlooked the difficulties faced, and overcome, by the thirteen states that formed the American Union. These states, although ethnically alike and speaking the same language, had to surmount many obstacles before union was achieved. How much more is this true of Europe, with many languages, sharp differences of religion, and the abiding political problem of the extreme left.

The supporters of federalism and supranationalism in Europe survive, although their numbers and influence have diminished. Their argument for their form of unity is that no international organization can function effectively unless it is guided by a higher authority. Decisions in this authority must be taken by majority vote, and the minority, as in any democratic organization, must go along with the majority's decision. The system of discussions at regular meetings proposed by the Fouchet Plan would be ineffective as a foundation for European unity, they contend, because each government would follow its own policies even though the majority of its allies opposed them. This is exactly the freedom De Gaulle wants for France.

As EEC moves toward greater economic integration, however, the Fouchet Plan or some development of it, as suggested by Spaak, remains the only substantive proposal before The Six. The clash between the supporters of this plan and the federalists recently has been compounded by a dispute between the European Commission, the highest authority in EEC, and the member governments over the extent of the Commission's political role in a united Europe. This dispute really is an extension of the fundamental conflict between the two ideas on how European political unity is to be organized.

All this is taking place in a Europe in which the present membership of EEC appears frozen. Discussions of political unity do not extend beyond the six original members. Yet there is a general acceptance that the question of the final geographical extent of united Europe must be dealt with in the future. To most Europeans this means Britain and the development of her relations with Europe.

Early in 1965 Europeans heard encouraging noises from Britain. The Labour government wanted to be friends, although it chose some highly original ways of demonstrating it, and the Conservative Opposition made it clear that once in power it would try again to enter EEC. All very cheering for those Europeans who had always wanted Britain in Europe. But as time wore on, they realized that the British had not kept pace with what was happening on the continent. Those incurably isolated islanders, having devoted the interval to scandal in high places, prime-minister-making, and elections, still appeared to think of the Community as it had been in 1963 when General de Gaulle slammed the door in their faces. The progress since should make it both easier and more difficult for Britain to enter Europe if a Conservative government comes to power and carries out its promise to do so.

Mechanically the process should be easier. The Community is more integrated and becoming more so with each passing month. This condition should provide a better focus and more attention for any British application. One of the difficulties that faced Edward Heath and his team of negotiators in 1962 has never really been understood in Britain and the United States. This was that while they were negotiating with The Six's representatives for entry, these same representatives also were negotiating among themselves on outstanding issues of economic cooperation within the Community. It was like planning an annex to a building before the main building itself is completed.

But the greater measure of integration also presents Britain with a new difficulty. The Community is more settled. Its member governments and peoples are becoming accustomed to it. Its machinery is running well. The way to industrial and agricultural common markets is fairly clear. No government wants to invite delays by new negotiations to bring Britain into Europe.

Labour, Europe takes for granted, will not try to join. But it does want to cooperate with EEC. Mr. Wilson's cabinet wants to increase Britain's trade with the continent. It would like to achieve an easier relationship between the Community and EFTA and a reduction of tariff barriers between the two groups. It wants to participate in all discussions of political unity; a position hotly opposed by the French. There is, however, no basic change in Labour's policy from what it was three years ago. It remains opposed to joining Europe. The change is in the atmosphere, with Labour politicians ceaselessly proclaiming that Britain is a part of Europe. But they are careful to point out that EEC is not Europe but only a part of it. Which is perfectly true.

In opposition, as in power, the Tories have favored British entry into Europe. But their support for the policy has been spotty. Once De Gaulle had blackballed the Macmillan government's bid, the party seemed to lose interest in EEC although Heath and a few stalwart "Europeans" kept the idea alive in the party. During the election campaign of 1964, Sir Alec Douglas-Home dismissed the European issue as "a dead duck." On the hustings or in its own conferences, the party as a whole showed a marked disinclination to discuss a project that, only two years before, had been a basic element of its foreign policy.

But as we have seen, the Tories returned to the battle in 1965. Their brave words about another bid to enter EEC were of more than passing interest to the members of the Community. They felt that the Labour government could not retain power for long. In Europe's eyes, even those of convinced socialists, the Wilson government had been timid about tackling the basic problem of the British economy. Europe saw trouble ahead for the Prime Minister. So the governments of The Six listened carefully to what the Tories were saying, for they appeared to many to be on their way back to power.

What was remarkable about the new Tory attitude, however, was the manner in which the bulk of informed public opinion appeared to swing behind it. As *The Sunday Times* pointed out, ". . . if the chance comes for Britain to resume negotiations for entry into the Common Market, it does not look this time as though General de Gaulle or anyone else will be able to claim, as he was justifiably able to do before, that opinion in Britain is so undecided as to make the validity of British membership a very dubious proposition."

The Six, however, remained suspicious of the Conservatives' motives. Some saw their emphasis on reentry as an attempt to score politically off a Labour government whose foreign policy showed a singular lack of imagination. Others regarded it as an attempt by Britain to escape the formidable domestic economic decisions that must be taken by joining Europe and letting free competition with The Six force labor and management to rationalize and modernize.

British stock in Europe is very low and not entirely because of the ineptitude of the Labour government. In the last three years a quiet reassessment of Britain has been going on among politicians, officials, and businessmen. Three years ago Europe was prepared to take Britain pretty much at her own rather inflated valuation. In the interval, the British image of political probity and stability has been marred, the country has gone through its most serious financial crisis since the war, and, most important, little or nothing has been done to shake the economy or the people out of their complacency.

At the same time the United States has demonstrated a steadily growing economic strength and drawn far ahead of any other Western power, or combination of powers, in the field of nuclear weaponry. This development combined with Britain's own internal weaknesses has dispersed any lingering impressions in Europe that Britain was, as she claimed to be, a world power. To Europeans, even to General de Gaulle, there is only one world power in the West, the United States, and there will not be another until political unity creates Europe as a third world power of the first magnitude.

Some British think that because of the war, Europe owes something to the United Kingdom. This was true fifteen or even ten years ago. It is no longer true. A Belgian, who spent the war years in London, was asked what EEC would do about Britain.

"We're not going to do anything, it's up to the British," he said. "They've got to do something. And, if they don't realize now that they must join Europe, then I fear they never will."

These considerations naturally do not affect General de Gaulle's firm opposition to British entry. He and France are perfectly willing to be friendly with Britain—as long as Britain doesn't knock on EEC's door. In fact, friendship on a bilateral basis with Labour seems much more to the General's taste than friendship with the Tories. Cooperation with Britain on the Concorde supersonic airliner and on the research, development, and production of an extensive range of aircraft has been agreed to by the two governments. But, as we have noted, France is implacably opposed to British participation, through WEU, in any talks on planning political unity.

Unwavering French hostility, the present weakness of the British economy, and the uncompleted state of agricultural and industrial cooperation within EEC all argue for a postponement of any new bid for entry by the United Kingdom, even if the Tories were to return to power this year or next. Some Europeans, who want Britain in, believe that 1968 is the year for a new approach. By then, they say, Europe will have completed its economic integration and the critical question of political unity will be paramount. It is in the political field that they expect to get the most from Britain's membership.

Britain's relations with its partners in EFTA deteriorated during the Labour government's first half year in office. The fifteen percent surcharge on imports may have been necessary if Britain was to escape temporarily from her financial difficulties. But it was announced and imposed in an awkward manner, and the situation was not improved by the early realization of the United Kingdom's partners that some of the Labour ministers didn't know the real purpose of EFTA. Some Labour ministers appeared to think that EFTA was a framework for future political union among its members and that, if it prospered as an economic group, it would attract to it some of the EEC countries. Neither idea was ever the intention of the founders of EFTA.

Moreover, Labour appeared to misunderstand the differences between EFTA and EEC. The former is economic and static. The latter, originally economic, is political and developing. Even if tariffs between the two are lowered, as the Labour government has suggested, EEC is bound to move farther away from EFTA as economic integration and political unity develop.

The British government also overlooked the attraction that the dynamism of EEC exerts on members of EFTA. Austria, a member of EFTA, is seeking association with EEC, and its government is negotiating the harmonization of its industrial tariffs with those of the Community. Should the negotiations succeed and make Austrian tariffs equal or nearly equal to those of EEC, this will imply Austria's withdrawal from the Free Trade Association. EFTA, consequently, is a rather rickety basis for a British policy in Europe. The Six are not impressed. They expect other members of EFTA to seek association with the Community.

It seems reasonable to assume, moreover, that when Britain does try again to enter Europe, the Commonwealth connection will not play so important a role in the negotiations as it did on the previous occasion. The Labour government and party place great emphasis on the Commonwealth. This is partly because of historical reasons—India and Pakistan were given their freedom by a Labour government—and partly because the dream of a great multiracial Commonwealth inspires many British socialists. In one of those sudden turnabouts of politics, the Labour party today cares more for the Commonwealth than the Tories, except for the Beaverbrook press and a sprinkling of diehard M.P.'s.

But whatever dreams are dreamt by the Labour party, it is evident that the Commonwealth is no answer to Britain's problems. Canada and Australia are moving into the American economic sphere; the former might be said to be there already. Ghana has deteriorated into a dictatorship that is steadily going broke. Nigeria is torn by internal differences. The countries of the Commonwealth are still a valuable market for Britain and a source of some raw materials. But as a substitute for British membership in Europe it does not make sense either economically or politically. From the economic standpoint the United Kingdom will get far more out of union with Europe than it will out of the Commonwealth. As Duncan Sandys, in and out of office a strong advocate of Britain's union with Europe, reminded his countrymen, the Commonwealth is not an alternative to EEC and the Commonwealth countries themselves are no longer as anxious about British entry into Europe as they were three or four years ago.

And what does the "political leadership" of the Commonwealth really mean? Politicians of both parties in the United Kingdom have made much of it in the past. But does India or Australia or Canada invariably follow British leads in international affairs? Suez provides the answer. India and

Canada were critical, Australia favorable. Any British claim to be a world power on the basis of "leadership" of the Commonwealth is an empty one. The realization of this should be part of the realistic appraisal the British must and will make of their role in the world.

Sir Winston Churchill, when he headed his last government, used to say that British foreign policy rested on three bases: the Commonwealth, the intimate relationship with the United States, and Europe. One sign of much-needed realism in British thinking is that the "Europeans" of the Tory party and the few hardy souls in the Labour ranks who share their views now understand that if Britain goes into Europe, the relationship with the United States will suffer to some extent. They also know that the closeness of this relationship was one of the reasons why De Gaulle kept Britain out in 1963. The "Trojan Horse" theory that saw the British in Europe as the spokesmen for the United States may not have been the only factor in making up the General's mind, but it was an important one.

Whether Britain joins Europe or not, events have conspired to change the relationship with the United States. Simply put, America has gone ahead since 1963, the British have slipped back. The United Kingdom is unlikely to make up the ground it has lost without a major national effort to correct its economic weaknesses. Under Labour there has been no sign that this will be done, although there has been a spate of high-flown arguments for action. Britain needs the shock of entry into Europe more now than she did five years ago.

The disenchantment with Europe experienced by Britain after her rejection has been reflected to some extent by the United States. The belief grew that De Gaulle's strident nationalism would block further economic integration and prevent any real progress toward political unity. Washington has been wrong about the first and, up to now, right about the second. The importance of the agreement on grain prices as a pilot to agricultural integration was discounted by the Administration at the outset. But one American authority in a paper on integration in the Community has said that "national officials estimate that seventy-five percent of the major political decisions of vital importance to agricultural policy [and indeed to general economic policy] have been taken out of the exclusive control of national governments and made the subject of bargaining in the community institutional system." *

American thinking, like British, clearly has exaggerated the impact of Gaullism on the economic aspects of EEC. Whatever America and Britain think, and whatever the latter does about joining, the Community's course between now and 1968 seems set.

This statement does not discount the potential dangers that lie in the path of the Community's development. France's tendency to slow progress toward political unity by insisting that European unity take the form of l'Europe des Patries or nothing reflects the General's opposition to integration and supranationalism in the political field. But the final lowering of industrial tariffs is likely to bring him face to face with an equally unpalatable result of integration in the economic field: the invasion of French markets by tariff-free German, Dutch, Italian, and Belgian products. Unless the General and his advisers are confident that French industry can meet this competition, EEC must expect a new and formidable challenge to its continued existence. This is most likely to arise when the Commission in Brussels sits down to write the new treaty covering the three communities. This will offer De

* Leon M. Lindberg, University of Wisconsin.

Gaulle the opportunity to delay progress and divert the course of development from integration of any kind.

France and the General, naturally, are not the only threats to the Community's development. Nationalism is reviving rapidly in Europe. How long will it be before it infects Germany? And when the Germans weigh the prospect of reuniting their country against continued membership in EEC, a choice they may have to make, which will they choose?

These are potential dangers. On the surface, the Community is moving steadily ahead toward economic and political unity and, consequently, toward a more important and powerful role within the Atlantic community. The task of statesmen, American as well as European, must be to insure that this role is one of cooperation with the United States, Britain, and the other non-members of EEC. The danger is that as the Community develops economic and political strength, and ultimately some degree of nuclear strength built around France's independent nuclear force, its policies will diverge increasingly from those of the United States.

The back-room boys of the Kennedy Administration evolved what they called the dumbbell theory back in the days when Britain's entry into Europe was confidently expected in Washington. The United States would be one globe of the dumbbell and a powerful, integrated Europe the other. What they did not foresee is what is quite likely to happen. This is that The Six, without Britain but under the influence of first nationalism and eventually Europeanism, would establish Europe as an independent third power. Frightened by propaganda, largely based on fact, of the dangers of an American economic takeover in Europe and worried by the prospect of being involved in the United States' wars elsewhere in the world, Europe could move very swiftly toward this sort of independence.

The damage that nationalism can do in France or Germany is not confined to those countries. It could infect all Europe and end by tearing the Atlantic community apart. An independent Europe, believing itself to be the third power and following its own policy in its relations with the Communist bloc, Africa, Asia, or Latin America, could destroy the foundations of Western partnership. This is the new dimension of the crisis in the transatlantic relationship. The shadow it casts is yet another reason why every effort must be made to unite the community before it is too late.

## Chapter IX

## EUROPE AND THE
## "MORE EQUAL" ALLY

NATO in Trouble: The Price of Success • America, the "More Equal" Ally • France, Germany, and the Nuclear Strategy Row • Herr Strauss and the European Nuclear Force • Patterns for Revival

The crisis in Western relations has reached the point where an effort must be made to restore purposeful cooperation. The success of NATO in the Fifties bought the West some time, nothing more. Time is running out. Europe is drifting into a state that will leave it vulnerable to internal dissension and external pressure. New forces and new issues that will affect directly the well-being of Europe are developing in Asia, Africa, and Latin America.

If cooperation is to be restored in the West, NATO clearly is the best available medium. The organization of fifteen members, spanning the Atlantic and extending deep into the Middle East, is served by an able, experienced secretariat. A NATO that has regained some of its old dynamism and purpose would be the most useful starting point, at once solid and flexible, for the West's effort to meet the new problems that confront us.

The middle of 1965 found NATO in very bad shape. General de Gaulle's methodical weakening of the alliance and its own failure, which, of course, represented the failure of the member governments, to solve the problem of strategic nuclear weapons weakened the alliance far more than most governments cared to admit. Indeed, the tendency of many of its foreign ministers (Secretary of State Dean Rusk was a notable offender) to discount in public the seriousness of NATO's situation encouraged a false optimism. Even those diplomats and officials who had served it most loyally were overcome by pessimism. In the spring of this year some of his colleagues gave a dinner party for an ambassador who had been a permanent representative on the North Atlantic Council for some time. His final remark, as he looked around the table at his colleagues, was, "I'm sorry to be leaving you all, but I'm very glad that I won't be here to see this great organization break up."

The decline of NATO is a dangerous development. The West has become so accustomed to the alliance that it has forgotten its great importance. NATO unites fifteen member nations in a collective security agreement under which "an attack on one country is regarded as an attack on all," and a permanent system of political and military planning is maintained. The members nations are: the United States, Britain, Canada, West Germany, France, Italy, the Netherlands, Belgium, Norway, Denmark, Portugal, Greece, Turkey, Luxembourg, and Iceland. The alliance is the core of a system of global military arrangements. For example, the United States, Britain, and France are linked with four Asian and Australasian countries in the Southeast Asia Treaty Organization (SEATO) and Britain is tied to three countries of the northern tier in the Middle East by the Central Treaty Organization (CENTO). The United States is joined to Australia and New Zealand by the ANZUS Pact under which the three countries would provide mutual defense in the event of an attack on any of them. America also has bilateral mutual defense treaties with Japan, Taiwan, and South Korea. The whole defensive system of "aligned" states established in the non-Communist world to contain the Communist powers in Europe and Asia thus begins with NATO.

The alliance comprises three military commands: Europe, the Atlantic, and the English Channel. The directives for these commands come from the Military Committee composed of the Chiefs-of-Staff of each member country except Iceland, which has no military forces. Its executive group is the Standing Group composed of American, British, and French representatives supported by German assistants. Allied Command Europe is unique in that it has national forces assigned to its operational control in peacetime. But all three NATO commands include other forces earmarked for assignment to the alliance commanders in the event of war.

However, the strategic nuclear forces of the United States, Britain, and France remain under national command and control. The United States, however, in an effort to give non-nuclear powers some participation in nuclear strategy, has created a Joint Strategic Planning System based on the Strategic Air Command where officers of other NATO powers participate in strategic planning. The United States since 1963 also has committed three Polaris submarines to the planning control of Supreme Headquarters Allied Powers Europe (SHAPE), and Britain has committed Bomber Command of the Royal Air Force in the same manner.

The center of NATO's military life is Allied Command Europe, covering the continent from Norway's North Cape to the eastern frontiers of Turkey. The command is integrated. This means that at SHAPE officers of all the member nations work together on the various staff sections; operations, intelligence, and so on. The Supreme Commander has been an American general since SHAPE was organized; General Eisenhower was the first and the present incumbent is General Lyman L. Lemnitzer.

What are the elements of NATO's military strength that have enabled it to reduce Soviet pressure on Western Europe? First there are the tactical nuclear weapons, whose number has risen by about sixty percent in the last three years. The "units of delivery," that is, missiles and aircraft, now number about 2,500. But the United States is the only member nation that has produced nuclear warheads for tactical use. Here is an important aspect of America's importance within the alliance. The United States retains control of the nuclear bombs and missile warheads that are to be used, in war, by the national forces of other members. This is called the "double key" arrangement. It is being augmented by the introduction of an electronic lock for larger nuclear weapons. Consequently the tactical nuclear weapons can be employed by the Supreme Commander only with the permission of the President of the United States and, very important, the agreement of the government whose forces have the means of delivery.

The basic conventional military strength of NATO in Europe is some sixty divisions assigned to it by the member governments. Should an emergency last long enough, another thirty divisions could be mobilized and deployed. Many of the divisions have Honest John missiles, and the American and German forces have the Sergeant and Pershing missiles as well; all these missiles have a nuclear capacity. The ground forces are supported by about 5,500 tactical airplanes based on 220 airfields.

The most important of NATO commands in Allied Command Europe is Allied Forces Central Europe with twenty-seven divisions assigned by eight countries. Almost all of these troops are based in West Germany; they are supported by 3,500 aircraft. An integrated early warning system covering Britain, West Germany, the Netherlands, Belgium, and northeast France has been developed, and twenty-two battalions of the Hawk ground-to-air missile are deployed in the command.

NATO's northern flank is covered by Allied Forces Northern Europe. This command is responsible for the defense of Norway, Denmark, Schleswig-Holstein, and the Baltic approaches. To it are assigned all the Norwegian and Danish land, sea, and tactical air forces plus one division, two air wings, and the Baltic fleet of West Germany.

Allied Forces Southern Europe, whose commander is also the commander of the United States Sixth Fleet, is responsible for the defense of Italy, Greece, and Turkey. Forces assigned to it include fourteen Turkish divisions, eight Greek and seven Italian, and the tactical air forces of these countries.

To keep NATO's military strength in perspective it should be noted that the Soviet Union has twenty-six divisions, well supported with tactical aircraft, in East Europe; twenty in East Germany, two in Poland, and four in Hungary. There are also seventy-five divisions in European Russia and twenty-two in central Russia. Supplementing the Soviet forces are those of the East European Communist states; sixty-two divisions and 3,000 aircraft. All the Soviet divisions have tactical nuclear weapons available.

NATO thus is a great deal more than a rather vague multilateral alliance whose members are given to somewhat tedious bickering over complicated problems. It is an effective military organization. But the alliance's military strength, which must be considered as a principal cause of the relaxation of

Soviet pressure in Europe, is only one, although the most important, aspect of NATO's place in the Atlantic community.

There has developed over the years out of the military cooperation a very real and effective political cooperation. At every juncture when it appeared that the Soviet Union might be preparing new action against Berlin or the German Federal Republic, NATO was prepared to give a firm, collective warning. A growing corporate sense among the diplomats and civil servants who served the alliance fostered a spirit of calm deliberation in the discussion of issues like the Congo, Cyprus, west Irian, Malaysia, and Vietnam, all of which lay outside the alliance's military area but which affected one or more of its members. The tendency among the permanent representatives of NATO to view these and other problems internationally has been of the utmost importance in a Europe where national aspirations increasingly have restricted the exchange of objective views among governments.

Cooperation in the military field inevitably led to cooperation in defense production, symbolized by NATO's Defense Production Committee. From the work of this committee emerged the "Atlantic" maritime patrol airplane. Five European members, Belgium, France, Germany, Italy, and the Netherlands, joined in the multinational production of the Hawk missile and eight countries in the production of another American missile, the Sidewinder. Belgium, Germany, Italy, the Netherlands, and the United States organized and supervised a joint production program for the American F-104-G fighter bomber.

From the start NATO has tried to achieve as much standardization as possible to ease the problems of supply in an alliance of fifteen powers. The flow of United States military aid to NATO in the early years of the alliance insured a considerable amount of standardization in weapons and materiel.

Since then agreements on standardization have been reached for vehicle components, electronic valves, electronic components, explosives, certain types of ammunition, and gun steels.

The creation of NATO's infrastructure, the fixed installations on which its forces deploy and operate, has been one of the triumphs of postwar collaboration. Under a system of cost sharing, which took into account the contributive capacity of the member countries, the advantages to the country using the installation, and the economic benefit for the host country, a vast system of military installations has been built in Western Europe. This includes about 250 airfields, 5,600 miles of pipelines, nearly 2,000,000 cubic meters of fuel storage, tens of thousands of miles of submarine and land cables and radio links, naval facilities, such as piers, breakwaters, and storage for oil and ammunition, valued at about $246,000,000, and a huge network of radar warning systems.

Through a Science Committee and a Science Adviser to the Secretary-General, NATO has encouraged cooperation in this field among the member governments. A Science Fellowship Program has been launched supported by NATO funds, as has an Advanced Study Institutes Program. Research in fields like oceanography is supported by a Research Grants Program, and NATO provides grants for special studies in the universities and laboratories of member countries.

NATO, as Dr. T. A. Margerison has pointed out, "spends about four million dollars per year for stimulating and supporting cooperation in the field of fundamental research. The independent tradition of Western science, which is sometimes described as wasteful, appears in this context as its strongest point."

The alliance, in sum, is a great deal more than meetings of ministers issuing emollient statements or diplomats and officials debating in the great, white building at the Porte Dauphine. It is the most powerful military alliance ever established in time of peace, a basis for the most intimate political cooperation, and an organization that has inspired and assumed serious responsibilities in industrial production and scientific research.

Consequently the danger that NATO may "break up," as the pessimistic ambassador phrased it, is a matter of the most desperate seriousness for the West. Before the member governments can mend the situation, they obviously must understand more clearly the internal differences that are in the process of destroying the unity and purpose of the alliance.

The basic cause of discord with the alliance is the present inequality of its structure. NATO, in theory, is an alliance of equals. But this equality cannot be reconciled, as NATO now is organized, with the fact of United States nuclear supremacy. America no longer enjoys a nuclear monopoly within the alliance. But the armory of missiles and bombs and bombers is so large that NATO could fight and win a nuclear war, if indeed anyone will be the victor in such a war, relying on American nuclear power alone.

This power, the prodigious contributions made by the United States over the years to NATO's conventional forces, and the dominant position occupied by Washington in organizing and leading the alliance understandably enough created a feeling of inferiority in European members once they had regained their national identity.

"The United States is much more than a mere *primus inter pares* in this collective alliance," Franz Josef Strauss noted in 1965.* "Essentially, the alliance is directed in a patriarchial manner from Washington. According to the text of the treaty,

* *International Affairs,* April 1965.

236

it is in America that the NATO states have to announce their accession or give notice of withdrawal from membership."

This inequality of strength in a theoretically equal alliance led directly to the present dispute on nuclear strategy. As long as the United States had a near monopoly on nuclear strength in NATO and the British nuclear force was tied tightly to the American forces in planning and strategy, Washington could dictate the general nuclear and conventional strategy for all the allies. Once, however, France had attained a truly independent nuclear status, the dispute developed. And although it is primarily about nuclear strategy, it also concerns political influence within NATO.

On one hand in this dispute we have the United States, supported by the United Kingdom, advocating the strategy of a graduated response to any Communist aggression in Europe. On the other side are the French, discreetly backed by some German politicians, diplomats, and general officers, advocating an immediate nuclear attack on targets in the Soviet Union at the outset of any aggression. This is the strategic doctrine to which the relatively small and weak French *force de frappe* is now committed.

The Americans, according to Pierre Messmer, General de Gaulle's Minister of Defense, are thinking of defending Europe in depth. But, he reasons, "there is no operational depth" in Europe for such a defense. The West, in the French view, cannot wait to discover the intentions and strength of any aggressive action by the East. It must "respond immediately with nuclear reprisals on the territory of the adversary," Messmer said. "Only that strategy is a 'deterrent.'" The American strategy, in the Minister's view, leaves the enemy the choice of time, place, and means of aggression and will lead to "the destruction of Europe."

This last has been an important factor in European criticism of the graduated response since the idea was first advanced by the Kennedy Administration. In its most exaggerated form it is expressed in the prediction that by the time the United States makes up its mind about the intentions and strength of a Communist attack, most of Western Europe will have been destroyed and large parts of West Germany overrun.

The argument over nuclear strategy does not involve the role of the tactical nuclear weapons under SHAPE's command. Some of these are "tactical" only by courtesy. With a range of seven hundred miles, they can hit targets deep in Communist territory. But General de Gaulle, an expert at having his cake and eating it, too, has never urged that these weapons be placed under independent French command or the national commands of the other countries holding them. He recognizes that the tactical nuclear weapons represent a very important part of the overall nuclear deterrent.

The fundamental nuclear inequality in NATO in regard to end weapons, that is, missiles and aircraft capable of delivering thermonuclear bombs, and the dispute over the proper strategy for their use has led to a delay in framing a new NATO purpose to fit the changed military and political situation in Europe and the world. Although the United States has made some minor changes in its position, this Administration's approach to the alliance is fundamentally akin to that of the Truman Administration that brought NATO into being.

In this situation there has been a drying up of governmental support for NATO. In part this is due to complacency; the alliance has outlived past crises and will surmount this one. In part it is due to the concentration of some of its leading members on other issues: the United States and the war in Vietnam, Britain and her economic and financial difficulties, France and the General's "Europe for the Europeans" policy, West Germany and unification.

Over the last six months there has been a perceptible weakening of governmental support for NATO among the major powers. The results have been the most serious in regard to the United States. The smaller members of the alliance have been the true believers through thick and thin, and they relied on American leadership to maintain NATO's drive and purpose. Some of them, notably the Norwegians and the Danes, were worried by the American proposal for a mixed manned nuclear force because they foresaw its disruptive effect on the alliance. But none of them welcomed the virtual withdrawal of United States leadership, leaving the field to De Gaulle.

The General's influence on NATO is negative and powerful. He has told Manlio Brosio, the Secretary-General, that France opposes any further integration within the alliance. Since it is highly unlikely that any further integrated conventional military commands will be established, De Gaulle means by this the creation of an integrated nuclear force such as the MLF or the British proposal for an Allied Nuclear Force.

De Gaulle also has informed the alliance that he believes it should be revised in 1969 to make it more a coalition of independent powers and less an integrated alliance. Behind this lies the definite possibility that the General will not wait, that he will demand a revision of the alliance well before 1969 when, under the North Atlantic Treaty, any member may denounce the pact. If this demand is refused, the French may well put out of NATO. And, although there are some who profess to believe that the alliance could survive this, the effect would be destructive.

France's conventional military forces are not conspicuously

powerful, although the government has done much to improve their weapons, training, and morale. Her atomic *force de frappe* is insignificant compared to the American nuclear armory. But, geographically, France is of vital importance to NATO and to the United States. As Hanson Baldwin has pointed out, the United States Army Communications Zone in Europe, about sixteen Army supply depots and facilities, eleven Air Force bases, and a huge complex of United States and NATO pipelines, communications, petroleum tank installations, and controlling headquarters are situated on French soil. Consequently if NATO and the United States were forced to forgo the use of French territory and French facilities, it would be extremely difficult to support and back up the American and other NATO forces in Germany.

General de Gaulle thus has a very high card to play. He can use it, as he has, to put pressure on the United States. He can also use it on his European allies. They realize that if France leaves the alliance, NATO will be seriously weakened. As a consequence of this indirect pressure, some NATO governments are inclined to go along with the General lest he wreck the alliance. The French President's challenge to NATO is related to West Germany's present position and future aspirations within the alliance. And both are the product of the first principle of NATO discord: the factual inequality between America and her allies.

De Gaulle wants no further integration, which means no German participation in a nuclear force planned and, at the outset, controlled by the United States. Germany, the principal European contributor to NATO's military strength and geographically the most vulnerable of the alliance's major powers, wants, if not nuclear equality, some participation in nuclear weapons. The General opposes this as long as the United States is the dominant nuclear power in Europe. He says it will impede progress toward European political unity, a development he has done his best to delay.

What prospects are open to the Germans? Two proposals, the MLF and the ANF, have been put forward. It may be possible to combine the two. Finally there is the shadowy, never clearly defined French idea of a European nuclear force. About the only thing the Germans have been able to learn about this "European" force is that it will be French, that France's European allies can provide financial and industrial support, and that control of the force will rest with the French government. European nuclear defense thus would be based on the weapons of one country, France, instead of the present arrangements under which the United States, Britain, and France would contribute their nuclear forces to NATO's use in the event of war. Until De Gaulle further defines his ideas about a European nuclear defense, the idea is likely to be unattractive to the Germans.

Yet a new bid by Bonn for nuclear status appears inevitable. It is most likely to develop in the winter of 1965–1966 when, if the present coalition of C.D.U./C.S.U. returns to power, Herr Strauss is expected to reenter the cabinet. This gifted but somewhat erratic politician has already begun to lay the groundwork for German participation in some form of European nuclear force. He believes that the United States no longer sees "the *principal* aim of its foreign policy as the promotion of Western European unity and autonomy," and has begun to "concentrate on reaching an agreement with the Soviet Union on the basis of a *status quo* in Europe."

The "passive" behavior of the continental powers, Herr Strauss argued, has made them "guilty of an offense against both the spirit and the letter of the NATO treaty. In Article 3 of the treaty, the contracting states are required to preserve and strengthen the defense capability of the alliance by *effective self-help* as well as by mutual support. Such self-help and cooperation were a necessity for the European countries from the moment that America found herself in a new position in relation to the Soviet Union, and finally in relation to mainland China also. Europe ought to have concentrated all its efforts on developing the defense of its territory on an independent basis." *

We have heard this argument before. It is the one General de Gaulle has advanced to justify the French nuclear force's independent strategic role. Now, however, it comes from an important German political figure at the moment when most European statesmen expect a renewal of the German bid for nuclear participation and when an increasing number believe that the Germans are justified.

The consequences of a negative answer by the United States will be serious. If the Administration again abandons its leadership in establishing some form of a nuclear force tied to NATO and leaves the matter to the Europeans, progress will be very slow. For, as Herr Strauss and other Germans realize, the Federal Republic remains committed by the A-B-C clauses of the 1954 treaty not to manufacture nuclear weapons. American leadership is essential if any integrated nuclear force, including West Germany, is to be created. Certainly this will provoke another Franco-American row. But just as certainly the issue of Germany's nuclear role, involving the whole future of NATO, must be resolved in the immediate future.

What can the Germans do? If the United States remains on the sidelines, they can turn to France and the General's ectoplasmic European nuclear force. Or, more likely in the long run, they can pursue their own nuclear independence. They have the industrial base and the technological skill.

* *Ibid.*

They can advance reasonable political arguments for independent action. These include Germany's position as the NATO front line with the majority of Soviet missiles already targeted on the Federal Republic, the massive German contribution to the conventional defense of Europe, and the fidelity of German governments to NATO and their support for the policies of its members outside Europe.

In this situation it is difficult to believe that any government in Bonn will be fobbed off with promises of "sharing" or participation in settling nuclear "guidelines." Once France, a weaker power in NATO than Germany, established her own nuclear forces, the German search for equality was only a matter of time. The problem of German nuclear forces, with all its emotional overtones in East and West, like the problem of German reunification must be faced—and soon.

The rationale for the German position is offered by Herr Strauss:

"The European NATO countries are justified in reading into the text of the Atlantic treaty an obligation to seek ways and means in the future of making their defense possible from within Europe itself, just as America is able directly to defend herself. For it is in any case the fact—an untenable fact—that the alliance presents an aggression with the chance, by means of a massive threat of annihilation against the European or American part of it, to render a coordinated Western strategy impossible and thus the treaty ineffective. Yet the security of Europe rests today solely on the threat of reprisals by the United States. The presence of American divisions in Western Europe, equipped with tactical nuclear weapons, strikes many people as a sufficient guarantee against an attack from the East, and one must regard the six nuclear-armed U. S. divisions as having more than a symbolic value, even if they could hardly withstand an attack by twenty or more nuclear-armed Soviet divisions.

"Western Europe is the target area for innumerable Soviet medium-range rockets, which of course have a higher degree of accuracy than intercontinental missiles; thus a 'balance of nuclear forces' does not in any sense exist within the borders of Europe, since Europe has not had, and does not have now, launching bases for medium-range rockets, either on land or at sea. It is only logical if, as a result, the Soviet threat to Europe is to some extent a more open one than it is to the United States."

Such arguments, as much European as German, underline the urgency of trying once again to establish a multilateral nuclear force. In view of the statements of Herr Strauss and others, the logic for American leadership in this process is stronger now than it was five years ago when Secretary of State Christian Herter first mooted such a force. Whether or not the United States will be able in any future NATO debate to maintain the three principles that have animated thinking in the past is doubtful. These were: the force must be complementary to and not a substitute for the American strategic nuclear forces, it must be under NATO, that is, SHAPE operational control, and it must preserve the fundamental political principle of integration. Only by adhering to the last of these can the alliance regain, at the highest level of modern weaponry, the cooperative dynamism that marked its earliest years.

Herr Strauss, at the moment, says he is thinking of a European rather than a German force, "the creation in Europe of a sufficiently strong defense system, of which the strategic nuclear forces of *Great Britain and France* should be a part.

"The states which are steering toward a political federation should create a *European nuclear council*," the former

German defense minister believes. This would be composed of the defense ministers of the individual countries.

"The nuclear council would be the body in which a common nuclear defense strategy would be determined. For the purpose of coordinating the planning of targets and dispositions within the framework of European territorial defense, the commander of the American NATO units in Europe would need to belong to this council, although his status in it would still have to be decided. Beyond that a *European nuclear arsenal* should be created on French territory and, if Great Britain takes part, on British territory as well. The development and manufacture of European nuclear weapons should be supported with scientific and financial contributions from the other states of the European union. As a beginning there must be a provision that in this first stage in the shaping of the community the order for the use of nuclear weapons may only be given by the really established authorities, that is, the French President and other heads of government on whose territory part of the nuclear arsenal is placed. In this way it would very soon be possible to achieve the establishment of two efficient Western strategic systems, complementary to each other and yet autonomous. The one would have its control-point in Washington, the other on the European mainland.

"I should like once again to stress that in such a European scheme—for the reasons I have already mentioned—Germany would not have any national control over nuclear weapons. The aim naturally remains the complete transfer of the power to order the use of nuclear weapons from a national to a communal authority." *

Progress within NATO toward settling these all-important issues has been impeded by the failure of the most important

* *Ibid.*

245

member governments, for reasons of preoccupation with other problems, in the case of the United States, or hostility to NATO's present organization, in the case of France, to negotiate differences and frame common policies.

In the absence of positive action, the North Atlantic Council has done what it could to sharpen the efficiency of NATO. There has been a successful effort to enhance the Council's importance by attracting to its meetings as many visitors of ministerial rank as possible. George W. Ball, the United States Under Secretary of State, Paul-Henri Spaak, Belgium's Foreign Minister, and other cabinet ministers in Europe periodically attend the Council's sessions. Secretary-General Brosio has visited capitals in Europe and America to solicit stronger support for the alliance. The permanent representatives have formed *ad hoc* committees to deal with specific problems within the alliance. The reconciliation of the diverging views on strategy and on NATO organization, however, will be accomplished only by the governments concerned. Here the position, if not hopeless, is desperate until some structural change is made in the alliance.

There is nothing novel about agitation for change in NATO. General de Gaulle suggested a tri-power directorate, France, Britain, and the United States, seven years ago. Since then other alterations have been suggested. But it was not until this year, when the alliance clearly was losing prestige and influence in Europe, that the need for change became urgent.

Any change that takes place must be an attempt to eliminate the basic source of discord within the alliance: the present inequality between America and the fourteen other allies, particularly the more powerful European partners. And, of course, change merely for the sake of change will serve no purpose unless the governments involved are prepared to make a real effort to reconcile their differences over the alliance's purpose and strategy.

Most of the proposals focus on the establishment of a central group of powers within NATO that would decide purpose and strategy and review the national commitments of the members. To this extent, although for different motives, they reflect De Gaulle's proposal of 1958. All the current proposals agree that West Germany must be a member of any inner circle. Most of them suggest that Italy, too, be included because of its strategic position as the southern anchor of the defense position in Europe.

Perhaps the most thoughtful proposal from outside government has been made by Dr. Henry A. Kissinger in his recent book *The Troubled Partnership*. He has suggested the creation of a NATO executive committee or council composed of five permanent members, the United States, the United Kingdom, West Germany, France, and Italy, and one rotating member elected by other ten smaller members of the alliance. Some NATO members have argued that the proposal does not provide adequate representation for the smaller powers. They have suggested the election of two rotating members; one representing the "northern" group, Norway, Denmark, the Netherlands, Belgium, Luxembourg, Canada, and Iceland, and the other speaking for the "southern" members, Italy, Greece, and Turkey.

Anthony Eden, Earl of Avon, who rescued NATO from the 1954 crisis over Germany's entry into the alliance, has suggested the creation of a federal political structure for the alliance, giving it fresh momentum. One of the primary tasks of such a federation would be to coordinate the aid efforts and other policies of the free nations across the world.

"Alliances don't stand still," Lord Avon warned. "They either put out fresh roots or wither. Our alliance is in need of a fresh momentum and it should come from a closer Atlantic union."

There is no disagreement, however, about the tasks that face any reorganized NATO. The most urgent need is the formulation of a common political policy and a common strategic doctrine. This will involve, inevitably, a long-over-due review by the governments concerned of the present military arrangements within the alliance. The tendency to reduce military commitments, understandable in this period of détente, could be rationalized, if not halted, by agreement on NATO's purpose in the changed circumstances of today. Once the alliance is agreed on the aims for the last years of this decade, it will be easier to conform the present military arrangements. But it is useless to urge greater efforts on laggard members while the present uncertainty about the objectives of the alliance prevails.

One necessary step in any reorganization would be the moving of the Military Committee and the Standing Group from Washington to Paris. This was suggested six years ago by Field Marshal Viscount Montgomery and was summarily dismissed as "just one of Monty's wild ideas." Admittedly, the Field Marshal threw off ideas like sparks from an emery wheel. But over the years this one has won wide support.

It seems incredible that, after nearly seventeen years of NATO's existence, the North Atlantic Council and the two senior military groups in the alliance conduct their affairs separated by the Atlantic. The general efficiency of the alliance would benefit if both its political and military nerve centers were in Paris, and the French and other European critics, who claim that the military side of NATO is dominated by the Pentagon, would be disarmed.

None of these structural changes will in themselves resolve the disputes at present weakening the alliance. But they should facilitate the substantive consultation that is the only means of settling these differences in the approach to allied cooperation.

On one hand there is the Anglo-American approach stated by President Eisenhower and Prime Minister Macmillan in October 1957: "The concept of national self-sufficiency is now out of date. The countries of the free world are interdependent and only in genuine partnership, by combining their resources and sharing tasks in many fields, can progress and safety be found."

Opposing this is General de Gaulle's conviction that a true European defense of Europe can be obtained only through the encouragement of national forces loyal at the outset to the interests of their own nation-states and ultimately to the Europe they are to protect.

It can be argued that these two diverging attitudes can never be reconciled until NATO assumes new responsibilities and, in the process, new members elsewhere in the world. This development will take on added importance if, as some fear, the Europe of EEC fails to grow into a federal political unit and remains a loose confederation of national states as De Gaulle wishes. NATO will then remain as the only effective organization for military, political, and economic cooperation in the Western world.

In the past three or four years the alliance has made some progress in embracing new interests—Cyprus, the Congo, Vietnam—if not new responsibilities. If NATO were to assume common responsibility for these and other areas of conflict in the world, it would be easier for its members to accept the guidance, if not the leadership, of those member nations most concerned.

The chances are that unless there is a structural reorganization of NATO the basic differences centered on strategic equality cannot be reconciled. Even if they are, Americans must expect that the outlook of the European members will differ from theirs on a number of salient points. There are, however, some fields in which the allies can and should negotiate a common policy as soon as possible.

One of these is commercial policy toward the countries of East Europe and the Soviet Union. This is an area where the European Commission, the governing body of EEC, has tried and failed as a result of France's desire to have the best of both worlds. The Commission tried to establish a common policy on trade relations with East Europe in certain sectors including export credits and import liberalization lists. The French refused to give any solid commitment because of their growing export trade, particularly in capital goods, with the East. The estimate is that nearly a third of French exports of such goods will go to the U.S.S.R. in the next few years and that if the exports to other East European countries are included the figure is closer to fifty percent.

Other nations, notably West Germany, Britain, and Italy, are avidly soliciting a share in this trade. The NATO argument is not against the trade itself. It is that in failing to be selective about the type of capital goods sold and the length of the credits extended—the old rule against five-year credits was abandoned in 1964—the Western powers have thrown away an important weapon for influencing the Communist powers. A common economic policy, therefore, would in the long run benefit the alliance's primary aim of maintaining a balance of military power, which is based on economic strength, in Europe.

The willingness of some governments to discount the importance of NATO and to doubt its relevance to the great problems of today blindly ignores the fact that the great objectives to which the Atlantic community subscribes are impossible to obtain unless that community is represented by a coherent alliance. It is both childish and dangerous to believe that, because NATO has worked to the extent that Soviet pressure has been relaxed, it has no important place in the world of the future.

Even if the alliance's activities are confined to the relatively minor geographical sphere of Europe, there are great tasks ahead that NATO, and only NATO, can perform. The obvious one is to maintain enough military strength to prevent any renewal of Communist pressure on Western Europe. Here European public opinion must be led to a more realistic view of the nature of Communism. The masses live for the hour, and the hour is calm and peaceful. A stream of Soviet visitors and emissaries from the Communist states of the East pours through the capitals of Europe encouraging the belief that the Communists have changed overnight, that capitalism is no longer their avowed enemy.

There is one method by which NATO can test the reality of these supposed changes in Communist outlook. It can ask for the views of the Warsaw Pact powers on disarmament in Europe. The issue is one in which all Europeans, East and West, and all members of the Atlantic community have an interest. NATO should raise the issue with all the diplomatic weight that an alliance of fifteen nations can mobilize. The West will soon learn how seriously the Communists' professions of coexistence can be taken.

The effort is necessary because the combination of nationalism and misguided optimism about the Communist danger in Western Europe has created an atmosphere that encourages appeasement. Already France's attitude toward China in Southeast Asia is perilously close to appeasement. How long will it be before she or other European nations are taking the same attitude toward Russia in Europe?

It is essential that the governments that contribute to NATO and the organization itself dispel the lethargy and the wishful thinking about Communism that has developed in Europe. Conflicts of national policies and the jealous protection of independence and sovereignty have brought NATO to its present low state. The changes that are urgently necessary in its structure, its strategic planning, and its attitude toward the unrelenting enemy beyond the Elbe must be made if the West is to cope with the coming problems. But they cannot be made unless they have the support of popular opinion in the countries concerned.

As an anonymous official of NATO has written, the alliance "should be able to count on the support of public opinion in each and every one of its member countries, for this is a factor which is vital to success in any community of free peoples. Hence the need for constant efforts better to acquaint the citizens of NATO countries with its aims and with its achievements, and to explain to them the actions they are called upon to approve if NATO is to complete its work. In this way they will become more aware of their partnership in an alliance whose destiny is linked with their own security and with their own freedom."

NATO is in fact a necessity for the West. The history of the last twenty years has demonstrated repeatedly that survival depends on some form of political and military union.

Warnings about what will occur if the present decay of the alliance continues have come from many pens. Perhaps the most persuasive was that of Donald Tyerman on his retirement as editor of *The Economist*.

"Because the big, decisive, apocalyptic bomb belongs to the Russians and the Americans, who will never dare to use it, we no longer need to bother about the taut alliance to defend us all; so we argue. We can kick our heels, even nuclearly; we can pretend that because the big deterrent has worked so well, for the first time in history, we can make our own national hay while its sun shines. The Western alliance thaws with the Eastern one, and we can all go safely on our own national way. Just because the structure of alliance, made this time in peacetime, has preserved us, we and the General would dismantle it. But the Russian or the Chinese national interest does not alter because the Communist monolith has split; our national interest in the freedom of us and others has not changed; let us indeed make peace and trade with all kinds of countries wherever we can (certainly including China as well as the Soviet Union) but never let us forget where the facts of power, and of ambition, still lie. Never let us mix up who are our friends and who, unless we guard our own and our friends' interests, may be our foes again."

These strong, wise words apply directly to the European members of NATO, including Britain, today. They will be no less relevant in the future when the West will face new challenges, different in their origin and in their direction, but no less dangerous. NATO remains the only Western organization with the experience, the strength, and the breadth of membership suitable to meet these challenges. Before it does, however, the alliance must be revived. And, to repeat, the initial impetus must come from the governments concerned, in America no less than France.

## Chapter X

# THE LARGER ALLIANCE

The Challenge to the West and New Machinery to Meet It
• American Leadership in the New Situation • How
Europe Sees the United States as Leader • The Con-
tinuing Struggle

A decline in the authority and influence of NATO, uncertainty about the future of political unity in Europe in the face
of revived nationalism, the magnitude of the social, economic,
and political problems that confront the West are aspects of
the Atlantic crisis that have induced a mood of pessimism and
negation. It is generally recognized that existing international
machinery will not suffice to meet the developing world crisis
in the remainder of this century. But there have been few
proposals for the creation of new international instruments,
which by uniting and utilizing the economic, political, and
military strength of the Western powers will enable them to
surmount the new challenge. Clearly a new international
organization that will respond to this challenge, that will do
for the world what NATO did for Europe in the Fifties, is
needed. All the existing organizations fall short in some
respect.

NATO is losing ground because it did the job it was organized to do: containing the Communist bloc in Europe. As

soon as the politico-military pressure of Communism on Western Europe began to relax, largely because NATO had made that area too tough a nut for Moscow to crack, the decline began. The speed of decline was accelerated by the revival of nationalism. But the trend was there long before General de Gaulle began to undermine the alliance's position in Europe.

The United States made one final attempt to revive NATO. It proposed the establishment of a multilateral nuclear force that would embody NATO's governing principle, that of military integration, in the field of nuclear weapons and that would give the non-nuclear powers a share in nuclear strategy. General de Gaulle's fierce opposition to this proposal and his willingness to extend his hostility to any NATO power willing to participate in the force led the United States to drop its support. The MLF had become a divisive rather than a unifying factor in NATO's affairs.

If the Administration sticks to its decision, NATO is left without a means of political revival as the critical year 1969 approaches. In that year, according to Article 13 of the North Atlantic Treaty, "any Party may cease to be a party" to the treaty "one year after its notice of denunciation has been given to the Government of the United States of America, which will inform the Governments of the other Parties of the deposit of each notice of denunciation."

General de Gaulle's opposition to any further extension of the principle of integration of military command, his belief in the superiority of national rather than international strategic planning, his reduction of the French forces committed to NATO all indicate that, if he is still in charge, France will demand basic changes in the structure and principles of the alliance in 1969 and that, if these are not accepted, France will leave NATO. By April of 1965, the General's hostility to

NATO and his confidence in the strength of his own position had reached the point where he felt able to inform the responsible authorities at NATO that France would not accept any further integration in the alliance because this would impede progress toward European unity. The sublime self-confidence of the man! There he was, citing European unity, which he was doing his best to replace with "cooperation" among The Six, as the basis for French opposition to a policy he found equally distasteful.

In the circumstances, the best that the West can expect as a result of De Gaulle's tactics is to salvage some form of interdependent defense system for NATO. The worst is that Europe will retrogress to a loose alliance of national armed forces, an alliance of the kind that was so singularly unsuccessful in preventing war in 1914 and 1939.

EEC cannot be expected to be the basis of a new international group that will enable the West to meet the problems of the future. Despite the efforts of other European nations to associate themselves with the Community in the economic field and the probability that Britain, under the next Tory government, will apply again for membership, any political entity that develops out of EEC is likely to be highly restrictive. Even if the Community develops politically, its geographical range is bound to be "Little Europe" rather than Europe.

The word "if" is used advisedly. The Community has made great strides. But it is no more immune to the disease of nationalism than NATO. Moreover, De Gaulle and France carry more weight in EEC than they ever did in NATO. The General is likely to shift his undermining activity from the Atlantic alliance to the Community once he understands the dangers to French independence of the nascent federalism in Brussels. The results can be disastrous.

No remarkable prescience is necessary, therefore, to foresee a series of crises for EEC in the near future as negotiations for political union develop.

The European Free Trade Area cannot be considered seriously as a framework for Western unity in the wider sense. It includes only one more country than EEC. It is purely economic. It is in trouble. In 1964 EFTA ran up a trade deficit of $6,300,000,000 largely due to a reduction in British exports to the United States and to the Association's failure to sell to EEC, where the increased tariff discrimination was beginning to affect trade. EFTA is a fading organization.

The Western European Union nowadays is important only as a channel for keeping Britain and through her the United States in touch with the development of European political unity. Because France is opposed to this function of WEU, it is unlikely that the Union will have any relevance to the future of Atlantic unity.

Nevertheless, the need for a new organization embracing the NATO allies and others becomes more evident every day. The containment of the Communist bloc in Europe is not the end of the conflict with Communism but only a temporary armistice on one battleground of that conflict. The West, on both sides of the Atlantic, now is engaged on a much wider front. The new theater of operations is not the narrow area of Central Europe divided by the front lines of NATO and the Warsaw Pact powers, but Africa, Asia, the Middle East, and Latin America. Here the fight will be primarily political and economic rather than military. There are bound, however, to be outbreaks of fighting, the so-called brush-fire wars; more if the Communist powers believe the West will not respond fully, less if Moscow and Peking are convinced that guerrilla action will be met promptly and effectively.

Whatever the character of the struggle, its length should not be doubted. This conflict will be fought by our children and our children's children. It must be won. It can be won only by a united alliance. Union can develop fully only if all the powers, including first of all the United States, recognize that the problems of the next twenty or thirty years will be too big, too complex, too widespread for any one nation or for any one of the present alliances to deal with successfully.

Even now these problems dwarf those that have vexed the West since 1945. The population explosion insures that by the end of the century the world will have to cope with the pressures arising from the existence of a billion Chinese. Throughout Asia, Africa, and Latin America populations multiply. Scientific agriculture has done its best, but there is at least a reasonable doubt that food supplies will fail to keep pace with population increases. Industrialization of a sort has been begun in the underdeveloped countries of these three continents. But industry in the advanced countries of North America and Europe is undergoing a revolution of its own that will raise production to new heights and, as automation and cybernetics develop, create new and grave social problems.

The conclusion must be that without a united effort on the part of the advanced nations, the poor will get poorer and the rich will get richer. This is certain to exacerbate the conflict, already spreading, between the colored and the white races. Only economic assistance, education, and enlightened statesmanship on both sides can prevent its spread around the world.

Americans must conclude that even if the United States had the will and resources to tackle these problems alone, they would prove too much for us. America must work with her allies. She cannot turn inward onto a Fortress America or neo-isolationism. Appealing although these ideas may be to many, they are out of question in a world that is shrinking with alarming rapidity, a world where the Republic is too involved with the economic and political survival of her allies to go it alone. There must be a new alliance on a broader geographical and political base. The criteria for membership should include an advanced technology coupled with an understanding of the problems and a desire to help. This phase of the world conflict will be fought in the class-rooms, the kitchens, the hospitals, and the government planning offices of the world. Economic and political contributions rather than military forces and equipment will be the weapons.

The military critic will say that we cannot be sure that the present nuclear stalemate will continue—what will happen when China begins to produce hydrogen bombs; won't there then be a renewed danger of nuclear war? We cannot be sure of anything in this dangerous century. We can reason that the possession of advanced nuclear weapons by the Chinese will impose upon them the same self-denying ordinance that possession has imposed upon the Soviet Union. If the history of the Russian revolution is any guide to future development in China, there is at least a reasonable prospect that the Chinese, while maintaining their aim of spreading world revolution among the peoples of Asia and Africa, will not employ nuclear weapons to further that aim. The Chinese will find, as the Russians have found, that they have too much to lose in a nuclear war. But the other, greater conflict will continue. To fight it successfully we must have a new alliance.

The fifteen members of the North Atlantic alliance offer a suitable nucleus of membership. As it stands today, NATO spans the Atlantic. It penetrates the eastern Mediterranean in Greece and Turkey and consequently is an instrument of

Western influence on the Middle East. The six members of EEC and four of the seven members of EFTA (Britain, Denmark, Norway, and Portugal) all are members of NATO.

The global extent of the new problems, however, demands a wider grouping. A start should be made in Europe by seeking the membership in the new group of the countries outside NATO, Sweden, Switzerland, Austria, and Spain. All four are anti-Communist, although this in itself is not the most important qualification in considering their membership. What counts is that all four belong to the mainstream of European civilization and each has something to contribute.

Spain's inclusion will offend those who detest Franco and his regime. But Franco will not live forever. Spain already is changing economically and politically. And Spain has influence among the Arab nations. The new alliance is going to need every favorable factor if it is to do its job.

Sweden, Switzerland, and Austria are democracies. However, this may not be as important in the struggle in Africa and Asia as the fact that they are untainted by colonialism. There are countries, there are whole sections of continents where the Swedes or the Swiss will be given a freer hand than, say, the British or the Belgians because no one would ever suspect them of what the Communists call "neo-colonialism." Finally, these are advanced nations with the technologies that are the basis for contributions in the underdeveloped world.

The three have been neutral in the cold war in Europe. There can be no neutrals in the next or global phase of that war. If the new nations are to be led away from Communism, they must be led by a united alliance that includes some of the hitherto uncommitted nations.

Nowhere is the West's position weaker than in Southeast Asia. No remarkable foresight is necessary to see what will happen if it continues to lose ground. We will see the same melancholy process that occurred in Europe thirty years ago. One by one the Chinese giant will gobble up the small, independent states that front on her southern borders until finally she is ready for the biggest prize of all, India. The process will be slower than it was in Europe in the Thirties. China is not yet a coherent, efficient military state comparable to Hitler's Germany. She will be subverting, too, societies that are much less organized than Czechoslovakia or Austria; the process of establishing Chinese domination will take longer because the new power will be operating in countries lacking modern communications. To check and contain this Chinese advance, the West's first requirement is bases. Not bases in the military sense, but national bases that can bring economic and political influence to bear on Southeast Asia as part of a worldwide alliance.

Australia and New Zealand, Japan, and the Philippines are the logical Far Eastern members of the new alliance in its first phase. All four have a deep interest in developments in Asia, not the least of which is the strong probability that, if China wins on the Asian mainland, they will be the next targets. All have something to offer Asia in the economic or industrial field. The Philippines offer a political example of an Asian nation that, emerging from colonialism, has been able to rule itself. The ultimate argument is that countries like these, neighbors of Asia, are more likely to be listened to by governments and peoples than are nations on the other side of the world. A good deal of national pride will have to be swallowed if Western civilization is to emerge in a recognizable form. A start could be made by seeing that economic aid from European and North American members of the alliance is channeled to Asia through these members of the alliance.

261

Latin America represents a difficult and distinctive problem. The economic and political influence of the United States has been so great and the inevitable anti-American reaction against it so powerful that wisdom dictates that the effort to develop its resources and strengthen democracy be carried on by others than Americans.

Spain and Portugal in Europe are linked to Latin America by culture, history, and language. France, under De Gaulle, has shown its interest in economic help and political guidance below the Rio Grande. Here is an area where these three European states could play a signal role in the coming years of economic and political conflict for the future of a continent. But again the outlook for victory would be improved if the new alliance numbers among its members countries of Latin America. Mexico and Chile are two that are on the way to filling the requirements for membership.

Mexico has a rapidly expanding economy and boasts a political stability unusual in Latin America. Chile, also politically stable, is moving toward the resumption of control of its own natural resources. If this process is successful in Chile, as it has been in Mexico, the country will be well suited for the role of pilot in the development of South America. Again the need is for countries in the battle area to represent an allied effort and to act as an operating base for the new alliance.

Africa, and particularly Africa south of the Sahara, poses the greatest problem. Poverty is greater, resources, including those known but untapped, are impressive, racial strife has already begun. The demand for education, public health services, and communications is imperative. Here, colonialism has lingered longer than in Asia or Latin America, here Communism, particularly Communism preached by a colored race, the Chinese, has its best chance and the advanced nations their heaviest responsibility.

Sub-Saharan Africa's development will call for a united effort by the new alliance or the countries there will go to Communism by default. It is easy enough to note the disintegration of countries like Ghana that were established by departing colonial powers and to argue that Europe and America should let the Chinese try and fail and then, after the failure, return and restore. These are counsels of despair. Too much is at stake. What has happened in the Congo may happen tomorrow in Angola and Mozambique. Chaos and racial strife can sweep the continent. The destruction of life and property will be on such a scale that the development of Africa and its peoples will be set back for twenty years.

The West has the economic means and should develop the political wisdom to avert this. But to do so it must have allies, in this case allies rather than bases, in Africa. These can be found, I believe, in those African states that have made the transfer from colonialism to independence with the least strain: Nigeria and the former French colonies on the west coast, Kenya in central Africa. Ethiopia, as an independent nation, must be brought into the contest. It will be argued that the new states of Africa are ruled by governments incompetent to use whatever is given them for development and deeply resentful of instruction from their former colonial rulers. This is true to a large extent. The alternative seems to be to use instructors and technical assistants from countries with no colonial record in Africa, indeed to go farther afield and ask trained personnel from Japan or the Philippines to help.

Every day's news emphasizes the extent and urgency of the widening conflict with Communism. In Asia, two Western powers, the United States and the United Kingdom, already

263

are engaged politically, militarily, and economically. In Africa, the challenge is developing rapidly. To take one example of vital importance to the future: the Soviet Union this year will establish a fourth air route into Africa. Four years ago the Russians had only one line into Africa and that reached only to Cairo. Now the routes may be traced across the map to show Aeroflot penetrating into the capitals of the new nations.

One line runs from the Yemen to Mogadishu, where a large and energetic Soviet Embassy foments trouble among the racial and tribal enmities of the Horn of Africa. Another flies by way of Algiers and Tunis to Bamako and Accra in west Africa. A third service, started in March of 1965, goes by Cairo and Khartoum to Brazzaville, linking Moscow, if not with the Congo itself, at least with the rebels just across the Congolese border. Applications for landing rights have been made for a fourth route that will connect the U.S.S.R. with the turbulent politics of central and east Africa. This route will open a regular service between Moscow, Cairo, Khartoum, Entebbe, Nairobi, and Dar es Salaam.

One consequence of this expansion is that it puts the Russians in a favorable position to sell airplanes to the African governments. But this is less important than the fact that wherever the Soviets sell an airplane or are given landing rights, they soon establish a sizable group of technicians who, of course, double in brass as spies, propagandists, and instructors in Communism. The American and British intelligence services, who are alive to the danger, have reported secret shipments of arms and propaganda material along the air routes already established. The Russians also use Aeroflot to carry Moscow-trained Africans back to their homelands without the knowledge of their governments.

This is a means of penetration at present denied to the

Chinese Communists in Africa. They, too, are ubiquitous and industrious. For a number of reasons they have been more successful than the Russians, who are white and who have a highly developed racial sense, in winning converts to *their* brand of Communism. Recent reports from Moscow and from the East European capitals indicate that Africans studying there resent Russian racialism and tend, when they return home, to favor the Chinese. This development is balanced to some extent by another. The Communist parties of Western Europe have been very successful in converting African students to Russian Communism.

In theory, of course, the majority of the new African governments are nonaligned. But their present leaders, after spending most of their lives defying and fighting colonialism, are slowly recognizing the danger of Communism to their independence. Listen to Tom Mboya, Minister for Economic Planning in the government of Kenya, warning against the "evil" that Communism would bring to Kenya:

"Much lip service has been paid in some Communist quarters to the idea of giving economic assistance to Kenya, but in fact most of our present-day developments are being greatly assisted through the friendly cooperation and understanding of some nations of the West, such as Britain, West Germany, and the United States. It must be made clear that merely because Communist countries have never had an African colony, it does not mean they have no cold war designs on Africa."

The same day President Jomo Kenyatta warned Bildad Kaggia against subversive propaganda. Kaggia is the head of the Lumumba Institute in Nairobi built with Communist funds and staffed partly by Russians.

In Zambia, President Kenneth Kaunda cautioned his people against participating in the ideological struggle between East and West. His government, he said, would assume dictatorial powers to eliminate foreign interference assisted by strikes that undermined Zambia's economy.

Men like Mboya and Kaunda are the first generation of African leaders. They are of the left but not the Communist left. They are the West's natural allies in the struggle for Africa's future with China and the Soviet Union. When the Communists challenge their authority, they challenge Africa's chances for peaceful progress.

The purely political difficulties in establishing the kind of global alliance demanded by the world situation are staggering. The only reason for outlining what should be done is the down-to-earth practical one that it must be done.

One major difficulty is the achievement of a joint initiative. The United States, Britain, and France have glimpsed the challenge that what General de Gaulle calls the third world holds for their future. But there has never been any impulse toward a joint attempt to marshal the advanced nations in support of a program for this area. Individual countries extend credits. Others build steel mills. Still others send teachers and doctors. Granted the magnitude of the problem such efforts, while praiseworthy, cannot be preferable to a program worked out by an alliance. In such an alliance the United States would be a major partner. But America would have to be a partner and not a leader. If the advanced countries are to meet this new challenge, the United States must appear as a participant rather than as the director-general. This means cutting connections with the past, with the establishment of NATO under American hegemony. It means, in short, remembering this is 1965, not 1945.

The first step toward forming this greater alliance for progress should be the creation of a council of ministers of all potential member governments. The task of this council should be to assemble and coordinate the information of the various governments on the economic and political situations in those countries—Tanzania, Burma, and the Congo—where the conflict with Communism is at or near a crisis and where a united non-Communist effort is urgently needed. This would be accomplished by a general review of the whole of the battlefront, from Southeast Asia westward across the world to South and Central America.

By the assemblage and publication of such information, a Western world grown tired of overseas aid would be taught the seriousness of the situation and the urgent need for action. The peoples, as well as the governments, must realize that there is not much time to lose.

Once the objectives have been agreed to, the resources must be identified, country by country, and the strategy for their use planned. This is a point where national interests will clash. No government wants to make available large sums or resources of men and material if they are to be used generally by an alliance and, as will prove necessary occasionally, distributed by another country whose position in the critical area is unsullied by memories of colonialism or neo-imperialism.

The burden of establishing the alliance will require enlightened statesmanship, especially in Washington. The United States will have to play a major role, although she must expect assistance from some countries whose overseas aid in the past has been limited as well as from those immediately concerned. If the alliance is to function efficiently, it will be important that the United States appear as one partner, not as a leader. For a number of reasons, some of them good, American leadership is under a cloud in Europe. And it is in Europe that the new alliance must levy on governments for help.

Criticism of the United States in Europe today is influenced by two currents of thought. The first, with General de Gaulle as its principal spokesman, takes the position that Europe does not need the United States except as the western element of the balance of nuclear power. In other words, the United States is useful, for the time being, as a protector of Europe, but otherwise the old continent can get along without American political interference and economic penetration.

The second current of thought, one that has gained ground remarkably in 1965, is that America is no longer interested in Europe, that she has abandoned the attempt to understand her problems and has lost interest in the alliances she fostered. This is the more dangerous attitude of the two because if the current continues to flow, more and more Europeans will accept the Gaullist argument. If America isn't interested in Europe any more, then Europe must fend for herself.

It is always salutary for an individual or a nation to see itself through other eyes. We are in many ways closer to the British than to any other European country; the British know more about us than the French or the Germans. Consequently the American image in Britain today is important to the United States. If America is to embark on a great international effort to win the battle in the third world, she must take account of how her potential partners feel about her now.

Few Americans understand the depth of their economy's penetration of the British Isles. Leave aside for a moment the superficial aspects of Britain's Americanization, hamburger stands and the like. Consider the manner in which big business has moved into Britain, buying into or taking over British companies, building factories, buying properties. There are from time to time shrill outcries against this development.

They would be far shriller were it not for the very considerable penetration of the American economy by major British
companies, which to some extent balances the American investment in the United Kingdom. Even so the process cannot
be called popular. From the small trader ruined by the super-
market, which, whether or not it is American-owned, is in his
mind an American innovation, to the industrialist who finds
his business in competition with a British company behind
which stand the limitless resources of an American commercial giant, the American invasion is highly unpopular.

The American businessman will argue that British criticisms are superficial. The British, he will say quite rightly,
are a commercial people and if the American invasion is good
business, the British will accept it. It would be dangerous to
subscribe too heavily to this rather complacent view. There
are strange currents working under the rather placid surface of
British life. An economic crash could lead to a transformation
of the British political system. Or, more likely, it would push
Britain into Europe at any price, a Europe already heavily
infected with anti-Americanism.

The left in Britain already argues that the American economic invasion is the prelude to American economic domination. The argument is gaining ground in the center and on
the right. When it is generally accepted, the United States
will face a crisis in her relations with her most intimate ally.

The effects of this economic invasion exacerbate basic
British attitudes toward the United States as much as what
is called the cultural invasion. This is the popularity in Britain
of American books, magazines, television programs, and pop
art and, equally important, their imitation by the British.
This is a fertile field for critics on the left who see their
country's cultural heritage drowned by a tidal wave sweeping in from across the Atlantic and by critics on the right

whose view is that the American cultural invasion exalts the cheap, the shoddy, and the pornographic. Both the left and the right are correct up to a point. Jazz is more popular than Welsh folk songs, and for every Briton who has read *Huckleberry Finn* a thousand have devoured *Peyton Place.*

What both extremes forget, however, is that a cultural cross-fertilization has been going on across the Atlantic almost from the birth of the Republic. British authors, playwrights, educators, scientists, actors, dancers, and critics continue to influence the American cultural scene to an extent greater than those of any other country. And, on the lower level, the Beatles are from Liverpool, England, not Liverpool, New York.

American domination is most controversial in the political field. Here it attracts the greatest amount of criticism. Yet most of this criticism, among the well-informed at least, is founded on the knowledge that Britain must continue to be the junior partner, a very junior partner some say unhappily, in the alliance.

The view from Whitehall under a Labour government is little different from what it was under the Tories. Michael Stewart, the foreign secretary, conceded early this year that Britain recognizes the United States as the leader of the West. This is the basic assumption beside which political slogans, such as the cry for new horizons for Britain, are relatively unimportant at the moment. The fact is that Britain no longer has the resources to establish new horizons; her economic power and consequently her political influence have declined while America's has leaped upward. Like it or not, and many Britons do not, the United Kingdom is inextricably linked with the United States on the larger issues of foreign policy, partly because interests coincide in many areas of the world, such as Southeast Asia, but mainly because Britain could not operate alone in these or other areas without the support of America.

Acceptance of this basic situation does not mean an absence of criticism, far from it. Precisely because Britain's future is now so closely linked to that of the United States, criticism is constant and, let us remember, often constructive. Naturally it varies. Discreet and sophisticated in the inner councils of government, it is shrill in the House of Commons and often violent in the political left and the left-wing weeklies.

The oldest and still the most prevalent single criticism of the United States and its policies is common to all three groups. It is that the Americans in successive administrations have thought of international affairs in terms of black and white, of good guys and bad guys. Even the most enlightened administration, it is argued, cannot seek the intermediate solution between total victory and defeat because the American people will accept nothing less than unconditional surrender. So deeply ingrained is this belief on the extreme left of the Labour party that President Johnson's offer to North Vietnam of negotiations without prior conditions was not believed. It is symptomatic of the decline of American prestige and of the strength of our adversaries on the left that the wildest interpretations of carefully-thought-out policies of the United States are circulated and accepted. The effect upon popular opinion far exceeds the limited political strength of those who circulate anti-American views, often the most articulate section of the electorate.

This primary criticism overlooks recent developments in United States thinking—the speeches and writings of Senator Fulbright, for example. But there is always an irritating lag in one country's recognition of changes of mood in another. The British see the American tendency to divide the world into those for us and those against us as a barrier to effective diplomatic efforts to achieve world stability. Their course, followed by both Tory and Labour governments, is to urge upon an administration the wisdom of the middle way and to interpret for Washington the world opinion of salient international issues.

A second criticism is that the United States, in times of crisis, pays less and less attention to its allies, by which the British mean primarily the United Kingdom. Even those most faithful to the alliance with the United States were disturbed by the failure of the Johnson Administration to give the British government a clear idea of American objectives in Southeast Asia.

"When it's not important or when they think we can help, we're told," one British politician said. "When it's very important to them, which automatically means it's equally important to us, we're told nothing until after the decision has been taken and implemented."

This is a serious criticism; in the coming years of global crisis the United States will need all the friendly help it can get. Yet the American tendency to act unilaterally is a natural enough consequence of the country's great and growing ascendancy in economic and nuclear strength compared to its allies. The United States apparently is reaching the point where it believes it doesn't need any help, a dangerous psychological state for any country.

Another general criticism is that American policy oscillates between internationalism and nationalism. The United States, the British charge, takes the broad international view when its own interests are not directly involved and when those of some of its closest allies, Britain and France during the Suez adventure, for example, are at stake. But it shifts quickly to a national attitude, summed up by one diplomat as "hands off, this for Americans only" when the interests of the United States are affected. The most understanding British view of this attitude is that an American government is acting naturally in the circumstances even though its action creates serious difficulties for its allies. The worst interpretation, favored by the left in British politics, is that American internationalism is a sham, that the United States is interested in alliances only when they can be dominated by Washington's policymakers.

American leadership at times has been all that British critics charge; too positive and self-righteous, headstrong, intolerant of advice, given to sudden shifts of attitude and policy. These criticisms come from an ally that is needed and one, moreover, that is no stranger to American criticism.

If an alliance to win the struggle in the third world takes shape, Britain should play an important role. If she is to do so, then something must be done to correct her present tendency toward what David Riesman has called "inward-directed" thinking. This preoccupation with Britain's problems, important though they are, could rob the West of a valued partner. Even the present lively comment about the United States could degenerate from informed criticism to a petty hope that the Americans will get on with the job and leave Britain alone. "Little Englandism" is dangerous to the whole Atlantic community as well as to Britain.

British criticism of the United States will be a constant factor in the relationship as long as the United Kingdom remains an independent but intimate ally. But it should not lead Americans to discount the real desire on the part of the majority of Britons to continue as America's closest partner and to accept United States leadership. Members of this group do not demonstrate in Trafalgar Square or in front of the American Embassy. They are often critical but, in addition to the familiar charges already noted, they sometimes complain that the United States leadership is not firm enough. These are people who, feeling free to criticize since they are free-born Britons, still believe that American leadership is their best insurance for the future. The American student of British attitudes in government, the civil service, the fighting services, and business also will note a welcome understanding of what the United States' present position involves. The British have been there themselves and not very long ago. They understand that worldwide responsibility cannot be divorced from worldwide leadership. They sometimes feel we should worry less about criticism from allies—they seldom did—and realize that respect is the most that will be accorded the successful leader.

In the present crisis of Atlantic affairs, the British on the whole are far more realistic than the French. There remain some vestiges of the Empire and Commonwealth traumas, but increasingly the British view of their position in the world is in accord with the facts. The world they discuss is recognizable as the one we live in. In recent years, however, most of the British criticisms of the United States have crossed the Channel to be augmented by peculiarly French criticisms and to be magnified and distorted in the odd atmosphere of France under the Fifth Republic. The French of the middle Sixties are living in an unrealistic world of national grandeur. How a people who proclaim themselves the most logical, and who habitually have been the most critical, in Europe can choose to live in this make-believe environment baffles understanding.

As the French government sees the world—and it is the French government and only the government that counts in direct high-level relations with Washington—the United States is a distant country whose policies, with one exception, have little relevance or importance to France. The exception is the fact, seldom advertised by Gaullist ministers, that France depends on American nuclear protection. Aside from that it is depressingly evident that the government, the Gaullist party, most civil servants, a portion of the press, all of radio and television, and a section of the French people no longer think of the United States as an ally.

Indeed on many vital issues in international affairs over the past few years—the recognition of Communist China, the importance to the West of NATO, and the ultimate solution for Southeast Asia—the French government has given its people the impression that General de Gaulle's farsighted wisdom has been unaccountably opposed by the hostile Americans. At the same time the General and his ministers have hammered away at the theme of independence for France.

The government's assiduous efforts to sell these related ideas to the French are making headway. The mass of the people may still be pro-American, as the United States Embassy believes, but there are signs that the government's propaganda, spread chiefly by radio and television, is having some effect. For example, a young Englishman studying at Grenoble University was told by French friends of his own age, "You and the Americans are allies, but France stands on her own feet; we are not allies with America or with you."

This is the true spirit of Gaullism, anticipated a century ago by Lord Palmerston's dictum about Britain: "We have no eternal allies and no perpetual enemies; our interests are eternal and those interests it is our duty to follow." Any Gaullist and most Frenchmen would applaud this probably without recognizing the wide difference between De Gaulle's France, a major power of the second rank, and Palmerston's

Britain, which, at the time he spoke, was the greatest power in the world.

The chief French criticism of the United States is that America does not understand what is happening in the world while France, or at least its infallible master, does. Because Washington does not understand that the cold war is over in Europe, she continues to attempt to run NATO. Because neither the American government nor the American people recognize the extent to which Europeans desire national independence, successive administrations have tried to tie European political and defense policies to those of Europe. Because the Americans have failed to understand the depth of the hostility to them in the third world, they continue to try to manipulate its policies. Because the United States does not understand the nuances of high-level diplomacy, it continues to ignore China's claim to recognition and membership in the United Nations. Because Europe's concern with its own problems is discounted in Washington, America insists on trying to settle great issues like German reunification instead of leaving them to the Europeans.

The burden of all this could be summed up as "Americans go home." Clearly this body of criticism, launched in the France of today, constitutes a major barrier to French cooperation with the United States in the next phase of the world conflict. These criticisms, moreover, are exacerbated by fears of an American economic and cultural invasion. On the whole this has been less prominent in France than in the United Kingdom because the process has not yet progressed as far. But to many Frenchmen, "our culture is in danger" is as moving an appeal as any amount of measured criticism of American foreign policy.

The French government's attitude toward the United States will not change while General de Gaulle is in power unless, of course, some renewal of Soviet pressure brings him back to reality. This poses a serious problem, both in respect to the contemporary problem of restoring some semblance of unity to the alliance and to the future problem of rallying Western forces for the next phase of the global contest with Communism. De Gaulle, alone among allied leaders, has made it plain that he wants neither American leadership nor partnership with the United States in building the future.

The problem is not susceptible to the ordinary negotiation of interallied difficulties. De Gaulle has gone beyond criticizing the United States. He has advocated policies in Europe and Asia that conflict with those of the Administration. He has established his doctrine as the rallying point for nationalist sentiment throughout Western Europe and as the basis for anti-American policies. He has in fact committed himself to the extent that neither he nor his government can withdraw. Consequently a discussion between the General and President Johnson would be highly unlikely to result in a modification of the French position. De Gaulle is not a man to be cajoled, bribed, or bullied. He will be moved only by events.

There is something awe-inspiring about the man's superb confidence, the breadth and depth of his outlook, his passionate aspirations for his country. Yet, having conceded all that, the objective onlooker in France often is struck by the ridiculous aspects of Gaullism. For example, the fight against the introduction of English words into French, the establishment of "Franglais," as it is called. Here the General is fighting the worldwide process by which one language, not necessarily French, infiltrates another. To Americans, and British, accustomed to taking convenient words from any language they encounter, the idea that national prestige could be involved is laughable. The thoughtful will recall, too, that in their time both Hitler and Stalin tried to prevent the use of foreign words where German or Russian ones would serve.

The grandeur that is De Gaulle, the almost monarchial aspects of his rule have an archaic flavor in twentieth-century Europe largely because they have no deep roots in the society over which he reigns. French satirists are fond of depicting the General as another Louis XIV. To some the Gaullist regime is closer to that of another ruler of that name, Louis Napoleon, Emperor of the French. The student of history will note a resemblance between the pretentions, the pomposities, the adventurousness mixed with caution of that day and this. And, if there is no Victor Hugo to criticize from exile, there are plenty of Mornys about. De Gaulle and Gaullism have reached the point where they are not susceptible to alien argument.

In this situation the wisest course probably is to leave De Gaulle alone—difficult tactics for Americans who for twenty years have been accustomed to a paternalistic leadership in Europe. But leaving the General to self-communion in the Elysée Palace is only a partial solution. The remainder is to be found in the renewal of American interest first in Europe and secondly in the struggle for the future of the third world. An American policy that enunciated clearly what the government wanted now in Europe and in the next ten years in Africa, Asia, and Latin America and that promised a revival of the dynamism displayed by the United States between 1945 and 1955 is the sort of event that would move De Gaulle and might even transform his successor from an imitator of the General to a leader in his own right prepared to make France's peace with America.

There is little sense in leaving Europe alone and allowing De Gaulle to do what he wishes; that is to delay European unity by interposing his intransigence and his dream of an independent France between the United States and the fulfillment of its role in world affairs.

The hostility the General feels for the United States and its policies has no counterpart in Federal Germany. Although there are politicians in both the major parties there who hearken to the call of the wild and flirt with nationalism, the link with the United States is the paramount fact of German foreign policy. To Americans in this difficult decade this is welcome. West Germany is the most prosperous of European states. It is an important customer of the United States. It has made a military contribution to NATO that daily becomes more important as France's coolness toward the alliance becomes more marked and Britain weighs the reduction of her Rhine Army. American reliance on Germany has reached the point where the Administration can believe in NATO's survival even if France becomes only a nominal member.

West Germany, in foreign policy at least, looks to the United States as the big brother. In such a relationship there are bound to be criticisms. For example, the Germans are hypersensitive to any suggestions that the American military commitments in Europe, which to them means West Germany, should be reduced. They also feel that, as one ambassador said frankly, "Washington doesn't understand the difficulty we have in reconciling our close relations with you and our Treaty of Cooperation with France."

Occasionally, too, Germans criticize Washington for asking too much political support from Bonn for American policies in areas like Southeast Asia that have almost no importance to the mass of the German people or indeed to many in the government. Germany's overseas experience, the period of colonialism before World War I, was unpopular then and the memory is distasteful now. Like every continental country, her main interest is Europe. Germans are dismayed, therefore, when they are asked to express publicly their backing for American policy all over the world. Their loyalty to the American connection forbids refusal, but they are not particularly happy about assent. What has Saigon to do with the Common Market? Where is the link between Venezuela's troubles and German reunification?

In the world situation of the next twenty years this German preoccupation with Europe will not be enough. West Germany should be led into contact with the larger problems of the third world, a world larger than EEC or NATO, a world that needs the energies and technical skill of the Germans. Once in contact with that world and helping to solve its difficulties, Germany's desire to check the spread of Communism will have found a more rewarding outlet than brooding about reunification. And a Germany that is involved in the wider world will be much better fitted, psychologically, to deal with its own principal political problem than a Germany that has thought of nothing but unity.

Anti-Communism alone is a sterile creed. It is particularly strong in Italy, where all but the Communists and their allies look upon the United States as the political and military protector against Communism. Again, as in Germany, this sentiment should be harnessed and used in the third world.

None of these countries, not even Germany, however, can be driven into the next phase of the struggle at our side. They must learn first why the struggle is important to them as much as to us. And finally they must be convinced that in the future they will be partners rather than vassals. This may be easier than it appears. NATO has been distorted from the outset by America's position as the only important nuclear power within the alliance. But this nuclear strength, while vital to the maintenance of what Winston Churchill called "the balance of terror," is not going to play as important a role in the struggle with Communism in other continents as it has in Europe. In these other areas the emphasis will be on technological assistance, education, and political guidance. In these fields Europe, which has accomplished an economic miracle and has in EEC contributed a new and striking political innovation to world politics, can make a full contribution.

To bring Europe out of itself, to make EEC meaningful and outward-looking in a world sense is to recreate in happier circumstances the role that Europe played from the close of the fifteenth century to the first quarter of the twentieth. This is a great challenge, much more important to the future of man than De Gaulle's parochial vision of The Six as a third force in the world.

But if this is to be accomplished, America herself must change. The recognition that the prestige and influence of the United States has declined in Europe is commonplace. What is not generally realized is that it has taken place in a remarkably short time. The starting date probably is the Cuban crisis, which, paradoxically enough, probably was America's greatest triumph in the cold war. The death of President Kennedy and to a lesser extent the manner of that death also hurt the American image. In Europe Kennedy stood for the understanding Americans, those who wanted to cooperate rather than to push, who said "come" rather than "go."

Of the American policies that have occupied Western Europe since his death none has aroused greater controversy than the Multilateral Nuclear Force. This was not a Kennedy project or a Johnson project. It originated first in the dying months of the second Eisenhower Administration. As it was developed by the two Democratic Presidents, the MLF was a bold and imaginative political instrument for reviving NATO. But, for reasons never fully explained, the project instead of being presented in that way wandered off down by ways of nuclear strategy. A noisy and trivial dispute arose over its effectiveness as a weapon. The cartoonists in every interested country had a field day depicting crews drawn from seven or eight different navies. Consequently the virtues of the force as a cooperative concept never were fully expounded to the interested people and its political value was obscured.

Washington's decision to reduce diplomatic support for the force was the result of the alarm in the Administration over the discord the proposal had created among the Atlantic allies. Whatever the reasoning in the White House, the decision reflected a profound lack of understanding of the European situation among President Johnson's advisers.

Discord between the United States and France arose from a number of factors: De Gaulle's nationalism, his belief that a "European Europe" could not be established if one of its members, Germany, remained dependent militarily on the United States, his resentment over Bonn's purchases of American rather than French arms and military material. De Gaulle chose to fight on MLF because it symbolized West Germany's military ties with America and, equally, because it could be considered an indication of the United States' sincerity in seeking a more equal nuclear role for her allies. When President Johnson backed down, President de Gaulle won a victory. He took care that France's allies noted it.

The American action left those allies that had been interested in the force with an uneasy suspicion that perhaps the United States had not been serious about MLF. Such suspicions of American policy and policy-makers are all too easy to arouse. Too often Washington brushes these suspicions aside as meaningless gossip, forgetful that although they may be gossip they are the topics of discussion in homes, political meetings, businessmen's groups all over Europe.

A striking example of these suspicions, and of America's failure to respond adequately, was the belief between 1961 and 1964 that the United States and the Soviet Union planned a bilateral settlement of Europe's problems, particularly German unity. Members of the Gaullist party, including deputies to the National Assembly, did their best to promote this idea, especially among the West Germans, always hypersensitive where unity is concerned. They pointed out that the State Department had been remarkably taciturn about Russo-American talks. They hinted that the United States was so interested in pulling the U.S.S.R. away from China that it would make a deal over Germany to achieve a realignment in the Communist world.

In the State Department such fears probably appeared puerile. They were nonetheless real. They could have been dispersed in a week either by a resounding statement on America's policy toward the Soviets or, if this was tactically out of the question, by providing full information to all interested governments through their embassies in Washington.

Western Europe also suspects, and has done so almost since 1945, the intimate relationship between the United States and Britain. This suspicion influenced De Gaulle's decision to keep Britain out of EEC. In a roundabout way it also has affected West Germany's attitude toward the United States. During Dr. Adenauer's long rule in Bonn, it was a matter of faith among the Chancellor and his advisers that the British were continually preaching appeasement of the Soviets, at Germany's expense, to Washington and that Washington was listening.

The change in the power relationship of Britain and America rather than careful explanations by Washington of its true status has reduced the importance of this suspicion. Accurately assessing the great and widening difference between British and American power, Europe now realizes that the United States is unlikely to be influenced by the British, who, however, are still credited in Bonn, Paris, and Rome with a good deal more subtlety and diplomatic expertise than they possess, although not, perhaps, more than *they* think they have.

Europe recently has become more realistic about the basis for the Anglo-American relationship, not, again, as the result of American explanations. Most continental governments understand that, because of the community of language, law, and culture, the British always will have a relationship with Americans that no other European nation is likely to have. The point is that nowadays the continentals don't worry about it.

The question of American foreign policy that provokes the greatest fear and suspicion, however, is the duration of the United States' military and political commitments in Western Europe. Again, General de Gaulle has encouraged the suspicion and the fear that someday, he obviously would prefer it to be soon, the United States will withdraw its military forces from Europe. But it is wrong to give the General all the blame for the existence of this troublesome factor in America's relations with the continent. The fault must be assigned to the curious interaction of European and American attitudes toward NATO.

This began with the reduction, first by France, of military commitments to NATO, a process that has been going on for the past five years among most European members of the alliance. Knowledge of this development moved members of

Congress to ask why the United States should bear the greatest part of the burden of defending Western Europe when the Europeans themselves should be, and were not, doing it. As always happens, there were loud cries of "bring the boys home" and when these were joined at one point by former President Eisenhower, NATO's first Supreme Commander, a tremor ran through the NATO capitals, except, of course, Paris. Europe reacted by concluding that the Americans were going or about to go.

Nothing that successive Secretaries of State have wearily said at NATO conferences has succeeded in eliminating this suspicion. Perhaps the only answer to it is a greater dynamism in American policy for Europe and an attempt to engage the continent's interests in an alliance that will deal with the global problems of the remainder of this century.

Europe's attitude toward the United States today is compounded of criticism and suspicion. There naturally are other themes of thinking abroad. Vestiges of gratitude for the economic assistance of the late Forties and Fifties are still encountered. A number of governments and political parties—the Tories in Britain, the Christian Democrats in Italy, for example—understand, although they are not always enthusiastic over, Europe's military dependence on the United States. But at this stage of Europe's postwar development, when she is regaining her old political dynamism and independence, it is perhaps natural that criticism and suspicion should be predominant.

The question Americans must ask is whether the United States can recover the ground it has lost in Europe since the revival of nationalism. Recovery is certainly possible provided Washington begins by admitting that Europe has changed and that it would be utterly futile to attempt to return to the policies of ten years ago. Unfortunately, American policy toward Europe since 1955 has consisted largely of an effort to adjust the power situation of that time, which involved undisputed United States military and political leadership, to a drastically altered situation on the continent.

Because the United States used NATO, the multilateral approach, as the vehicle for adjusting its relations within the new power structure, the alliance lost some of its standing even among its most loyal adherents. This was largely because the American policy sought to alter the alliance's strategic concepts without first leading an all-embracing review of its strategic purposes. When this was finally agreed upon, the damage had been done.

The Germans, for example, clearly were not to be satisfied by promises of "sharing" in the establishment of "nuclear guidelines," and it is arguable whether or not they will ultimately be satisfied by a role in any multilateral nuclear force that does not give them more than simply participation in the force. A German government that includes the aggressive Herr Strauss is likely to ask for much more.

The change in the European situation is not due exclusively to the revival of nationalism, although that is its most spectacular expression. The balance in nuclear weapons has created a situation that gives individual allied governments in Europe all the advantages of an alliance in the form of protection with the freedom to act as independently as they wish on matters of national interest. It is a reasonably safe bet, for instance, that De Gaulle would be far more solicitous of American feelings if he were not sure that the United States, to protect itself, would come immediately to the protection of Europe. He reasons that France need not contribute much to the alliance because, in his inner mind, he knows that the United States' nuclear power *is* the alliance.

Any future United States effort toward the reestablishment of leadership must take into account this strategic concept, which is increasingly popular among European military experts, as well as the changes in attitude toward the United States among European political leaders and voters. America must in fact almost start all over again, this time not with impoverished, shell-shocked client nations as our partners but with a group of states with stable governments and remarkable confidence in their economic future.

Europe, it cannot be emphasized too often, no longer is interested, as it was in the first decade after the war, in influencing American policy to help Europe or the individual policies of its governments. Rather, European governments are concentrating on inducing the United States to accept their national policies.

The American approach in restoring the Atlantic community to its old vigor in joint responsibility, an indispensable first step toward a future alliance, must be positive. It cannot dwell too heavily on "reviving" NATO, although clearly if Europe is to be secure, the alliance must recover some of its former coherence and purpose. European nationalism, which is the biggest obstacle to community action, must be met not with solemn warnings about the inadequacy of a French or even a European nuclear force but with proposals for a more vigorous form of internationalism that will serve the future. The American policies to be offered Europe must be relevant to the political, economic, and social problems of the Seventies and Eighties rather than those of the Fifties.

The major roadblock the United States will face on the path back to union and stability in the West is psychological. It centers upon the conviction that the United States will not join in any international enterprise unless it is to be the acknowledged leader. Any American President who summons Europe to new mutual effort must *mean* partnership as well as talk about it. And he must be able to offer proof that the United States is prepared to act in concert with its allies in meeting the challenge implicit in the emergence of the new states of Africa and Asia with something more than sermons.

The period of preparation will be important. In the last ten years the European colonial powers with the single exception of Portugal have gradually divested themselves of most of their overseas possessions. The consequence has been a concentration upon Europe that has had, thus far, happy results at home but that has reduced European responsibilities abroad.

What Europe must be brought to realize now is that its present economic security and safety is not the end but only one phase of a continuous struggle. In this informative function, the United States should play a key role. It will lie with the Administration in Washington to convince its friends in Europe and the other continents of the seriousness of the developing situation and to make them realize that Europe cannot, no matter how much she would like to, forget the wider world and live happily ever after.

All this will impose new and heavy burdens on a Western world that within little more than a quarter of a century has lived through a world war, the Korean War, a cold war, and the disruptive period in which great empires were dismantled and new and often contentious states emerged. It is a world that has seen the high hopes placed upon the United Nations lost in prolonged wrangles and disputes over procedures.

Ultimately there is a single argument for restoring the Atlantic community and progressing in partnership toward the problems of the future: the world does not stand still, and if the countries with the greatest economic strength, political stability, and technological achievement do not act together the game will be lost by default.

The struggle will be a long one. It must be begun now if generations yet unborn, in the valleys of the Mississippi or the Ganges or the Congo, are to know peace and security.

# INDEX

move toward independent parties, 45
propaganda of, 195–196
in the satellite nations, 172–205
schism in China, 181, 183–185, 199
US attitude toward, 6–8, 34
Congo, 263, 267
Council for Mutual Economic Aid (COMENCON), 183
  Czechoslovakia and, 183
  *International Life* (journal) on, 198–199
  Rumania and, 187, 190
Cousins, Frank, 93
Cuba, 33–34, 62, 185, 204, 281
Cyprus, 9, 249
Cyprus
  NATO and, 30, 31
Czechoslovak Putsch, the, 112
Czechoslovakia, 15, 29, 42, 173, 174
  COMENCON and, 183
  economy of, 199
  multilateral trade and, 191
  opposition to German unity by, 119–120
  refugees from, 132–133


De Gaulle, Charles, 48–80
  attitude toward Communism, 6
  birth of, 49
  Communist China recognized by, 16, 54, 61–62
  conception of Europe, 58, 64
  criticism of US, 268, 274–279
  on the defense program, 77
  dictatorship aspect of, 62
  education of, 49
  Erhard and, 126, 213
  EEC and, 25–26, 28–29, 64–65, 81–82, 97, 256
  on European unity, 57, 66–67
  the Fouchet Plan and, 209–211

  on the Italian plan for political unity, 212–213
  Latin America and, 262
  Macmillan and, 97
  marriage of, 50
  method of reaching decisions, 52
  on multilateral force, 14
  the National Assembly and, 52–53
  nationalism of, 34, 35, 36, 42
  news conferences of, 52
  NATO and, 32, 52, 67, 230, 238–241, 246, 247, 249, 255–256
  on nuclear power, 46
  opposition to, 54
  on parliaments, 52–53
  on political unity, 32–33
  popularity of, 56
  possible developments following death of, 26, 63–64, 79
  power of, 52, 62–63
  the press and, 53–54
  on reunification of Germany, 201–202
  on supranationalism, 57, 208
  system of justice and, 63
  Treaty of Cooperation and, 60
  on the Treaty of Rome, 58–59
  on USSR, 58
  on a United States of Europe, 27
  veto of Great Britain by, 25–26, 28–29, 64–65, 81–82, 97
  on Vietnam, 58, 62
  on West Germany, 112, 116–124, 126, 127, 132, 139–142, 144
  Wilson and, 98
  on the world monetary system, 71
  in World War I, 49–50
  in World War II, 50–51
  *See also* France

294

McCarthy, Joseph, 141
McCloy, John J., 137
MacLeod, Iain, 99
Macmillan, Harold, 24, 25, 38, 60, 96, 109, 249
  De Gaulle and, 57, 97
  on the EEC, 82
Malaysia, 5, 12, 31, 39, 204
Malenkov, Georgi, 177
Malinovsky, Marshal, 185
Mansholt, Sicco, 208
Mao Tse Tung, 183
Margerison, T. A., 235
Marshall, George C., 137
Maudling, Reginald, 93, 99
Mboya, Tom, 265, 266
Messmer, Pierre, 237
Mexico, 262
*Mezzogiorno* (southern Italy), 152–159, 161
*Monde, Le* (newspaper), 54, 62
Monnet, Jean, 34, 55
Montgomery, Viscount, 248
Moore, Sir John, 22
Moro, Aldo, 151, 167
Morocco, 171
Morrison, Herbert, 93–94
Mozambique, 263
Multilateral force, 239, 241, 255
  Erhard on, 61
  Johnson on, 13–14
Multilateral Nuclear Force, 281–282
Murville, Maurice Couve de, 25, 62, 67, 130, 212
Mussolini, Benito, 162

Napoleon I, 22
National Hydrocarbon Board (ENI), 156
Nationalism
  in France, 36–37, 42, 48–49, 55
  in Great Britain, 37–41, 106–107

growth in Europe, 227–228
  in Italy, 168, 171
  in USSR, 200
  in US, 272–273
  unity vs., 22–47
  in West Germany, 41–45, 115, 144
NATO, *see* North Atlantic Treaty Organization
Nazi party, the, 41, 42
Nelson, Horatio, 22
Netherlands, the, 3, 25
  defense set-up for, 233
  on Great Britain's entry into the EEC, 25
  NATO and, 230, 233, 234, 247
  urban population of, 34–35
New Zealand, 99, 100, 261
  US influence in, 104
Nigeria, 100, 224, 263
North Atlantic Treaty, 239, 255
North Atlantic Treaty Organization (NATO), 229–253
  Belgium and, 230, 233, 234, 247
  Canada and, 230, 247
  Cyprus and, 30, 31
  decline of, 229–230, 236–255
  Defense Production Committee of, 234
  defense set-up of, 232–233
  Denmark and, 230, 233, 239, 247
  economy and, 31
  establishment of, 8
  France and, 32, 52, 67, 230, 231, 233, 234, 237–241, 243–47, 249, 253, 255–256
  the German-American alliance and, 112
  Great Britain and, 230–233, 237, 241, 244–247, 249, 253
  Greece and, 30, 31, 230, 233, 247
  Iceland and, 230, 247

301